DATE DUE

DE 1 8 '99			

DEMCO 38-296

The Comedy
of
Democracy

THE COMEDY
OF
DEMOCRACY

James E. Combs
and
Dan Nimmo

PRAEGER

**Westport, Connecticut
London**

Library of Congress Cataloging-in-Publication Data

Combs, James E.
    The comedy of democracy / James E. Combs and Dan Nimmo.
      p. cm.
    Includes bibliographical references and index.
    ISBN 0–275–94979–6 (alk. paper)
    1. Democracy—Humor. 2. Political science—Humor. I. Nimmo,
Dan. II. Title.
JC423.C6493   1996
321.8—dc20   95–34411

British Library Cataloguing in Publication Data is available.

Library of Congress Catalog Card Number: 95–34411
ISBN: 0–275–94979–6

First published in 1996

Praeger Publishers, 88 Post Road West, Westport, CT 06881
An imprint of Greenwood Publishing Group, Inc.

Printed in the United States of America

The paper used in this book complies with the
Permanent Paper Standard issued by the National
Information Standards Organization (Z39.48–1984).

10 9 8 7 6 5 4 3 2 1

To
Max Bialystock and Leo Bloom,
who understood the serious in the frivolous
and the frivolity in the seriousness of
Liebkind's approach to politics

Contents

Introduction: Wit's End—
Taking Political Comedy Seriously

Star Trek is a remarkable phenomenon of American popular culture. Born in the 1960s, it lives on through original episodes and reruns of four TV series, profitable movies, paperback books, and countless memorabilia. *Star Trek: The Next Generation*, the successor to the original TV series, proved especially successful. There were many reasons. One was the array of beguiling characters. One of the most intriguing was an android, Data, a machine designed to look and interact like a humanoid. As episodes unfolded, Data was like Pinocchio, the wooden puppet trying hard to be a real boy, for one of the charming aspects of Data's character is that he never quite "gets it." He can't grasp why humans act oddly, that is, their lovers' spats, displays of gloom or anger, and readiness to say things contrary to what they mean. Data seems to think, "Oh, to be human so I could explain humans' puzzling ways."

In the first movie spin-off featuring characters from *The Next Generation*, the 1994 film *Star Trek: Generations*, Data comes a step closer to realizing his Pinocchio-like wish to be human. He has installed an "emotion chip." The chip allows Data to feel human emotions, crossing the line from being just a reasoning machine to a feeling being. In the course of the story, he feels fear, remorse, exhilaration, relief, satisfaction, and grief. Perhaps the truest evidence of his new human status is that he acquires a sense of humor. He recalls a joke someone told him in the past. When he first heard it, he found the joke incomprehensible. Suddenly, thanks to the emotion chip, he bursts out in laughter, "Now I get it!," much to the bewilderment of his fellow crew members.

As Aristotle long ago defined humankind, Data had become a "laughing animal," albeit a mechanical one. We know not how the pre-emotional Data might have tried to make sense out of American democracy. But we suspect that as he developed, courtesy of the chip, into a laughing animal he would be far more capable of understanding human politics than as a purely reasoning machine. The contention of this book is that it takes a sense of humor to "get it" when "it" is politics. A humanized Data would see democratic politics as comedy. Indeed, he would come to understand that comedy may well be the most insightful and penetrating perspective from which to fully grasp that Aristotle's "political animal" and "laughing animal" are the same.

Those of us who don't need to have emotion chips installed, since as humans we have emotions, should follow the laughing Data's lead. To be sure, to understand politics we can turn to serious political science, analysis, commentary, and punditry. But to really get it we also need to turn to political comics. Think, for example, of Mark Twain, Will Rogers, and W. C. Fields: all handled serious matters from a comic standpoint. And, more to the point of this book, they all treated politics as comedy. Thus did Mark Twain, a bard of the first order, ridicule U.S. intervention in the Philippines as making a burlesque out of the American flag: "the white stripes painted black and the stars replaced by the skull and crossbones."[1] Will Rogers, master of the pre-TV sound bite, had a one-liner for everything political. On Congress: "Congress met. I was afraid they would." On candidates: "It's like a campaign promise. It's too good to be true." On the vice presidency: "A Vice-President answers about the same purpose as a rear cinch on a saddle. If you break the front one, you are worse off than if you had no other." And on political integrity: "Corruption and golf is two things we might just as well make up our minds to take up, for they are both going to be with us."[2] And W. C. Fields, Rogers' fellow *Ziegfeld Follies* headliner, was no slouch at political comedy either. Like Rogers in 1928 as "The Bunkless Candidate," W. C. in 1940 announced his own facetious candidacy in *Fields for President*; he too was a pre–sound bite master. Comparing himself to bottle-scarred President Ulysses S. Grant, who had a penchant for alcohol, Fields quipped, "Well, of all the Presidents' hobbies, I think General Grant came nearest to my ideas and ideals—excepting that I was never a great cigar smoker."[3]

Political humorists they were, wits who shared a conviction: politics is so serious it must be taken humorously. Politics, like life, is too important a thing to take seriously. Mark Twain, Rogers, and Fields were not the only ones; add, for example, H. L. Mencken, the Marx Brothers, Mort Sahl,

Gracie Allen, Walt Kelly, Erma Bombeck, Russell Baker. The playbill is lengthy. Add us as well. Juvenal, the first century Roman poet, said he lived in times when he found it hard *not* to write satire. On the threshold of the twenty-first century many of us find it hard not to invoke the comic muse. So we shall. Beware! The aim herein is not to try to be funny, but more modestly to offer insights gained by looking at American politics as comedy, so that the reader may come away from the book with a heightened comic sense about democratic politics. Like Data, we hope the reader will learn to get it about politics as comedy.

DEMOCRACY: CRYING, LAUGHING, LAUGHING THROUGH TEARS

Given the litany of woes peoples of the earth witnessed in the twentieth century, is it not insensitive to suggest that we might find comedy in politics? Major economic upheavals left people homeless, starving, diseased, and dying. Add two world wars and countless, endless armed conflicts between nations, and within nations pitting religion against religion, faction against faction, tyrant against tyrant, drug lord against drug lord. Throw in the Holocaust, ethnic cleansing, mass murders. All of that in a world of diminishing resources, fouled air, polluted waters, and exploding populations. So what's so funny? Given the wretched practices and prospects of the human race, it is tempting to say, perhaps nothing. Then again, maybe more than one might think.

The Sour and Dour of Power

In the face of the twentieth century's apocalyptic politics of war, famine, pestilence, and death, the human drama raises vital questions about human existence, morality, and our essential social and psychological relationships. These matters are surely tragic, not comic. And not just in the twentieth century: as far back as ancient Greece a tragic view of humans and their recurring species-threatening problems became an important dramatic perspective. Ancient tragedies pitted cosmic and human forces against one another. Greek dramas told of gods exerting a supernatural power independent of human conditions, a power counting as much, even more, in the outcome of religious and civic affairs as human factors. Tragedy through the ages has had a dreadful message: even the greatest of mortals has limited power to control and rule the world, and all of us are subject to the logic of tragic endings, because of our excesses (*hubris*) or simply because of the mortality of all things. Oedipus, Medea, Lear, Faust, Willy Loman are tragic figures of the theater; but in the realm of modern politics, we are aware of the awesome grimness of tragedy too—the Holocaust, Vietnam, the fall of great but flawed princes such as Woodrow Wilson and Richard

Nixon. Life and politics become the theater for the enactment of great human wrongs and falls from grace and power, and mighty is the fated fall.

In his *Poetics* Aristotle (384–322 B.C.) taught that epic poetry and tragedy, as well as comedy, were imitations of life.[4] For example, the epic tragedy imitates how humans adapt to political conditions, say war, coming to accept warlike conditions and feeling at home in them. Tragic epics accomplish this by magnifying the glory, and the mighty fall, of a warlike hero. The epic hero teaches the virtues of individual courage and self-sacrifice; every one of us, from the master to the slave, from the haughty to the humble, becomes vicariously heroic by identifying with the hero, who triumphs by transcending overwhelming odds in a struggle with godlike and natural forces. In epics each citizen can be Patrick Henry demanding liberty or death, George Washington crossing the Delaware, Ol' Hickory winning the Battle of New Orleans, Harriet Tubman risking her life to rescue slaves, Franklin D. Roosevelt slaying the Great Depression.

Today, however, heroes don't reside on every "fruited plain," or even in a presidential primary. The ancient tragic epic demanding heroic victories of good or evil seems not to apply in an urbanized, sophisticated setting. When moms no longer raise their sons to be cowboys, the tragic view of life must be adjusted to changing times. The ingredients for tragedy are still there. After all, modern sophistication is simply another form of the false pride (*hubris*) that has always been the fatal flaw in humans that leads to tragic consequences.

So tragedies remain. But instead of telling us to resign ourselves to our miserable condition by vicariously enjoying the fruits of heroic victory over evil, contemporary tragedy teaches us to resign ourselves to living within our limits while pursuing aspirations that are limitless. Pride tells us we deserve to have what we covet. Everyone deserves a palatial home, a swimming pool, a sporty car, a college education, a lucrative and fulfilling vocation, an endless vacation. The tragic muse says, "Hold on. Beware the evil of self-indulgence." Its message: Each of us, not some abstract hero, must exercise self-restraint and even accept self-sacrifice.[5]

U.S. Presidents still preach the tragic gospel of self-restraint: Jimmy Carter's energy conservation, the moral equivalent of war; Ronald Reagan's cuts in domestic programs to beef up defense and defeat the Evil Empire; George Bush's kinder, gentler nation of citizens volunteering in a thousand points of light; and Bill Clinton's plea to sacrifice for health care reform because it's the "right thing to do."

The tragic muse tells us to get with the program, not change it. Either vicariously or by recognizing our tragic flaws, we must accept our fate, not laugh at it. Life is real and life is earnest, calling for high seriousness that is no laughing matter. But an irreverent question insistently arises: What if we laugh at it all instead?

Comedy Tonight

A song written by Stephen Sondheim for the farcical Broadway musical that became a 1966 Hollywood film, *A Funny Thing Happened on the Way to the Forum*, is full of promises: Something Exciting, Something Inviting, Something for Everyone, A Comedy Tonight! The promises are fulfilled. Hilarity abounds: gladiators practice head-smashing skills on live targets, slaves mock their masters, and a heroic soldier relishes a drink of wine only to discover it is horse sweat. We find ourselves laughing at pretty rough stuff: the tortures a master threatens a slave with, a boy threatening to kill himself over a slave girl, a pompous general bragging in song of his many slaughters.

The source for the production was the work of an ancient Roman playwright, Titus Maccius Plautus (c.254–184 B.C.). Plautus' works derived from ancient Greek New Comedy. One characteristic that distinguished the New Comedy of the fourth century B.C. from the Old Comedy of the fifth was subject matter. Old Comedy ridiculed matters of great import—the fickleness of the gods, politics, rulers and ruled, war and peace. By contrast, New Comedy, like most TV sitcoms, was concerned not with political and civic questions but with everyday life: petty misunderstandings, mistaken identities, white lies, harmless deceptions.[6] The plots of Old Comedy poet Aristophanes (c.448–380 B.C.) made fun of life, for instance, in *The Knights* and *Peace*. Aristophanes did so in a manner akin to a twentieth century Will Rogers chiding Congress or warring nations. Similarly, Plautus' *The Menaechmi*, with its plot about quarreling husbands and wives, courtesans, and mistaken identities, foreshadowed situation comedies like *I Love Lucy*.

There was a reason why the New replaced the Old in Greek comedy. In the fourth century-B.C., the Macedonians conquered Greece, and Athens and the Greek territories fell under the rule of Alexander the Great. With self-rule gone the freedom of citizens to criticize rulers, seek redress of grievances, and demand reforms went with it. Old comic Aristophanes looked at Greek city-state democracy, depicted it as ridiculous, and called for political change; later the New comic Plautus looked at Roman imperial politics, resigned himself to it, and found fun in everyday domesticity. There's comedy tonight so long as it doesn't threaten the imperial powers that be. Early in the history of civilization it became very clear to those in authority that political comedy was dangerous, something that needed to be suppressed or displaced.

Making Fun, Taking the Fun Out, and Being Funny

In his *Poetics* Aristotle taught that the development of tragedy as a poetic form was easy to trace. Not so for comedy: "it was not as yet taken up in a serious way."[7] When it was taken seriously, at least by the Old School, comedy became a means of *making fun* of human ways, especially politics and political rulers. Making fun pointed out the ridiculous in human affairs, what Aristotle called a "mistake or deformity not productive of pain or harm to others."[8] Making fun was not being nasty. Rather, making fun of mistakes called attention to them in order to seek a corrective. New Comedy resigned itself to political misrule; Old Comedy was diagnostic and therapeutic for healthy political rule.

As we have seen, the old comic muse died early. The New Comedy *took the fun out* of democratic politics by the simple device of ignoring it, by making fun not of political life but of personal life. Thus began a long comedic tradition, not only of taking some of the fun out of politics but out of politically potent comedy as well. That tradition is kept alive in a host of approaches to political humor current in social science research.[9] Social and behavioral science treatises examine, for example, the origins of laughter and humor. Studies identify such factors as superiority (humans make fun of others' infirmities, ignorance, pomposity, and silliness), conflict (we find humor in the unexpected, the incongruous), and relief (people laugh to ease pain, reduce stress, avoid embarrassment, and express the euphoria of being triumphant in some contest).

Scientific studies also catalogue the social functions of humor. We learn, for example, that humor establishes social distance between us and others: sharing a joke can bring people together; ridicule may drive them apart. Or by making fun of things in a social situation, we broach topics that otherwise might be avoided (Other than that, how did you like the play, Mrs. Lincoln?). And humor helps deflate pomposity (as in the Marx Brothers or W. C. Fields) while helping one to act like an ordinary person who doesn't take oneself too seriously.

The science of comedy also explores why some of us find things funny when others do not, and why jokes, puns, double entendres, and other comic situations affect different people in different ways. Scholarly studies offer a litany of reasons in differing personalities, motivations, ambitions, repressed desires, prejudices, and sensitivities; our social positions, occupations, incomes, and achievements are not the same; our ethnic, racial, religious, and cultural backgrounds are diverse; and some of us are simply able to be wittier more often, in more places, and more persuasively than others. The science of comedy also studies why some people have a sense of humor and others do not; we have all experienced the grimness of being around a humorless person.

Scientific studies have also inventoried basic joke types and techniques of humor.[10] So, for example, we laugh at accidents (bloopers), as when President Jimmy Carter at the 1980 Democratic National Convention introduced former Vice President Hubert [middle name Horatio] Humphrey as Hubert Horatio Hornblower. Or unexpected utterances: "Take my wife, PLEASE!" cracked comic Henny Youngman. Or ethnic, racial, or gender stereotypes ("Heard a good Polish joke lately?" "Heard the one about the feminist who . . . ").

Although "humor can be dissected, as a frog can . . . the thing dies in the process and the innards are discouraging to any but the pure scientific mind."[11] Perhaps social and behavioral scientists find genuine fun in probing the origins, sources, functions, types, and techniques of comic humor. Yet, seeing comedy in a clinical way takes the fun out of it for most of us. We want to say to the vivisecting analysts, "Get a life!" Moreover, by jumping off the analytical deep end one runs the risk of seeing comedy by seeing *through* it, missing its overall significance. The pages that follow will try not to be so clinical. Sometimes, as the great clinician Sigmund Freud said, even a cigar is just a cigar—rather than a phallic symbol, a substitute for a master's riding crop, or the bludgeoning weapon of a tyrant. Sometimes, too, comedy is to be accepted on its own terms.

What are those terms? They consist neither of taking the fun out of comedy (the clinician's style) nor of making fun of things simply to make fun (the debunker's style). Dealing as it did with the absurdities of daily living rather than with matters of civic life, New Comedy debunked human affairs. Debunking, however, can violate Aristotle's basic injunction of comedy, namely, point to the ridiculous without pain or harm.

Satire, a form of debunking, is an example. If noted literary critic Kenneth Burke is correct, "the satirist attacks *in others* the weaknesses and temptations that are really *within himself*."[12] Like any attack, satire can be mean-spirited; Plato, in his Socratic dialogue *Gorgias*, understood; he had Gorgias rebuke Socrates with a biting "Kill your opponent's jest with your earnestness and his earnestness with your jest."[13] Negative political campaigning is an ancient practice.

Satire can produce either pain or harm, often both, and not only to those who are ridiculed, the targets of the satirist's spleen. For since the satirist is a person unhappy *within*, the pain projected on others is painful to one's self. Burke observed that Jonathan Swift, the author of every schoolchild's fairy tale—and a model of satire—*Gulliver's Travels*, was really beating up on himself unmercifully in his writing. It was a self-flagellation that Burke surmised proved disastrous for Swift.[14] Yet, Swift's bitter satires—his "Modest Proposal" on how to control the famine in Ireland—did project his inner pain onto political objects quite effectively. For great political comics like Aristophanes and Swift, the ability to provoke laughter is no laughing matter; satire is funny business about serious business.

Burlesque as a comedic device also carries potential for pain and harm. Burlesque focuses on the things we readily witness in human beings, such as one's posture, tics of the eye, body configuration, voice, dialect, and so on. A burlesque ridicules those signs by reducing them to absurdity, by ignoring all mitigating circumstances that would put the person being burlesqued in a better light. In Burke's phrase, the writer of burlesque "hilariously . . . converts a manner into a mannerism." But because such characterization is partial, it is "partisan" and "incomplete."[15] Thus, for instance, one could argue that the whole of President Richard Nixon's career was burlesqued by those fixated on his complexion and posture: a five o'clock shadow, shifty eyes, slightly stooped figure, arms spread-eagled above his head, two fingers of each hand signaling a V-for-Victory salute. Here was the very essence of the humpbacked, diabolical child murderer of legend, Richard III—scarcely a flattering portrait, or a complete one, yet a public persona easy to burlesque by impressionists and columnists, who cut Nixon down to size.

One of America's most celebrated debunkers was H. L. Mencken. His wit was sharp, his satire vitriolic, and his burlesque unrelenting. One of many politicians who was a butt of his humor was William Jennings Bryan, three-time party candidate for president, Woodrow Wilson's secretary of state, noted orator, populist, and religious fundamentalist. In 1925 Bryan traveled to Dayton, Tennessee, to argue against the teaching of evolution in public schools, the issue surrounding the infamous "Monkey Trial" of John T. Scopes. Cross-examined by famed trial lawyer Clarence Darrow, Bryan sweated profusely, swatted at flies in the stifling heat, and furiously wiped his brow. After the straining trial, Bryan died in Dayton. Mencken, who had been in the southern village covering the trial, published "In Memoriam: W.J.B." in the Baltimore *Evening Sun*. Mencken who had no love for Bryan but loved to burlesque politicians, satirized: "[Bryan's] imbecilities were excused by his earnestness—that under his clowning, as under that of the juggler of Notre Dame, there was the zeal of a steadfast soul." (This from a Mencken whose critics also thought him guilty of imbecilities, but still an earnest newspaperman.) And Mencken burlesqued:

Bryan's last secular act on this globe of sin was to catch flies. . . . He was the most sedulous fly-catcher in American history, and in many ways the most successful. His quarry, of course, was not *Musca domestica* [the common fly] but *Homo neandertalenis* [the uneducated rural simpletons or "Neanderthals" Mencken hated].[16]

Debunking by satire and burlesque, making fun while inflicting pain and harm, is not the whole of a comic perspective, at least not of comic minds like Aristophanes and Mencken; in fact, it runs the risk of violating that perspective. Hence, we should not equate comedy merely with making fun of, or taking the fun out of, political life. Nor do we equate the comic perspective with simply *being funny*. To be sure, comedy and tragedy are dramatic forms. Indeed, Kenneth Burke thought comedy "the most civilized form of art."[17] As a dramatic form comedy is often distinguished by the comic art of its actors, and many American politicians, from Ben Franklin to Bob Dole, have been comic artists in their own right. Compendia of their jokes, parables, and one-liners make amusing reading. And we will occasionally refer to the witty products of such comic art. But a comic perspective requires more than being funny. President John F. Kennedy, no neophyte at being funny, understood that: "There are three things which are real—God, human folly, and laughter. The first two are beyond our comprehension, so we must do what we can with the third."[18] Let us turn to doing just that.

We Have Met the Enemy and He Is Us! Fun as Subversion

To grasp the character of a comic perspective on democracy we must take one more look at the roots of Old Comedy in ancient Greece. The Greeks first presented dramas in conjunction with festivals honoring Dionysus, the god of wine and fertility. According to Greek mythology, Dionysus was the son of the greatest of all gods, Zeus; Dionysus' mother was a mortal, Semele. After Dionysus was killed and dismembered, he was brought back to life by Zeus. The Greeks held religious festivals throughout the year; by 534 B.C. the festival of the City Dionysia, held at the end of March, included drama contests. For half a century the festival featured only tragedies; then, in 487 B.C. comedy appeared, and thereafter one day of each festival was set aside for comedic presentations.

Out of the folklore surrounding Zeus and his resurrected son grew legends of Dionysus (introduced to Greece from Asia Minor as early as the thirteenth century B.C.) connected to the life cycle of birth, growth, decay, and rebirth. To celebrate Dionysus was to celebrate rebirth; it was to embrace the return of spring after the passage of summer, fall, and winter. With spring came fertility, grapes, wine, and celebratory *fun*.

Traditional tragic performances at City Dionysia were not fun. As a dramatic form tragedy suppressed the magic surrounding fertility, concentrating instead on the portrayal of the suffering and death of a hero, king, or god.[19] Tragedy's form is fixed and orderly; a plot with beginning, middle, and end provides unified action. And as tragedy suppresses fun in favor of suffering, it suppresses the unique qualities of individual character to the plot's unfolding. People are at the mercy of the story. In Aristotle's words, "A tragedy, then, is the imitation of an action [plot] that is serious [suffering] and also, as having magnitude, complete in itself [there is no escape!]."[20]

With its stress on suffering and restricted freedom, pain, and captivity, tragic action, "however inspiring and however perfect in artistic form, runs through only one arc of the full cycle of drama: for the entire ceremonial cycle is birth: struggle: death: resurrection. The tragic arc is only birth: struggle: death. Consequently, the range of comedy is wider than the tragic range—perhaps more fearless."[21] It is fearless in part because a comic perspective accepts human beings as imperfect, as fallible creatures that, even in their most serious moments, engage in folly. Tragedy recognizes imperfection, but holds out the promise of perfectibility and, in the end, punishes the tragic flaws embedded in character that block humans from achieving perfection. Submit to the program, says the tragic perspective; accept the social order, thereby ending doubt, easing pain, and overriding the flaws of free-wheeling character.

In contrast with acceptance of social order, comedy refuses to pay "the price of banishing doubt and question."[22] Indeed, the focus of the comic perspective is not order but *deviation* from order, recognizing that the widely used phrase, "That's just the way things are done," is a sham; in most cases that's *not* the way things are done. Behind the facade or mask of how things are done in an orderly, correct manner is likely to be a far more chaotic, mistake-prone revel of getting-along-in-the-world. The impiety of comedy challenges the accepted in subversive, even revolutionary ways. As Walt Kelly's cartoon character, Pogo, was wont to say, "We have met the enemy and he is us!" Through comedy we are fearless enough to subvert our own folly.

Comedy is also fearless in its improvisation. Missing is the tragic triad of beginning, middle, and end that yields a comforting, even when horrifying, predictability. Comedy's form is formless, a loose structure of logic-in-use that tolerates surprise, chance, changes in fortune, and people with all of their character flaws acting in irreverent ways. Because they don't know what to revere? No, because reverence is for birth, struggle, death, but not for fecund resurrection. As Kenneth Burke argued, tragedy deals with *"cosmic man,"* but comedy deals with *"man in society."* Like tragedy, comedy warns against pride, but the comic perspective shifts the emphasis from *"crime* to *stupidity"*:

The progress of human enlightenment can go no further than in picturing people not as *vicious*, but as *mistaken*. When you add that people are *necessarily* mistaken, that *all* people are exposed to situations in which they must act as fools, that *every* insight contains its own special kind of blindness, you complete the comic circle, returning to the lesson of humility that underlies great tragedy.[23]

Fearless in accepting human imperfection, subverting social order, and prizing improvisation, comedy is fearless in another way. Societies collapse. Organizations break down. Families split up. Marriages dissolve. When they do, people get hurt. Individuals face, either literally or figuratively, death provoked by the disintegration of the very social order that gave them an identity. A comic perspective fights off the fear of that death; it says: "Hold on. There is a chance to live." How? Humor offers a way of *distancing* ourselves from disintegration, of retaining individual identity in the face of societal chaos.

The very act of laughter is an example. We speak here of spontaneous laughter, not the contrived laughter of giggling at the joke the boss makes, or of the guffaw aimed at convincing others that you are enjoying yourself when you are miserable. When we laugh we draw aside, exhale, toss back our heads, and revel in Falstaffian merriment. We stand apart. Comedy makes us laugh and live. It is fearless because it removes our fear to

approach the most dangerous, most disruptive aspects of existence, such as sex and death, which are commonly its topics . . . comedy makes a person aware of [a] social phenomenon's potential disintegration but distances one's self from it to preserve one's integrity; tragedy also makes one aware of the social phenomenon's potential disorganization but so involves the self in it that one suffers the agony of being pulled apart personally along with it.[24]

Victims of the Holocaust interned in concentration camps, there to slave and ultimately die, employed jokes, funny stories, and ridicule to distance themselves from the Nazi torment imposed on them. That they had to give voice to their humor behind their captors' backs illustrates again the subversive character of comedy. The victims' laughing at the ridiculous may not have been intended to pain or harm, using Aristotle's phrase, the Nazi tormentors. But try telling that to anyone of a fascist mentality committed to a tragic view of life. Keep your wit to yourself and don't joke around with the school hall monitor or the local policeman who stops you, advice not to fool around with prudish figures bordering on the tyrannical.

Comedy thus becomes a form of "internal exile," of withdrawing from the "public-forum-turned-public-madhouse into one's own private life" where one through ridicule of authority can live to fight another day. Dissidents in Eastern Europe and the Soviet Union (Vaclav Havel in Czechoslovakia, Andrei Sakharov in Russia, Polish intellectuals), barred from voicing protests in public, retreated into themselves. They lived as exiles within their own land, there to smile and laugh, and "live as if we were free."[25] Their underground humor sustained them through years of oppression and imprisonment, eventually bringing down a system the dissident intellectuals regarded as more preposterous than sinister, totalitarianism as a big joke.

When we stand back, employ a comic perspective, and observe the fits, folly, and foibles in even the most serious of political matters, we use what Kenneth Burke called a "perspective by incongruity."[26] We see Aristotle's ridiculous, the clash and strife between even our best intentions—that when things are what they are, then they are *not* actually what we thought we were bringing about by our well-intentioned actions. By distancing us from what we are doing, comedy highlights the limits of our intelligence, knowledge, and success.

Burke offers an example, one replete with irony. It applies to transportation policy. It could as easily be health care reform, wars against drugs, programs for energy independence, or any other contemporary national crusade. We build roadways. Travel increases; so too do the hazards of travel. Out of public obligation we must insure travelers against increased hazards. Since public money built the roads, "the *increased insurability* is a *public liability.*" But no, "*private* insurance companies are organized to exploit it as a *private asset.*"[27] Thus does the carnival of public policy create a public problem capitalized on by private interests as a surefire money-maker! Rather than problems creating solutions, solutions create problems, which call for more solutions, and so on, in an endless comic cycle.

A comic perspective, then, makes a game of "serious" matters, not to debunk them but to point out the errors of our ways. The *errors*, not the sins. The mistakes, not the crimes. Once the grave becomes gravy, what Burke labels "comic correctives" (reform, revolution, rebirth, resurrection) are possible. The comically correct (but decidedly not politically correct) view is amused and bemused by the antics of humankind, and able to understand the infinite folly of our fellow creatures because we all commit the same errors, make the same stupid mistakes, and make as much a mess of things as the people in the social games we observe who make a few hits, fewer runs, and *lots* of errors.

In sum, the argument of this book is that whatever politics may be, political analysis had best be comic, and indeed is at its best when it is conducted as comic. A comic perspective fearlessly diagnoses the ridiculous in politics, including but not endorsing the harm or pain; it is irreverent, even subversive, but not doctrinaire, since doctrine is just another part of the political comedy; it assumes that politics is as much improvisation as plan, that politicians are fallible and certainly not perfectible; it stands apart from political folly through humorous reflection; and it celebrates the Dionysian cycle with hope for rebirth beyond birth, growth, decay, and death. Comedy offers a hopeful and larger view of things: beyond every winter chill is a fertile new spring, where death is carried away and there are new human tangles for our comic pleasure.

MACHIAVELLI: A WIT'S PERSPECTIVE ON DEMOCRACY

In an instant we travel forward two millennia from ancient Greece to the Italian Renaissance, a culture competing with Periclean Athens as a Golden Age of enlightenment. As the saying goes, however, "you can't make an omelette without breaking a few eggs." Renascent genius was born not in a slow cooker but in a sizzling frying pan of disintegrating social order and crackling political turmoil. Great Ideas flourished, but so also did petty skirmishes, destructive wars, political torture, assassinations, intrigue, and skullduggery. (As the character Harry Lime jokes in the movie *The Third Man*, the Italy of the Borgias and Medicis produced the Renaissance, while the centuries of stable government next door in Switzerland produced—the cuckoo clock.) In this world of intermingled humanistic creativity and political mendacity resided Niccolo Machiavelli (1469–1527), a wry political artist, a comic observer of democracy. We look to him as an exemplar of the comic perspective on politics. He grasped that the practice of democracy is comic.

Laughing in Hell

Machiavelli was both a diplomat for the Florentine republic and a humanistic scholar and writer; he was an exemplar of the Renaissance Man, a scholar-activist equally at home in a library or a chancery. He acquired his comic, playful view of life both through streetwise political experience and bookwise reflection. He knew firsthand the vagaries, insanities, and inanities of politics. He was indefatigable in his travels as a diplomat for the city-state of Florence. As secretary to the Council of Ten, the ruling body of Florentine politics, he was an eyewitness to all key decisions. So much so, in fact, that when the Council fell from power, Florence's new regime imprisoned Machiavelli, put him on the rack (from his viewpoint stretching things a bit too far), and eventually sent him into exile, where he both reflected on, and schemed to become again a player in, the comic drama of politics that so gripped him.

A glimpse of his comic amazement at political life appears in his diplomatic dispatches. They are both informative and funny: he is both political actor and author, acting in a bubbling political cauldron, and thinking and writing about the stew he was so much a part of. He finds it all fascinating, but is not so immersed that he cannot maintain a perspective on it. He is both in it and distanced from it, able to act in it and also to analyze dispassionately what is happening. He is no special pleader and has no ax to grind. Yet, he not only reports events, he speculates on motives and possible responses, what outcomes might be expected, what moves might be made next.

Even though he is hard at work on the road for the Florentine government (his friends composed a mock epitaph for him: "Niccolo Machiavelli / for love of country 'pissed in many a snow' "), he cannot help but express his delight at what he sees: he is witnessing a theatrical drama as a marginal character viewing with a high degree of detached amusement the antics of other players who strut and fret their hour upon the political and social stage.[28] His experience helped develop his comic perspective on the rough-and-tumble politics he was witness to.

Although Machiavelli's reputation as a political thinker rests largely on allegedly serious works, most notably *The Prince* and *The Discourses of Livy*, he was a comic playwright as well. A body of drama labeled the "theater of life"—plays about generic life in the tradition of Greek New Comedy—was very popular in Renaissance Italy: romantic melodramas, farces about sexual peccadillos, slapstick family situations, and so on. This was not a time for tragic dramas of sin, suffering, and sacrifice. Playwrights no longer faced life as a wearisome burden, like the medieval pilgrim, but in the optimistic, cheerful, and vigorous conquests of sensual Renaissance men and women, reviving the pagan spirit of the classical world.

Machiavelli's dramas involved frank sexual adventures, flouting of social conventions, ulterior and base motives, hypocritical portrayals of authority (priests, parents, the nobility, etc.), and portrayals of opportunism, adultery, conspiracy, and lying as accepted, effective ways of behaving. Yet, although Machiavelli was using the form of Greek New Comedy with its emphasis on private lives, his target was not private citizens in their mundane, albeit hilarious, daily existence; rather, he used the *form* of New Comedy to achieve an Old Comedy purpose, for example, Aristotle's ridicule, neither "productive of pain or harm," and Aristophanes' aim to let the politicians have it. Machiavelli's plots were of the boudoir, but his target was the public, political life and the politicians who live it.

For example, Machiavelli's most famous play, *Mandragola* (*The Mandrake Root*), is a portrayal of elaborate deception perpetrated by a nobleman who exploits the hypocrisy, stupidity, or self-serving aims of others. On the surface the work in a playful way teaches a useful moral, namely, the ethical doctrines professed by the play's characters, as with humans generally, are wholly at odds with what they do to attain their various ends. *The Mandrake Root* is a hilarious romp about professing one thing, doing another. In short, we ain't what we appear to be.

And neither is Machiavelli. Oh, he says to the audience in his prologue to the play, with false humility, that "its author has no great repute . . . he's reduced to indolence"; a sad condition for "a man of serious pretense." But, no longer with humility, he assures that "if you don't laugh while we essay it, he'll treat you to a flask of wine."[29] Yet, Machiavelli's *Mandragola* offers far more than a homily about false pretensions. For his subject is not the private lives of self-centered persons, it is the politics of contemporary Florence. That is a politics of deals and double-deals, of foxiness and fraud, or *forda*. Machiavelli's streetwise and bookwise understanding was that no regime, certainly not a democratic one, could survive by chance. Indeed, chance, *fortuna*, undermines political rule. Still, even though fortune may govern half our actions, Machiavelli wrote in *The Prince*, the other half is in our power to control. That control requires professionals who put aside private ambitions in the name of a wider, inclusive civic good.

But princely politicians are rare. When they appear they must be richly rewarded, lest they depart or, worse, turn to deceit, pretense, and deception, thus *appearing* to serve the civic interest while privately feathering their own nests. The political moral of *The Mandrake Root* is that Florentine political corruption was "due fundamentally to the absence of rewards for political ambition resulting from a general disposition to blame rather than to praise or honor."[30] As in Aristophanes' Athens, bickering and backbiting ruined the republic.

In Machiavelli's comic perspective a drama has two purposes, to *delight* and to *instruct*. He spells them out in his prologue to another comedy, *Clizia*. First, "comedies are made to help and delight the spectator . . . to delight it is necessary to move the spectators to laughter, which one cannot do [by] keeping speech serious and severe; because the words that make for laughter are either silly or harmful or amorous. It is thus necessary to represent silly, ill-spoken of, or enamored persons." Second, comedies also help to instruct: "It helps greatly to any man, and most of all the young, to know the avarice of an old man, the frenzy of a lover, the tricks of a servant, the gluttony of a parasite, the misery of a poor man, the ambitions of a rich man, the flatteries of a harlot," and of course, "the little faith [ingratitude, untrustworthiness, dishonesty, and so on] of all men." Comedies "represent all those things with great honesty."[31] Here, then, lies the essential ingredient—the springtime of rebirth and resurrection that is comedy: "Machiavelli's political vision . . . has an affinity with comedy if one understands by comedy the archetypical celebration of the triumph of youth and desire over age, authority, and duty."[32] What the Florentines needed, like the Athenians, was the revitalization of youth, with new energy, hope, and even trust.

Comedy, then, may superficially deal with trivial matters, but even the most momentous aspects of political and social life are themselves subject to human triviality. The honesty of spontaneous laughter reduces them to their proper size:

Humor is the opposite of the heroic. The heroic promotes acceptance by *magnification*, making the hero's character as great as the situation he confronts, and fortifying the non-heroic individual vicariously, by identification with the hero; but humor reverses the process: it takes up the slack between the momentousness of the situation and the feebleness of those in the situation by *dwarfing the situation*.[33]

Machiavelli's private letters offer us much the same comic perspective on life as his plays. One of his most famous letters uses incongruity to deflate pomposity. He prefaces it with a salutation of pompous and bogus titles attributed to his correspondent ("Magnificent Master," "Governor," "most worthy and especially to be most honored"). Then comes the opening zinger: "I was on the privy seat when your messenger came, and just then I was thinking of the absurdities of the world."[34] In a word, Machiavelli's attitude toward life, love, and politics is one of jocosity. Jocundity and jocularity are related terms, but jocosity derives from the Latin *jocus*, jest or joke, capturing the notion that Machiavelli is joking around, being serious in a playful way. In both his private and public letters, he rarely displays bitterness or petulance, and is, on the contrary, usually characterized by good humor, facetiousness, joy, merriment, gaiety, and playfulness.

Since, as Machiavelli wrote in *Clizia*, "comedy can teach the 'little faith of all men,' then it, too, can do what serious works of politics and moral philosophy do."[35] Here Machiavelli doubled in brass. As a playwright he

penned comedies. As a thinker he wrote "serious works" of political philosophy. Yet, informing these serious works there is a playful attitude, a
winking of the eye, a lilt of laughter, an air of impiety. *The Prince*, for
instance, is written in a familiar, almost offhand and matter-of-fact way, as
if the exiled secretary is in a conversation with a confidant.

Indeed, for all its ferocity, its recommendation of deceit, *The Prince* is
much like the author's plays. He plays with an "as if" world, pointing to
precepts learned from political history and experience; the text, like the play,
can "represent all these things with great honesty," including, again, "the
little faith of all men." Machiavelli's style in *The Prince* is jocose to the point
of sprightly lightheartedness: the serious business of Renaissance politics
he treats as a comic drama, a comedy of errors (including "all those princes
who have done everything they possibly could to get us in such a mess");
he both delights and instructs. Machiavelli as a veteran political functionary
knows politics as a playground of human insanity and inanity, activity to
be approached by sane persons with horror and revulsion—if it weren't so
inevitable, and thereby so funny.

An attitude of political jocosity helps us understand and appreciate
political practice as a comic art, one that requires both political and
aesthetic perspicacity. Machiavelli gives the reader a demystified, insider's
view of politics, demonstrating that what goes on is not only important, it
is also funny. Like love and war, of which Machiavelli also wrote, politics
may be hellish, but this does not mean it is not humorous. There may be
no laughter in Heaven, as Mark Twain said, but there is plenty of reason
for laughter in hell.

Machiavelli's jocose air is not frivolous. True, he shares the frivolity of
the court jester telling truth to power; he tells truth *about* power. But his
perspective is not one of simple amusement. His muse is Thalia, to be sure,
but his "play of musement" is a combination of engrossment in, and
astonishment of, the political life that he lived and watched. His is a
perspective of *comic sagacity*. The play of the comic muse "cures folly by
folly," making sport of the "serious" world revealed to us in all of its
intemperate madness and temperate insanity.

The jocosity of Machiavelli's comic musing returns us to Dionysian
origins of comedy. As with all Dionysian comedy, Machiavelli's perspective
is by nature impious, a reflection, on the "privy of life" where one sits and
contemplates the absurdities of the world. He reminds us that the comic
mythos stresses a world misruled, or perhaps better, *unruled*, by surprise,
chance, and misadventure. Hence, Machiavelli viewed a chaotic world
"under the auspices of Fortuna,"[36] decidedly not under the rule of a lawful
or orderly authority or structure.

The comic world is shifting, dynamic, untidy, and devoid of stability or
predictability; it is comic precisely because it is a world in indeterminate
flux. Comedy, unlike tragedy, has no place in a fixed, closed, determinate

or predestined universe. We laugh because free will makes for hilarious consequences, not criminal consequences but foolish ones. The things that make all of us as human beings comic—our pride, ambition, greed, lust, pretension, stupidity, indecision, prejudice, and so on—are more richly comic if seen on a large and visible political stage where the gigantic nature of mistakes and calamities, foolishness and disasters, *hubris* and catastrophes opens before us in the full glory of comic hilarity.

Four centuries after Machiavelli, Will Rogers, in his innocent yet insightful manner, made Machiavelli's view vivid for Americans. Speaking of jokes, Rogers said, "The thing about my jokes is they don't hurt anybody." After all, "you can say, well, they're funny, or they're terrible, or they're good, or whatever, but they don't do any harm." Then, the punch line: "But with Congress, every time they make a joke it's a law! And every time they make a law, it's a joke."[37]

In Machiavelli's eyes all comedy is political, all politics is comedy. A Lord of Misrule presided majestically (yes, ma*jest*ically), over Dionysian rites of comedy. The celebrants understood that they were making fun of—unmasking—the fundamental pretense of power and authority, returning us to the profanity of the alleged politically sacral, and the sacrilege in profanation of all that is thought holy. Having traveled much and seen much of the exalted and mighty, the powerful and the power-hungry, Old Nick was conversant with the comic perspective by incongruity that sees the jest in majesty. He could see politics from the outside as a grand and astonishing comic pageant, and from the inside as a comedy of familiar actors, the actual lords of misrule who presided over the very real political feast of unreason, conducted the liturgies of political folly, and worshiped asses. His open-eyed comic perspective and firsthand knowledge of the actors involved let him see through the facades and duplicities of politics, and enjoy much the marvelous fool's parade that spread before him.

The political truth in comedy is in its subversion of the symbolic clothing of power and right, desecration of the majesty of rule, reminding us of the wrong of what is asserted as right. The comic truth is that all vested authority is phony, and that all power is rife with danger for those who are powerless. Politics is inherently comic because of its futile attempt to lord it over the unruly, repeating once again the ritual drama of misrule. Rather than bear this with Apollonian sorrow at the eternal tragedy of wrong forever enthroned, however, with a comic perspective we can celebrate the Dionysian song of comic joy, finding delight and rebirth in the mad spectacle of politics that unfolds before us. Observing with Machiavelli's eye the absurdity of politics brings us not to hopeless despair but to truth revealed in the mischievous and irreverent laugh of the comic mask. For the comic political philosopher, perhaps the ultimate political idol is King Canute, the mythical ruler who took the illustrative comic step of setting his throne on the beach and majestically ordering the waves to halt. The Machiavellian comic knows, as most politicians do not (or pretend so), that all the king's horses and all the king's men cannot command the waves of time and chance, yet it is certainly hilarious to watch them try.

So, What's Funny About Democracy?

With Machiavelli's eyes, what do we find in democracies that is comic? Machiavelli admired republics, although he was skeptical enough to see the potential dangers in democratic self-rule: irrationality, demagoguery, vacillation, stalemate, commonness, and many, many more. The seeds of these threats lie in our capacity for self-delusion, an outgrowth of human fallibility. For Machiavelli, democracy cries out for comic analysis because democracy *is* comedy; democratic politics possesses all the flaws of folly depicted in comedy, and all the promises of seasonal resurrection. Yet, there is little comic political analysis, that is, viewing functions, institutions, and processes of democracy from a comic perspective. Rarely are Machiavelli's questions put: (1) What about democracy makes it so comic? (2) What about comedy makes it so democratic?

Democracy, like comedy, exemplifies irony, especially ironic humility. A president dies in office. The vice president assumes the presidency, grieved by the tragedy of the hero's death. The VP ritually adds a dose of self-deprecating humility about not being worthy of the office, of assuming the mantle of the Great One, and of daunting challenges serving a Great People. But the VP protests too much. Ironic humility Kenneth Burke likens to a "gentleman's subtle form of boasting": "He practices long and hard, he becomes an adept, he assures you that he is a veritable tyro—and then you play and he beats you." And "in case you win, that also has been taken care of."[38]

Ironic humility is an essential feature of democracy: politicians proclaim that democracy is rule "of the people, by the people, and for the people." Yet, the results are anything but popular governance. The irony is that the people who rule in democracies do just that: they *rule*—no improvisation, no tolerated imperfection, no fallibility. Ruling is at heart incongruent with democratic aspirations and ideals. No matter what politicians do in the democratic drama, they can never achieve the democratic ideal of popular self-government, for it is politicians who govern. Or even if people did *rule*, that is taken care of too by reneging on the fundamental promise of democracy. Comic irony reigns, that happy sense of contradiction felt by spectators of a drama who see characters acting in innocent yet hilarious ignorance of their condition. Audience members achieve a sense of smug superiority at first—we see the characters' misfortunes even if they don't. But before long the smugness vanishes. We see ourselves in their plights. And with Puck, we think, "What fools these (and we) mortals be."

Hence, the comedy of democracy resides in an ironic incongruity that eternally characterizes popular self-government, always making it less than it could be, bedeviling our hopes for human political fulfillment of the New Man beyond the cursedness of the Old Adam. The drama of "rule of the people" plays out over and over again in ignorance of its own comic flaw, the flaw being not so much that democracy doesn't work as that *it never gets tried*. The ultimate irony of democracy is that, as practiced, democracy rests on a flaw: *democracy can only work if it doesn't work, survive and endure only if its principles are violated*. Democracy asks too much of us, so we pass the buck; consequently, as always, the few still rule the many, even in democracies, not by force, but by manipulating and undermining the consent of the governed.

And what are those democratic principles of which we speak? They are, as Niccolo Machiavelli mused, the same principles on which comedy rests: accept human fallibility and imperfection; accept that humans make errors and are involved in a comedy of errors; apply the corrective of standing back, being fearlessly tolerant, viewing things from all angles, and exercising civility; be irreverent toward all "perfect" solutions; ridicule politicians, without inflicting pain, not because they claim to commit heroic, albeit horrendous, deeds, but because they are foolish; recognize that in the merriment of civil discourse all things may be born again; and above all, enjoy the wondrous spectacle.

Yet, these very comedic and democratic principles generate suspicion, and certainly contempt. Why? A simple reason. If human beings are fallible creatures addicted to folly, merrymaking, and improvising in making their private lives tolerable—if they are clowns—then how can weighty public matters be left to *them?? The noted debunker of democracy, H. L. Mencken, expressed the fatal flaw aphoristically: "Democracy is the theory that the common people know what they want, and deserve to get it good and hard . . . the art and science of running the circus from the monkey-cage."*[39] The sneaking suspicion of the comic is that the rulers of democracies, the people, make democracy into what it is, a democratic comedy that ironically undermines itself by the foolish limitations and decisions of its rulers. People choose to rule their own personal lives with varying degrees of maturity and competence; but when it comes to collective rule of a democratic state, this always seems to be outside the ken of people's lives and purviews. *Thus someone else, often themselves fools or scoundrels, rule in the people's stead.*

In the end, "serious" democracy is not tried for the same reason that comedy is frequently dismissed as frivolous and trivial: *both are subversive.* Each ridicules the histrionics of thespian political elites who regard their elaborate productions and stagings as deadly serious: to preserve democracy against the threat of the fools not competent to practice it. How? By assuring that it is not practiced at all! People are told, and come to believe, that the only way to preserve democracy is to refrain from practicing it.

People are in favor of freedom of speech, for instance, until someone tries to practice it. And one can imagine, from the point of view of power structures, how terrifying the prospect of "full participation" is; if everyone voted, and articulated demands at party meetings and congressional hearings, the system would be in danger. If we demanded that schools, corporations, unions, hospitals, media outlets, and governments be truly democratic, then these systems of power would be in danger. In other words, *if democracy worked, it would not work; and to the extent it doesn't work, it does*. That arrangement makes for a comedy of democracy, a persistent ideal never tried.

RAISING THE COMIC CURTAIN

Hereafter we take a comic stance toward the institutions, processes, rituals, and policies of contemporary democracy in the United States. However, since the authors are not comedians, nor writing comedy per se, the improvisation is restricted. Comic musings adhere to a plot. The plot unfolds in two acts. Act One plays out "The Political Comedies of Citizenship." It is divided into a quartet of scenes, each scene constituting a separate chapter of this book. Respectively the chapters depict the comic side of how citizens take part in politics, vote in elections, voice public opinions, and strive to become politically informed. Act Two presents "The Political Comedies of Policy Makers." Its four chapters deal respectively with the comic aspects of the presidency, legislative deliberation, government bureaucracy, and American justice. No comedy of democracy would be complete without an epilogue. "Exit Laughing" reminds readers of the importance of taking seriously both comic democracy and democratic comedy.

To paraphrase the closing couplet of Machiavelli's prologue to *Clizia*: Dear readers, adieu, you've heard our plot: Now let our tangled thread unknot.

NOTES

1. Quoted in J. Tebbel, *The Media in America*. (New York: New American Library/Mentor Books, 1974), p. 300.

2. Quoted in Bryan B. Sterling and Frances N. Sterling, *Will Rogers' World*. (New York: M. Evans and Co., 1989), pp. 66, 81, 137, 155.

3. W. C. Fields, *Fields for President* (New York: Dodd, Mead, 1940), p. 17.

4. Aristotle, *De Poetica*, in Richard McKeon, ed., *Introduction to Aristotle* (New York: Modern Library, 1947), p. 624.

5. Kenneth Burke, *Attitudes Toward History*, 3rd ed. (Berkeley: University of California Press, 1989), pp. 34–39.

6. Oscar G. Brockett, *The Theatre: An Introduction* (New York: Holt, Rinehart and Winston, 1964), pp. 50–93.

7. Aristotle, *De Poetica*, p. 630.

8. Ibid.

9. Among the numerous efforts by social and behavioral scientists to define the nature, origins, and functions of laughter, humor, and comedy, consult the following: Jeffrey H. Goldstein and Paul E. McGhee, eds., *The Psychology of Humor* (New York: Academic Press, 1972); Arthur Asa Berger, *An Anatomy of Humor* (New Brunswick, NJ: Transaction, 1993); D. E. Berlyne, "Laughter, Humor and Play," in Gardner Lindzey and Elliot Aronson, eds., *The Handbook of Social Psychology*, 5 vols., 2nd ed. (Reading, MA: Addison Wesley, 1969), 3: 795–852; M. Charney, *Comedy High and Low: An Introduction to the Experience of Comedy* (New York: Oxford University Press, 1978); A. Roy Eckardt, *Sitting in the Earth and Laughing* (New Brunswick, NJ: Transaction, 1992); Charles R. Gruner, *Understanding Laughter: The Workings of Wit and Humor* (Chicago: Nelson-Hall, 1978); and, of course, Sigmund Freud, *Jokes and Their Relation to the Unconscious*, trans. and ed. James Strachey (New York: W. W. Norton, 1960).

10. Thus, for example, Eckardt, *Sitting in the Earth*, pp. 1–11, catalogues "Ten Primordial Jokes"; and Berger, *Anatomy of Humor*, pp. 18–55, elaborates over forty specific techniques of humor.

11. E. B. White, *The Second Tree from the Corner* (New York: Harper and Row Perennial Library, 1989), p. 173.

12. Burke, *Attitudes*, p. 49. Emphasis in original.

13. B. Jowett, *The Dialogues of Plato*, in Mortimer Adler, ed., *Great Books of the Western World* (Chicago: Encyclopedia Britannica, 1952), 7: 255.

14. Although he lived to be seventy-eight, Swift was long plagued with giddiness and deafness. He suffered a paralytic stroke, sank into total mental apathy, and died in 1745. His fortune he left to found a lunatic asylum. He dictated that the inscription on his tombstone memorialize the "savage indignation" that could no longer "lacerate his heart." Disastrous consequences indeed. "Biographical Note: Jonathan Swift, 1667–1745," in Adler, *Great Books of the Western World* (Chicago: Encyclopedia Britannica, 1952), 36: x.

15. Burke, *Attitudes*, p. 55.

16. H. L. Mencken, *A Mencken Chrestomathy* (New York: Alfred A. Knopf, 1956), pp. 243–248.

17. Burke, *Attitudes, p. 39.*

18. John F. Kennedy, quoted in William Safire, *Safire's Political Dictionary* (New York: Ballantine Books, 1980), p. 315.

19. Wylie Sypher, "The Meanings of Comedy," in Robert W. Corrigan, ed., *Comedy: Meaning and Form (San Francisco: Chandler, 1965), pp. 18–60; also Francis Cornford, The Origin of Attic Comedy* (Cambridge: Cambridge University Press, 1914).

20. Aristotle, *De Poetica*, p. 631.

21. Sypher, "Meanings of Comedy," p. 36.

22. Hugh D. Duncan, *Communication and Social Order* (New York: Oxford University Press, 1962), p. 406.

23. Burke, *Attitudes,* pp. 41–42. Emphasis in original.

24. Murray S. Davis, "Sociology Through Humor," *Symbolic Interaction* 2 (Spring 1979): 107.

25. Georgie Anne Geyer, "Our 'Internal Exile,' " *Dallas Morning News*, December 7, 1993, p. 13A.

26. Burke, *Attitudes*, p. 173.

27. Ibid., p. 168.

28. See "Machiavelli the Working Democrat," in Robert M. Adams, ed. and trans., *The Prince* (New York: W. W. Norton, 1977), pp. 79–92.

29. Niccolo Machiavelli, *The Mandrake Root*, in David Sices and James B. Atkinson, eds., *The Comedies of Machiavelli* (London: University Press of New England, 1985), p. 159.

30. Carnes Lord, "On Machiavelli's *Mandragola*," *Journal of Politics* 41 (1979): 810.

31. Niccolo Machiavelli, *Clizia*, in Sices and Atkinson, *Comedies of Machiavelli*, pp. 283–284.

32. Lord, "Machiavelli's *Mandragola*," p. 807.

33. Burke, *Attitudes*, p. 43. Emphasis in original.

34. "Machiavelli the Correspondent," in Adams, *The Prince*, pp. 133–134.

35. Sabastian de Grazia, *Machiavelli in Hell* (Princeton: Princeton University Press, 1989), pp. 325–326.

36. Sypher, "Meanings of Comedy," p. 49.

37. Quoted in Sterling and Sterling, *Will Rogers' World*, pp. 49–50.

38. Burke, *Attitudes*, p. 48.

39. H. L. Mencken, *Chrestomathy*, p. 622.

PART I

The Political Comedies of
Citizenship

CHAPTER 1

The Citizen's Role in Democracy:
A Romantic Comedy

As Niccolo Machiavelli was writing his comedy, *The Mandrake Root* (c. 1504–1520), a drama of a different sort was popular with audiences elsewhere. In the late fifteenth and early sixteenth centuries morality plays flourished. These works celebrated the religious and spiritual trials of average people, much as the New Comedy celebrated human foibles. Although the title may today appear politically incorrect, one of the most enduring of such plays has been *Everyman* (c. 1500). It dealt with a problem all persons, regardless of gender, face: the inevitability of death. The lead character, Everyman, prepares for death by searching among his lifetime companions for someone to travel with him down death's road. Kindred, Goods, Beauty, Strength, Discretion, Five Wits—not one of his old chums will take the journey. Each declares no, no, I will not go. Only Good Deeds goes with Everyman to help prepare for salvation, that is, rebirth through death.

Few would label the plot of *Everyman* as comic. A fable about a person preparing to die is scarcely cheerful, as Dirty Harry made clear when he made his macho declaration, "Make my day." Yet, in certain respects *Everyman* possesses comic elements. Clearly there is irony in finding that our bosom buddies in whom we take so much pride in life, especially Beauty and Strength, forsake us when the going gets tough. And what can be more comic in tone than to replay again the entire cycle of Everyman's dilemma of fertility? For beyond birth, growth, and death, he seeks resurrection, the defining ingredient of Dionysian comedy. As with all good comedy, there is the promise in *Everyman* that Everyone, warts and all, survives foibles, errors, imperfections, and absurdities.

Such optimism embraces a romantic feature. How readily the giddy-headed lover overlooks the flaws in the beloved, and in oneself as well. Love, after all, conquers all. As the oft-quoted homily from a wildly popular Hollywood film of the 1960s, *Love Story*, said, "Love is never having to say you're sorry." There is nothing to be sorry about! We all know the celluloid fantasy of romance: lovers in slow motion, aching and frantic, racing . . . toward . . . one . . . another . . . along . . . the . . . beach . . . toward . . . fertile touching . . . and . . . the magic of fulfilling EMBRACE. Permanence without change. Life everlasting. If *Democracy* as a romantic comedy were now playing at a theater near you, what would its citizens cum characters look like?

THE COMEDY OF CIVIL ROMANCE

William Shakespeare died in 1616. One of his many lasting contributions to drama was the romantic comedy. Although he did not invent this particular form, he perfected and glorified it for Elizabethan audiences. *Love's Labours Lost, Twelfth Night,* and *As You Like It* became exemplars of romantic comedy for generations of future playwrights. Shakespeare's comedies depict lovers pursuing their courtship; suddenly, and due to no malice of their own, they find their happiness threatened by the ridiculous misunderstandings and boisterous shenanigans of well-meaning but erring friends, family, and servants. By making the lovers themselves so maddeningly lovable, Shakespeare impels audiences to sympathize with the *romantic* amours of the leading actors; the ridicule of the audience is heaped on the *comic* bumblings of the minor characters. Hence the term "romantic comedy" for the dramatic form.[1]

Two centuries after Shakespeare, roughly between 1800 and 1850, a new sense of romantic longing swept the artistic world. Many of the writers who were part of this Romantic movement yearned to throw off the restraints on imagination and intuition that they believed marked eithteenth century thinking; moreover, they questioned the rightness of the reigning social and political order. So they sought new dramatic forms that would give free flow to the creative juices. In Shakespeare's works, especially the romantic comedies, they found the freedom from restraint they sought.

What this period of romantic musing helped to introduce to thinking about Everyman was an emphasis on the individual as the center of all life and experience. The romantic belief stressed that each individual should be guided by natural instincts; those instincts would lead each person to right feelings and right actions. Just as Shakespeare's lovers were good, sympathetic characters foiled by the foolish interferences of outsiders, so too would the laudable goals of Everyman be achieved by liberating the individual from the meddling restrictions of forms, laws, institutions, and customs imposed by a doddering, decaying, and dying social and political order.

There is clearly a strain of the sentimental in all of this, if by sentimental we mean "an overemphasis upon arousing sympathetic response to the misfortune of others."[2] The principals in romantic comedies, whether the lovers depicted by Shakespeare or the liberated individuals in the comedies of the Romantic movement, are good and righteous people. We have no problem identifying with them as sympathetic characters. We commiserate with their plights. The minor characters—neighbors, parents, butlers, maids, press agents, and assorted hangers-on—draw our guffaws. Well before there was a Hollywood, romantic comedy projected a conception of Happy Endings with Good People free to frolic on the Beach of Life. They never had to say they were sorry; only the comic meddlers apologize. It is a comic vision readily transferred to democracy.

A Sentimental View of the Good Citizen

The romantic comedy portrays sympathetic lead characters in all their sentimental goodness. Good People populate romantic comedies, their natural righteousness stymied only by buffooneries not of their own creation. The comedy of democracy assigns precisely such a sympathetic, and sentimentalized, role to the Good Citizen. Consider this sentiment-laced comment by Alexis de Tocqueville after his travels through the frontier democracy of Andrew Jackson. Tocqueville is addressing the topic "Why it can strictly be said that the people govern in the United States." In America, he writes, "the people appoint both those who make the laws and those who execute them; the people form the jury which punishes breaches of the law." Americans directly nominate their representatives and choose them, generally annually, "so as to hold them more completely dependent."

Then, in a sympathetic vein, Tocqueville speaks of happy endings:

So direction really comes from the people, and though the form of government is representative, it is clear that the opinions, prejudices, interests, and even passions of the people can find no lasting obstacles preventing them from being manifest in the daily conduct of society.

Finally, the "majority rules in the name of the people." It is a majority "chiefly composed of," like Shakespearean lovers, "peaceful citizens who by taste or interest sincerely desire the well-being of the country." And, also like Shakespeare's lovers "they are surrounded by the constant agitation of parties seeking to draw them in and to enlist their support."[3]

Tocqueville's portrayal, however, is not the ode to democratic civics that it appears. With his unique brand of wry, dry wit, the visitor from France to Jacksonian America was having some fun. The "strictly" in his announced intentions tips off Tocqueville's ironic agenda. Strict implies precise, absolute, give-no-quarter rigidity. To be sure, there are some parents, teachers, military martinets, hanging judges, and guardians of etiquette who brook no violations of the Law. But more often than not, strictly belongs with the "could'aves, would'aves, and should'aves" of life.

A synonym of strict is "unerring." But who can say errors don't invade democratic politics? If they didn't we would not have had former U.S. Senator Gary Hart, after the press publicized his extramarital affair with Donna Rice in 1987, telling the decreasing numbers who cared to listen that, strictly speaking, without the publicity he could have, would have, and should have been elected president in 1988. And, yes, strictly speaking the hare should have beaten the tortoise.

Tocqueville's use of "strictly" keys his audience to the fact that what he is about to say is *not* the way it is. He's letting us in on the joke. And what's the joke? It is that Tocqueville knows, and his wink at the audience permits *us* to know, that the people he describes *don't* govern in the United States. Why? Because the democratic view of the Good Citizen is a romanticized, sentimentalized fantasy. That Good Citizens, like lovers in romantic comedy, are "peaceful citizens who by taste or interest sincerely desire the well-being of the country" is a laudable romantic notion. However, the fiction masks the fact that if these peaceful citizens are truly to govern, they must form majorities, for in the United States, as Tocqueville has said, the majority rules. Therein lies the rub. For majority rule, according to de Tocqueville, is the antithesis of popular rule by the Good Citizen: "What I find most repulsive in America is not the extreme freedom reigning there but the shortage of guarantees against tyranny."[4]

What is a majority, in its collective capacity, if not an *individual* with opinions, and usually with interests, contrary to those of another *individual*, called the minority? Now if you admit that a man vested with omnipotence can abuse it against his adversaries, why not admit the same concerning a majority? Have men by joining together become more patient of obstacles? For my part, I cannot believe that, and I will never grant to several that power to do everything which I refuse to a single man.[5]

Hence, the comic incongruity: American democracy, like romantic comedy, celebrates the individual. The individual is the peaceful citizen sincere in a desire for the "well-being of the country." To advance that well-being citizens form ruling majorities in response to "the constant agitation" (i.e., boisterous, comic behavior) of political parties who seek support. But, as Tocqueville asks, "how can one deny that a party" can be tyrannical "toward a another party?"[6] (Or, in comic terms, how can one deny the political party is anything more than a well-meaning yet error-prone bunch of bumbling meddlers, akin to the families and friends who stick their noses into the affairs of Shakespeare's guileless lovers?) America's peaceful citizens grant power to the several that they would refuse to grant to a single citizen. Hence, the irony: the Good Citizen is not the subject of the Good Citizen, but is subject to the more whimsical rule of a ruling majority of meddlers.

If all citizens were the Good Citizen, of course, there would be no need for democracy; rather, power could be shared equally, an isocracy. Or, as James Madison wrote in *The Federalist Papers*, Number 51, "If men were angels no government would be necessary."[7] Tocqueville, however, went beyond Madison; he understood Pascal's comic view of human nature: "Man is neither angel nor brute; and the misfortune is that he who would act the angel acts the brute."[8] So, too, in a democracy one who would act the angel, namely, the Good Citizen, acts instead the brute, through majority rule.

So Tocqueville was not alone in pointing out the ironic contradictions between the romantic ideals of democratic citizenship and the comic realities. In the mid-twentieth century when political scientists started to take themselves seriously as scientists rather than as just another garden variety of historians, legal scholars, or philosophers, they grew perplexed at the gulf between the Good Citizens required, in democratic theory, to make American democracy work, and the kind of Indifferent Citizens they kept stumbling across in their empirical research. *Strictly* speaking, given the kinds of citizens found to be populating America, democracy could not, should not, and would not exist.[9]

For example, in principle, "the democratic citizen is expected to be interested and to participate in political affairs."[10] That means that citizens argue politics, get involved in electoral campaigns, join political groups, donate money, and vote. In practice, most Americans don't even get a political itch, let alone scratch it: less than half try to influence the political views of other citizens through discussion. Not even one in ten take part in political campaigns. To be sure, Tocqueville was right when he wrote, "Americans of all ages, all conditions, and all dispositions constantly form associations," but those groups are rarely political; they "make associations to give entertainments, to found seminaries, to build inns, to construct churches, to diffuse books, to send missionaries to the antipodes . . . [to] found hospitals, prisons, schools."[11] Yet, actual membership in a political club or organization appeals to only a fraction (2–5 percent).

Americans are generous with their dollars; in 1991 almost three-quarters of American households gave to charitable causes; the average amount was $900.[12] But when it comes to coughing up money to political causes, think again, for only one in ten open their pockets to specific candidates and parties. Moreover, the income tax checkoff instituted in 1971 scarcely collects sufficient revenue from volunteering citizens to meet the federal obligation to allocate funds to qualifying presidential candidates and political parties. Finally, America's Good Citizens are nonvoters: about one-half vote in presidential contests, lower proportions still in the plethora of federal, state, and local elections.

In the strict sense the Good Citizen is knowledgeable and informed about politics. So too, in the strict sense, any baseball thrown over home plate between a batter's knees and armpits is a strike. Umpires seldom call anything above the beltline (some of which are ample) a strike; so, also, citizens seldom are bookwise about politics. Periodically major polling organizations measure the level of political knowledge of Americans. The loud sound heard after the release of the findings of those surveys is that of the Founding Fathers whirling in their graves. One of the deals the Fathers were forced to cut in order to get the 1787 Constitution ratified was to add a Bill of Rights. Today surveys indicate that less than half (in some polls only a third) of Americans know that the first ten amendments to the Constitution are called the Bill of Rights. Fewer than a third of Americans can name the two U.S. Senators from their state; fewer than a third can name their own U.S. congressional representative.[13] Imagine how James Madison's bones rattle when a Gallup Poll announces that large portions of Americans think the three branches of government are the President, House of Representatives, and Senate!

Nor are citizens likely to be any more knowledgeable when it comes to selecting their public officials, a gap between democratic ideals and practices that contributes to the comedy of humors surrounding elections. (See Chapter 2.) For instance, *two days after* the 1976 presidential election only 58 percent of respondents in a nationwide survey knew the names of the two major political parties' candidates for vice president.[14] Will Rogers prophesied this state of ignorance and indifference decades earlier: "No voter can remember back a year. What happened in the last six months is as far as his mind can grasp."[15] (Things apparently have gotten worse since Will left us.)

The litany of specific differences between the Good Citizen of theory and the Indifferent Citizen of practice goes on and on: the democratic citizen is supposed to cast votes on the basis of principle, but chooses instead on the basis of impulse and habit; the democratic citizen should have a strong motivation to take part in political life, but motivation is more typically weak or nonexistent; the democratic citizen must grapple with key issues and reach decisions, but opinion polls show large blocs who don't know or don't care; and the democratic citizen should act in the name of the common good, not, as most do, for selfish interests. In the end we have a parody of the popular TV game show, *Family Feud*. It goes, "Democratic theory says . . . " and "Our surveys say. . . ." A loud horn sounds and an X crosses the game board. Lost again!

Why Good Citizens Are Politically Indifferent:
The Sentimental View

Faced with the discrepancies between theory and research, political scientists invented clever, and romantically comical, ways to preserve a sympathetic vision of the citizen. One was to say that the qualities that citizens actually possess as characters in the democratic plot are far less important than the plot itself. In scholarly jargon, so long as the system was democratic, citizens did not need to be democratic themselves. A second approach to salvaging a romantic view of democratic civics was to identify the specific minor characters and flaws in the plot, the buffoons, that force otherwise outrageously lovable citizens to be disappointments in the first place.

In the first instance researchers argued that, strictly speaking, if all citizens acted consistently as Good Citizens it might actually constitute a *threat* to democratic survival:

How could a mass democracy work if all the people were deeply involved in politics? Lack of interest by some people is not without its benefits too. . . . Extreme interest goes with extreme partisanship and might culminate in rigid fanaticism that could destroy democratic processes if generalized throughout the community . . . an important balance between action motivated by strong sentiments and action with little passion . . . is, in practice, met by a distribution of voters rather than a homogeneous collection of "ideal" citizens.[16]

What a blessing! And it is even more bountiful. When people are occupied by matters other than politics—mowing the lawn, coaching Little League, hitting the Las Vegas Strip, jostling about at Disney World, pigging out at McDonalds—there is a social bonding that lends stability to the polity. Add to this the fact that Americans are not "deeply concerned, well-integrated, consistently-principled ideal citizens"[17] and there is another benefit: they may pig out, but they're not pig-headed. The bad news is that people are politically indifferent. The good news is that indifference makes possible political flexibility. Indifference promises progress amid conservation (or conservation amid progress), consensus amid conflict (or conflict amid consensus).

Needless to say, this discovery of a silver lining in a cloudbank of disappointment did not set well with all political observers. It worked a happy ending to the romantic comedy of the Good Citizen that was just a tad too facile, a comic *deus ex machina*. So other political savants and reformers looked elsewhere, striving to rehabilitate a sympathetic view of the democratic citizen so ravaged by empirical findings. Turning a line from Shakespeare's *Julius Caesar* on its axis, they found that the fault lies not in the heirs of Brutus but in the stars. The obstacles to the romantic happiness of citizenship resided in factors over which the citizen had no control: one's age, gender, socioeconomic class, ethnicity, race, health, wealth, education, family ties, locale of residence, etc., etc., etc.—the cast of characters that fouled up democratic romance grew endless.

Thus, for example, citizens are buffeted by the times, good and bad. Like romantic lovers in Hollywood's screwball comedies in the Great Depression, citizens are "ragged and funny" even if they "ain't got a barrel of money." Will Rogers opined, with respect to the times, that "voters go to the polls and if their stomachs are full, they keep the guy that's already in; and if the old stomach is empty, they vote to chuck him out."[18] That says something about how times affect voting *if* people vote. But do the times keep people from voting at all, or even caring about politics?

By probing extensive sources of data regarding how people respond to the stress of the times, using the most sophisticated legerdemain of statistical analysis, political researchers confirmed what film addicts suspected: personal problems, such as economic adversity, lead people to pay less attention to politics. Bad times alienate us; "data suggest a depoliticization effect of personal stresses." Now that's the bad news about the bad times. Here's the bad news about the good times: when things are going well, people don't need to worry, so they go after private pleasures and achievement, and turn away from politics to leisure. "Thus a nice irony. Bad times and good times alike can affect people and assist them in paying less attention to politics."[19] Hence, as Machiavelli argued, fickle *fortuna*, which he thought governed half of everything in our lives, cuts both ways. And either way it works to reduce the cadre of Good Citizens.

Three decades of political research have also corroborated that there are other children of *fortuna* that rob democratic citizenship of romance, namely, bad health and death. Will Rogers was making fun when he said voters go one way with full stomachs, another when hungry. Yet, there is more than a gram of truth in his observation. Nutrition and citizenship are related. Political interest, participation, efficacy—all decline as nutritional levels drop. (Good nutrition, however, is not gluttony. No one has yet established that an appreciable increase in political participation in the United States belches forth as a result of billions and billions of burgers served.) The evidence from political research is, not surprisingly, convincing that people with serious health problems don't worry a great deal about politics. And, again not surprisingly, lingering anxieties about one's death are associated with increased feelings about life's meaninglessness and one's own powerlessness, not with political involvement. So, had Good Citizen been among Everyman's lifelong comrades, that crony too would have declined to tag along to death.

Certainly one could argue with conviction that the times people live in, how they eat, their medical histories, and their share of life-threatening calamities are not completely matters of comedy's fickle fortune. There is research to support the argument. The "haves" not only weather the times

well, eat well, are relatively healthy, and survive disasters, they also conform to the image of the Good Citizen: politically interested, involved,
informed, motivated, principled, and so on. Stress, malnutrition, illness,
and death anxiety come with being "have-nots." So too does being an
Indifferent Citizen. The inventory of factors in people's everyday lives that
make them personal and political have-nots is well documented. The
caricature is almost romantic in its empirical simplicity. It too reminds us
of Everyman's companions (Goods, Strength, Beauty, Discretion, Five Wits)
refusing to accompany him on his trip to death. Everyhave-not, preparing
for politics, suffers rejection from Uneducated, Low Class, Unemployed,
Low Income, Female, Black, Hispanic, Rural, Inner City, and Broken Family.
Only Indifference travels the road with Everyhave-not.

Yet, a Machiavellian muse would say, "Wait. Count *Fortuna*, in the visage
of Misfortune, as a companion of Everyhave-not." For one of the most
primordial of jokes, the basis of so much comedy—especially romantic
comedy—is "The Absence of Any Say in One's Birth." After all, no one asks
to be born. ("It would be odd if one *could* so ask—a joke against the Joke."[20])
And certainly no one asks to be born a have-not. The have-not, along with
anyone else, has the trial of making the best of things. One way to do it is
to weep at one's misfortunes. Another is to laugh at the folly of it all, at the
tricks of companions like Uneducated or Unemployed. It is the stuff of
romantic comedy to choose the latter, for thereby the basic incongruities
that comprise the comedy of democracy are exposed in all their Marx
Brothers' clarity.

There are, however, a couple of difficulties with conjectures that the Good
Citizen, like a Shakespearean lover, is admirable, romantic, and sympathetic, and that indifference springs from the jokes played by dicey birth
and social circumstance. One is that Americans don't actually think of
society as composed of haves and have-nots. Seven in ten Americans see
their nation as one of haves; and fewer than two in ten Americans think of
themselves as have-nots.[21] The obvious response to that fact is that perhaps
people simply don't know how miserable they are. Maybe that very ignorance of their objective condition makes them indifferent. After all, Will
Rogers said, "When ignorance gets started, it knows no bounds."[22] Yet,
fingering Ignorance as the comic sprite who makes Good Citizens indifferent is but another *deus ex machina* in the romantic fantasy. (It also produces
a double bind: "The reason you are indifferent is that you don't know how
bad off you are; if you *knew* how bad off you are, you would be indifferent!)

A second difficulty is that regardless of circumstances of fortuitous
nativity, for good or ill, both Good and Indifferent Citizens are made as well
as born. It would be ironic if it were the case, but is it possible that Americans
grow up being taught that to be a good citizen one should be indifferent?
Perhaps so. The plot that is the romantic comedy of U.S. citizenship assigns
minor, but certainly comical, roles to what political scientists call "agents"

of political socialization. These are the character actors who teach citizens, from cradle to grave, what citizenship is all about. What do they teach? Harkening back to Tocqueville, it can *strictly* be said that it is a catechism of the Good Citizen; it can *ironically* be said that it is a guidebook on becoming an Indifferent.

We'll confine ourselves for the moment to the political catechism of the family and schools, delaying consideration of what the news media teach until Chapter 3. Decades of research identifying what children learn about politics from Mom, Dad, Bro, and Sis painted an admirable, and romantic, almost a "Father Knows Best" picture of political learning. Haves and have-nots differed in specifics, but the overall findings were that children learn basics from their families: a sense of what it is to be a patriotic American rather than British, French, and so on; that the president personifies abstract "Government," the policeman embodies abstract "Law"—and good citizens respect both. Children also acquire an emotional loyalty to a political party, Democratic or Republican, in the loving confines of the family cocoon. The irony is that each of these fundamentals indoctrinates children in a defensive, not active, political role.

For example, long before there was scientific evidence to support him, Tocqueville understood that the "irritable patriotism of the Americans" derived more from selfish than community interest: the American "feels a duty to defend anything criticized there, for it is not only his country that is being attacked, but himself; hence one finds that his national pride has recourse to every artifice and descends to every childishness of personal vanity."[23] Respect for governing authority and the law, embodied in presidents and police, emphasizes the value of deferential, conformist politics, not the involved pursuit of change. Moreover, an electorate voting out of party loyalty is scarcely the principled, rational electorate of democratic theory.

Formal schooling strictly posits a romantic vision of citizenship while actually teaching indifference. In the elementary years civics courses assign importance to respect for political persons—chiefly the president, governor, mayor, and legislator. And although H. L. Mencken noted satirically that "there are no institutions in America: there are only fashions,"[24] American school children do learn about Congress, the Supreme Court, and other institutions. However, the romantic emphasis in political learning remains on individual, rather than collective, politics: "Children's evaluation of pressure groups is generally negative, and knowledge of the most efficient channels of influence is limited. They believe in *individualized* access to power—an unrealistic viewpoint, particularly in a rapidly expanding society."[25] As students enter secondary schools, the civics curriculum, with its required textbooks approved for adoption by higher authority, offers additional indoctrination in "don't rock the boat" politics. Textbooks, here and at the college level, are much like sex manuals—in the name of romance all is sanitized and mechanized.

Perhaps, then, agents of political socialization, more so than circumstances of birth, health, socioeconomic status, or other attributes, warrant star billing as the mischievous sprites of citizenship's romantic comedy just as Puck was of Shakespeare's *Midsummer Night's Dream*. If so, they are not alone, for politicians are spritely little Ariels as well.

COMIC EMBARRASSMENT IN AMERICAN POLITICS

The romantic comedy of democratic citizenship masks more incongruities than those between the romanticized Good Citizens of theory and the prosaic Indifferents of practiced politics. It also addresses the incongruities inherent in the relationship between political actors and audiences, between politicians and citizens in a democracy. If citizens can be convinced that they are Good, not Indifferent, then politicians as representatives of Good Citizens are thereby Good too. A romanticized version of citizenship is essential to the democratic politician's longevity, just as a romanticized notion of lovers is essential to the continued employment of meddling, intrusive, bumbling servants.

In one political critic's view, the relationship between democratic politicians and citizens constitutes a "Theatre of Embarrassment," where an audiences is made to *feel* it is "participating or overhearing the extremely painful scene taking place on the stage."[26] Pain in tragic plots appears as sorrow or remorse, but in comic staging pain can be the ludicrous or ridiculous. When a close and dear friend, for example, commits a public faux pas (tsk, tsk, say, gets a little tipsy and knocks over the wineglass, spilling chablis on the boss), one may feel embarrassed at the misfortune. It is the ludicrous, not pathetic, quality in the situation that provokes our mortification.

To be sure, many would prefer that politics inspire, that it elevate citizens to lofty and heroic heights. Sometimes, especially during times of crisis, politicians put out such a call. That was so during the Battle of Britain in World War II; Prime Minister Winston Churchill asked for self-sacrifice from the English, in their "finest hour." And in his inaugural address, President John F. Kennedy won rave notices for his clarion call to Americans: "Ask not what your country can do for you; ask what you can do for your country." But more often than not, the "local scale of our concerns gives an earthy symmetry to our reactions" to "appeals to the collective soul." On a regular basis such inspirational appeals "appear cheap or positively fraudulent," falling on one's ears like the pleas of the little boy who cried "Wolf!" The day-to-day grind of politics is less heroic than embarrassing. Politicians, however, can't admit that, at least not in public: "Only bad art produces the unfiltered 'slices of life,' dumped raw and fetid in our laps."[27]

What politicians can do in approaching citizens for their enthusiastic support, without spilling the beans and cheapening appeals to the collective soul, is to mask embarrassment as romance. Humor, Kenneth Burke notes, is the opposite of the heroic. The heroic works through "magnification," that is, it makes the hero's character as expansive as the situation faced. Humor, says Burke, reverses the process by dwarfing the situation to the feeble capacities of those who cope with it. Romantic humor achieves dwarfing by claiming that the situations that threaten the amorous goals of lovers (or Good Citizens) are not only no fault of the lovers, but are actually no big deal; they derive instead from ridiculous antics flowing from the happy stupidity of friends, servants, family, and other childish actors.

Romantic humor is "close to sentimentality";[28] no one need be embarrassed by indifferent citizenship since that is not really the problem. The politicians' message is that the problems of democracy stem from the skylarking and escapades of the hillbillies in Beverly Hills or the inmates on Gilligan's Island. The gravity of life may fail to register on these happy fools, but that does not mean the democratic citizen is any less virtuous, or more indifferent, than democratic ideals say.

In his bid for the presidency in 1976, Jimmy Carter (at first derided in the press as "Jimmy Who?") restaged the drama of American politics from theater of embarrassment to theater of romantic comedy. What with the pain of the Vietnam War and the torment of the Watergate scandal, the 1970s had witnessed an ample ration of the politics of embarrassment. The slices of life, war, and corruption that were dumped raw and fetid in citizens' laps in the seventies left them embarrassed but humiliated. Carter's message: America's citizens are intrinsically good; they should suffer no hangdog sorrow. The feeble folly of America's leaders, servants of the people, had indeed produced threatening times. But not to worry and not to fear, for conditions were not so grave that they could not be cut down to size by a government of Good Citizens rather than Bad Politicians. Carter promised "a government as good as its people," a two-pack that sentimentally elevated the worth of citizens and dwarfed the embarrassment provoked by a demoralizing war and a cancerous scandal.

One thing people want, which they feel they miss, is being spoken for. They want to hear their hopes crystallized into words, dramatised, if you like, made tangible.
     They want to hear a tune they can whistle . . . a tune that makes sense in their life, and the life of their country.[29]

By converting embarrassment into romance Carter gave Americans a tune they could whistle in 1976. But comedy involves irony and the very coupling of romance with comedy intensifies the irony. A short three years after his courtship of Good Citizens in his presidential bid, President Jimmy Carter turned from being suitor to scold. Roundly criticized by members of the opposition party, his own party, and pundits in the news media as ineffective and incompetent, Carter used a major speech to unmask the Goodness of Citizenship of 1976 as the Indifference of Malaise in 1979. Here was citizenry suffering from a "crisis of confidence"—distrustful of government, politically suspicious, self-centered, and alienated. Unfortunately for his aims of rallying support, Carter's tune proved embarrassing and, in 1980, went unwhistled by the electorate. Instead, they harkened to Ronald Reagan's pipings of a resurrected economy and reborn patriotism; like the Seven Dwarfs, they whistled while they worked.

DEMOCRATIC CIVICS AND COMIC INDIFFERENCE

There is another way to look at the romantic comedy of democratic citizenship. It is to envision indifferent citizenship as an admirable, rational, indeed *essential* quality of popular democracy. How can such comic civics be justified?

A romantic requirement of democratic civics is that citizens and government in the comic drama love one another. Jimmy Carter voiced the sentimental principle that the relationship between citizens and government should be amorous; America should have a government as good as its people, and a people as good as its government. Americans, however, as Carter was to learn, are not enamored with government; nor do they believe governing officials are enamored with them. If public opinion polls are correct, three of every four Americans "trust government in Washington to do the right thing" not always, but "only some of the time." Three-fourths of Americans say government is "pretty much run by a few big interests"; 60 percent say government is often incompetent. Four in ten Americans think congressional officials spend more time worrying about their future than they do passing wise legislation, and seven in ten disapprove of the way Congress is handling its job. Finally, well over half express the view that "I'm mad as hell about the way things are going in this country these days."[30]

If this is how Americans think of government as a lover, why should citizens continue the assignation? Why date someone who continually disappoints, even abuses? Why yield to the amorous seductions of a gigolo? Of course, citizens could be wrong; government as a suitor might not be the good for nothing, no account, ne'er-do-well, two-timing brute that Americans think. But that matters not. In love and politics, "W. I. Thomas' sociological theorem—'If men define situations as real, they are real in their consequences'—has been repeatedly verified."[31]

The consequences for comic civics are clear. Having been left standing at the altar by politicians far too often, citizens do the rational thing. They turn their attention to other wooers. There are many from which to choose, and citizens are free to amuse themselves as they wish. Since it is a democracy, after all, citizens have a legitimate right to spend their leisure time as they freely choose.

An irony of democracy is that such free choice is essential to democratic citizenship. Good Citizens have a right to be Indifferent Citizens. On the one hand, we expect Good Citizens to take part in politics. Yet, on the other, there is no imposed obligation to take part in politics. Indeed, such a formal requirement would violate the principle of individual liberty inherent in democracy. Given Americans' disappointment with the perceived performance of government and politicians, a requirement to take part would add to the comedy, like forcing Prince Charles and Princess Diana to remain together when they can't stand each other.

Rather, if there is really an obligation in democratic citizenship it is to respond rationally, and the rational response to an abusive swain is to distance oneself from the abuser, cut one's losses, and turn elsewere in the pursuit of self-interest. One political scholar has theorized that in democracy this is precisely what rational citizens do. In discussing the Good Citizen, political scientist Robert Lane argues that when a citizen has the task of searching "for information and guidance" relevant to the "pursuit of self-interest," that citizen "must develop a strategy that maximizes a number of values and minimizes cost."[32]

What, then, is the appropriate strategy for the Good Citizen to become informed? It is not to know everything, but to know selected things, that is, to be indifferent about most matters, and, by passing the buck, informed about few. For example, in a classic analysis Anthony Downs pondered the costs to voters of acquiring information. Information gathering carries a cost, namely, the deflection of scarce resources—the time it takes to learn about candidates, issues, parties, and so on. One way to reduce that cost is to transfer it. A rational citizen, that is, a Good Citizen, delegates much of the cost of acquiring raw data, assimilating it, and weighing it to someone else.

Moreover, "information is necessarily gathered by certain *principles of selection*: rules employed to determine what to make use of and what not to." The Good Citizen faces "a situation of economic choice: from among those many sources of information, he must select only a few to tap." In this process "rationality decrees that they [citizens] select those reporters who provide them with versions of events that closely approximate the versions they would formulate themselves were they expert on-the-spot witnesses." Good Citizens, being rational, "choose reporters whose selection principles are as nearly identical with their own as possible." As in romantic love, passion is crucial: "the reporters' inevitable biases will aid [citizens'] decision-making rather than hinder it."[33] So, like jilted paramours who remain curious about a lost love, Good Citizens rationally pursue political information not through face-to-face trysts, but by turning to trusted friends who proffer secondhand reports, gossip, and rumors.

Thus does comic civics, like many a broken love affair, shift from interpersonal intimacy to impersonal forms of influence. In America politics has for a long time been peripheral to most citizens' everyday concerns. Politics and government are abstractions, "things out there" that are divorced from most citizens' daily experience. Increasingly, rational citizens turn to impersonal, anonymous surrogates for guidance—"media-derived impressions of the nation as a whole."[34] As Americans increasingly delegate the tasks of citizenship to impersonal third parties, most notably the news and entertainment media (Chapter 3), the character of democratic citizenship as romantic comedy magnifies. For remember that in romantic comedy the tomfoolery stems not from star-struck lovers. No, they are acting rationally and responsibly. Instead the monkeyshines and highjinks lie in the antics of foolish third parties.

One of the most trite of romantic comedy formulae is the boy meets girl, boy wins girl, boy loses girl, boy regains girl, happy-ever-after plot. As many a Fred Astaire and Ginger Rogers film will attest, meeting, winning, and losing are matters of interpersonal intimacy. When it comes to boy regains girl, however, Fred and Ginger rarely sit down, face to face, and air their misunderstandings. Reconciliation depends upon the cooperation of the dancers' sidekicks, who messed things up in the first place.

Their film *Shall We Dance* (1937) typified the genre. We have Fred playing the role of a ballet dancer, Petrov, from St. Petersburg, Russia. (Actually, Petrov was born Pete Peters in Pittsburgh.) Ginger plays Linda Keene, singer and actress. Due to a bunch of mishaps that derive from the foolery of character actors, the perpetually flustered Edward Everett Horton and the snotty but always in a snit Eric Blore, everybody who counts thinks Petrov and Keene are married. The mise-en-scène: to prove they're *not* married, the dancers do marry so that they can divorce and thus no longer be married! It all goes awry, they fall in love, win and lose one another, and Pete straightens it out not with Linda directly, but with images of her. Whether as in politics or not, one image turns out to be real, and they are reconciled. Triumph over and with the help of fools.

The romantic comedy of democratic civics plays out much the same way. Without colluding with the clowns, whether in comic love or comic civics, there may be a rollicking good time. But will there be a happy-ever-after? That may depend less on what images citizens bring to politics than what they do in politics. Will Rogers said, "Us voters are more smart-aleck than we ever were, but we are no smarter."[35] Let's see if Rogers was right by turning to another comedy of democracy, that of humors.

NOTES

1. Oscar G. Brockett, *The Theatre: An Introduction* (New York: Holt, Rinehart and Winston, 1964); William Flint Thrall, Addison Hibbard, and C. Hugh Holman, *A Handbook to Literature* (New York: Odyssey Press, 1960).

2. Brockett, *The Theatre*, p. 197.

3. Alexis de Tocqueville, *Democracy in America*, ed. J. P. Mayer, trans. George Lawrence (Garden City, NY: Anchor Books, 1969), p. 173.

4. Ibid., p. 252.

5. Ibid., p. 251.

6. Ibid.

7. Alexander Hamilton, John Jay, and James Madison, *The Federalist* (New York: Modern Library, 1937), p. 337.

8. Blaise Pascal, *Pensées* Everyman Edition (New York: E. P. Dutton, 1906), Sect. II, No. 347.

9. Countless thoughts have been penned, typed, and word processed contrasting the kinds of citizens democracy requires and the types that actually populate America. The classic remains Bernard Berelson, "Democratic Theory and Public Opinion," 16 *Public Opinion Quarterly* 16 (Fall 1952): 313–330. A more specific view of Berelson's argument appears in his chapter entitled "Democratic Practice and Democratic Theory," in Bernard R. Berelson, Paul F. Lazarsfeld, and William N. McPhee, *Voting* Chicago: University of Chicago Press, 1954, pp. 305–323.

10. Berelson, "Democratic Practice," p. 307.

11. de Tocqueville, *Democracy in America*, p. 513.

12. Helmut K. Anheier, Lester M. Salamon, and Edith Archambault, "Participating Citizens: U.S.-Europe Comparisons in Volunteer Action," *The Public Perspective* 5 (March/April 1994): 16–18, 34.

13. Michael X. Delli Carpini and Scott Keeter, "The Gender Gap in Political Knowledge," *Public Perspective* 3 (July/August 1992): 23–26.

14. Samuel L. Popkin, *The Reasoning Voter* (Chicago: University of Chicago Press, 1991), p. 41.

15. Bryan B. Sterling and Frances N. Sterling, *Will Rogers' World* (New York: M. Evans and Co., 1989), p. 84.

16. Berelson, "Democratic Practice,", pp. 314–315.

17. Ibid., p. 316.

18. Sterling and Sterling, *Will Rogers' World*, p. 84.

19. Steven A. Peterson, *Political Behavior* (Newbury Park, CA: Sage, 1990), pp. 79–80.

20. A. Roy Eckardt, *Sitting in the Earth and Laughing* (New Brunswick, NJ: Transaction, 1992), p. 2. Emphasis in original.

21. *Public Opinion and Demographic Report*, May/June 1993, p. 85. Roper Center for Public Opinion Research, University of Connecticut.

22. Sterling and Sterling, *Will Rogers' World*, p. 29.

23. de Tocqueville, *Democracy in America*, p. 237.

24. H. L. Mencken, *A Mencken Chrestomathy* (New York: Alfred A. Knopf, 1956), p. 622.

25. Robert D. Hess and Judith V. Torney, *The Development of Political Attitudes* (Chicago: Aldine, 1967), p. 67. Emphasis in original.

26. Ferdinand Mount, *The Theatre of Politics* (New York: Schocken Books, 1973), p. 56. Emphasis in original.

27. Ibid., pp. 59–60.

28. Kenneth Burke, *Attitudes Toward History* (Berkeley: University of California Press), 1959, p. 43.

29. Enoch Powell, quoted in Mount, *Theatre of Politics*, p. 225.

30. *Public Opinion and Demographic Report*, March/April 1994, p. 88. Roper Center for Public Opinion Research, University of Connecticut.

31. Robert K. Merton, *Social Theory and Social Structure* (Glencoe, IL: Free Press, 1957), p. 545.

32. Robert E. Lane, *Political Life* (New York: Free Press, 1972), p. 310.

33. Anthony Downs, *An Economic Theory of Democracy* (New York: Harper and Row, 1957), pp. 212–213. Emphasis in original.

34. Diana Mutz, "Impersonal Influence in American Politics," *Public Perspective* 4 (November/December 1992): 20.

35. Steven K. Gragert, ed., *He Chews to Run: Will Rogers' Life Magazine Articles, 1928* (Stillwater: Oklahoma State University Press, 1982), p. 75.

CHAPTER 2

Candidates, Campaigns, and Voters: Comedies of Farce and Humors in Electoral Politics

It happens every four years. Americans go about choosing one of them-selves to be Chief of Everyone. "Hail to the Chief" doesn't have the ring to it of "All Hail Caesar!" But so what? It still makes for glorious spectacle. Moreover, just deciding who wins the office of president can be entertain-ing. And if one likes slapstick, it can be uproariously funny as well.

The presidential election of 1992 certainly had its boisterous twinklings. None, however, was quite so rib-tickling as the October 15 televised presi-dential debate between incumbent George Bush and his two challengers, Bill Clinton and Ross Perot. It didn't measure up to Larry, Curly, and Moe, but it had its moments. Political observers and media critics praised the confrontation as innovative, a breakthrough in running for the highest office in the land, and the most revealing, significant, and fascinating of debates since 1960. Here were the three contenders, sometimes seated on stools, sometimes strolling around the stage, squaring off against one another in a theater-in-the-round in their verbal "altogether," fielding spon-taneous, unfiltered questions from members of a live audience. Only mod-erator Carole Simpson of ABC News, imported to act as traffic cop for the Keystone Kids, was buffer to the one-on-one exchanges between the sea-soned candidates themselves, and between the contenders and their inter-locutors in the studio audience.

Aristotle taught that, compared to grave theatrical pieces such as tragedy, comedy is relatively unstructured; the freewheeling pandemonium lacks the progression of introduction, rising action, turning point, falling action, and climax of the serious mise-en-scènes. Comedy thrives on spontaneity. We always walk in during the middle of things, not quite prepared for the incongruities of what happens next. So, on the surface, the unrehearsed quality of the Bush-Clinton-Perot spectacle possessed a potential for the unexpected, incredulous, and ridiculous.

Granted, not everything was left to fortune in the staging; one could not expect a wrestlemania free-for-all. The debate format itself was selected by Clinton, the same TV talk-show gig he had used throughout his campaign, a format that he welcomed, since he modestly claimed during the confrontation that he had "created" it. The audience, allegedly composed of uncommitted voters, was as carefully screened as it was frisked; the spontaneous questions received preliminary scrutiny prior to air time. With notable exceptions, the majority of candidates' responses, in spite of the setting, were the oft-rehearsed utterings they had repeated in catatonic ways in numerous out-of-town tryouts as they criss-crossed the country for stump speeches and appearances on other radio/TV talk shows and forums.

The term "slapstick" derives from a stick, switch, or lath that comic performers once used to strike one another. The loud, unexpected crack of slaps, smacks, smites, and wallops provoked laughter from audiences. The presidential debate in Richmond, Virginia, had scarcely started before the first smack, crackle, and pop were heard. Bush took a swipe at Clinton with a verbal lath, questioning the Arkansas governor's credibility. Suddenly there was the sound of another stick. This one was not, however, brandished by Clinton in a defensive joust with the president. The blow came from an unexpected quarter, an audience member. Whack. Don't talk trash, said a white female. Whack. Focus on issues and needs, said a white male. Whack. Would the candidates cross their hearts and take a pledge to behave themselves, said another female?

Chastised and chastened, the candidates sulked through the remainder of the ninety-minute performance with, if not syruplike civility, at least a show of tolerance. Perot perked up his ears, Clinton smiled and strolled around, Bush checked his watch. Vaudeville was never too far away. Bush made a remark about the deplorable state of the state of Arkansas; Texarkana-born Perot countered that Arkansas was not deplorable, just irrelevant; and, whack, Weepin' Willie gave a heart-rending defense of his beloved home state. However, most such exchanges passed unnoticed. What political observers, commentators, and spin doctors featured most in their post-debate reviews was a bizarre exchange, provoked by a whack at all three candidates from a young black woman. Unfortunately for him, it landed first on George Bush. Perhaps sensing the president might dodge the lash, the moderator wielded the lash with implacability:

Woman: How has the national debt personally affected each of your lives? And if it hasn't, how can you honestly find a cure for the economic problems of the common people if you have no experience in what's ailing them?

George Bush: Well, I think the national debt affects everybody.

Carole Simpson: You personally.

Bush: Obviously it has a lot to do with interest rates.

Simpson: She's saying, "You personally." You, on a personal basis. How has it affected you?

Bush: I'm sure it has. I love my grandchildren.

Simpson: How?

Bush: I want to think that they're going to be able to afford an education. I think that that's an important part of being a parent. If the question . . . maybe I . . . get it wrong. Are you suggesting that if somebody has means that the national debt doesn't affect them?

Woman: What I'm saying is . . .

Bush: I'm not sure I get—help me with the question and I'll try to answer it.

Woman: Well, I've had friends that have been laid off from jobs.

Bush: Yeah.

Simpson: I know people who cannot afford to pay the mortgage on their homes, their car payment. But how has it affected *you*, and if you have no experience in it, how can you help *us*, if you don't know what *we're* feeling?

Bush soldiered on, bobbing and weaving, reeling, speaking of mail received in the White House, talks with parents, ending with a line worthy of one of the Three Stooges after having been cuffed senseless by the other two: "I don't think it's fair to say, you haven't had cancer, therefore you don't know what it's like."

Suppose that Alexis de Tocqueville had returned to America, circa 1992, and wandered into Richmond on that night in October and witnessed the scene. Even his wry acumen would have been put to the test. "What is going on here?" he might have asked. One answer: What always goes on in all election campaigns in American democracy—farce mixes with humor.

FARCE AND HUMOR IN COMEDIES AND CAMPAIGNS

Although engaged in not-so-lofty political debate, Bush, Clinton, and Perot were playing roles in a dramatic form that dates back to the Middle Ages. The farce as performed in the fifteenth century proclaimed "the ridiculous depravity of man."[1] Performances portrayed that depravity by depending less on the plot or the complexities of the characters than by exciting laughter through exaggerated, unlikely situations, coarse wit, and horseplay. (Remember, this is more than four centuries before the 1992 presidential debates perfected the form!)

Pierre Patelin, a farce by an unknown writer, is typical of the fifteenth century form; it is still performed today, even outside presidential politics. Patelin, the lead character, is a lawyer facing financial ruin. Yet, Patelin scrapes together the wherewithal to purchase a fine piece of cloth. A merchant gives Patelin the cloth, then agrees to come to Pierre's house to collect the money. The merchant arrives. Patelin is in bed, swears he has not been out of the house all day, and refuses to pay for the cloth. Patelin then feigns madness, beats the merchant, and runs him off. Later Patelin meets a shepherd and agrees to defend him in court on a charge of stealing sheep. He advises the client, a genuine simpleton, to say only "baa" in response to all questions. Lo and behold, the shepherd's accuser turns out to be the cloth merchant. The ensuing wave of charges and countercharges confuses the judge, so he dismisses the case. Patelin tries to collect his fee from the shepherd; but the shepherd calls out "baa" and runs away. Three knaves—a lawyer, a merchant, and a simpleton—have thus spent all their time outwitting one another. Any relation to Clinton, Perot, and Bush is purely coincidental, but the outcome of the story has been changed to protect the innocent.

Farce is not the only variety of comedy at work in election campaigns. For the most part the farcical roles go to the candidates. There are also roles for voters. These are the humorous roles. Playwright Ben Jonson (1572–1637) popularized the *comedy of humors*. Centuries ago there was a widely accepted physiological theory that the human body was governed by four chief liquids, called "humors": blood, phlegm, yellow bile, and black bile. These four humors were allied with four elements thought to comprise the world—air, fire, water, and earth. Hence, like air, blood was hot and moist; like fire, yellow bile was hot and dry; like water, phlegm was cold and moist; and like earth, black bile was cold and dry. If a person was to be healthy there had to be a balance among these bodily fluids; if there was an imbalance, and if one humor dominated the body, physical disease, mental illness, and moral "temperaments" were dreaded outcomes. Carried to its logical consequences the theory of humors provided a typology of human temperaments:[2]

Healthy: all liquids in balance.

Sanguine: dominance of blood; beneficent, joyful, amorous.

Choleric: dominance of yellow bile; angry, impatient, obstinate, vengeful.

Melancholic: dominance of black bile; gluttonous, backward, indifferent.

Phlegmatic: dominance of phlegm; dull, pale, cowardly.

A physician treating an imbalance of humors typically purged the patient to rid the body of excessive bile or phlegm, or used leeches to bleed and remove excessive blood. In the 1770s an inventive scam artist, Franz Anton Mesmer, came up with an intriguing variation on treatments. He tried to control health and human potential by passing a magnet over the body to redirect the flow of liquids. In the late eighteenth century it was fashionable to be "mesmerized" to health and well-being. Mesmer's claims, however, did not go unchallenged. A blue-ribbon panel (Benjamin Franklin was a member) investigated claims for the success of such "cures," but found them wanting in evidence.

Yet, even today one still comes across post-election analyses of voters "mesmerized" by a victorious candidate. Unlikely. Yet, the word *influence* derives from *influent*, the "in-flow" of fluid, or fluency. Perhaps being glib and facile does mesmerize the voter. Or does it simply drain the voter's vital fluids? Be that as it may, later we explore how the theory of humors and its attendant typology matches theories of voting in a democracy. For the nonce, however, play with this thought derived from Chapter 1: the Good Citizen is sanguine, the Indifferent Citizen is melancholic, the principled is choleric, and the alienated is phlegmatic.

By 1600 many playwrights frequently based their characters on the psychology of humors. Typical is Jonson's comedy of humors, *Volpone*. What *Pierre Patelin* is to electoral farce, *Volpone* is to electoral humors. Like many a politician promising to fulfill every constituent's wishes, Volpone pretends to be rich. Since he has no heirs, each of several characters (like a candidate's sycophantic advisers) thinks that by being in Volpone's good graces he will inherit the fortune. Each lavishes expensive gifts on Volpone (similar to flattery showered on candidates by sycophants). Volpone tires of it all, leaves his wealth to a servant, Mosca, and pretends to die. When Volpone returns from the dead, Mosca refuses to surrender the fortune. In the end everyone is exposed as a fraud and punished.

In *Volpone* Jonson uses humor to stereotype the characters by giving each the name of a predatory creature: Volpone is a fox, Mosca a fly, Voltore a vulture, and so on. Like humorous fluids, the names are descriptive of each member of the cast of corrupt characters. Thus, Jonson's comedy of humors parallels closely the burlesque discussed in this book's Prologue. Kenneth Burke might have been speaking of any writer of a comedy of humors when he wrote, "Hilariously, he converts a manner into a mannerism." This method of polemic through caricature is "partisan" in the sense that it is partial and in its incompleteness. Applying burlesque, or a comedy of humors, to electoral politics we must heed Burke's advice: "We can use it for the ends of wisdom only insofar as we ourselves provide the ways of making allowances for it . . . to be able to "discount" what it says."[3]

Without stretching the analogy too far, candidates and their handlers— sometimes because of their handlers—render much of the electoral drama into farce. And more often than not, they appeal to the electorate as though voters suffer from blood, phlegm, and bile imbalances—the sanguine middle-class, choleric minorities, melancholic unemployed, phlegmatic opposition, and so on. Keeping Burke's Law in mind, consider the farcical and humorous in American elections.

THE DEMOCRATIC CAMPAIGN: NOT AN AMERICAN TRAGEDY, AN AMERICAN FARCE

"Campaigns have ruined more men than they have ever made," said Will Rogers. Perhaps that is because, to paraphrase what Rogers went on to say about radio, nothing in the world exposes how little you have to say.[4] With so little to say, and so much time to say it, campaigners forget the plot and just whack, smack, and hack away.

We say "campaigners" rather than simply "candidates." Running for office today not only pits candidates against one another, it pits entourage against entourage, retinue against retinue. Surrounding each opposing candidate is a cortege of courtiers and guards that would make the mighty Julius Caesar envious: managers, media consultants, pollsters, speech writers, electronic wizards, advertising specialists; doctors, lawyers, merchants, chiefs; rich, few who are poor, but several sycophantic beggars and thieves. With so many hangers-on, a gathering akin to the characters in *A Funny Thing Happened on the Way to the Forum*, the potential for farce is overwhelming.

Campaigns were not always so specialized or gluttonous. Or at least gluttony was of a different sort. George Washington ran for the Virginia House of Burgesses in 1758. He was his own campaign staff. The only hint in his campaign of what was to come two centuries later was that he made sure that the 391 voters, along with their friends, were served 160 gallons of rum, beer, and cider on election day. Vote buying? No, simply an early celebration of certain victory.

Playing to Voters with Farce and Humor

It is difficult to say when American elections introduced the farce as a scenario, but it probably was around the time when contests for the presidency centered on appeals for a broad base of popular support. With a large audience to play to, the temptations for tomfoolery were too strong to ignore. The presidential election of 1840 is a case in point. It followed a decade of changes in election laws that lowered or abolished requirements that voters meet property qualifications or pay taxes to qualify. By 1840 "presidential contests ceased to be the private preserve of the rich and well-born" and instead became "great entertainments in which even people who could not vote joined in on the fun."[5]

Since farce relies on the loud blow of the lath rather than either the plot or the characters, the presidential election of 1840 aptly qualified as farcical. Moreover, humors appealed to by the candidates were out of kilter. If a campaign's plot consists of an unfolding dispute over matters of political substance, 1840 had no plot. The Whigs' only issue was that they wanted their candidate in the White House and the Democrats' Martin Van Buren out. The Democrats had no issues either; they simply denigrated the Whigs' candidate, William Henry Harrison.

If there was no plot to 1840, were there characters? Scarcely. The candidates were not characters; they were caricatures manufactured by faking mannerisms, and exaggerating the mannerisms into manners. The Whigs sought a candidate with a popular, "people's candidate" air. After all, that had put Andy "By God" Jackson in the White House in 1828; perhaps it would do the same for the Whigs. Harrison, however, was not to that manner born but was to the manor born. He came from a relatively affluent background, was college educated, and lived on a pleasant farm in Ohio. No, as a humor his blood was not royal blue, but it surely bore no faded populist tinge.

Harrison's Whig handlers overcame that liability by ignoring it. They focused instead on a critical remark about Harrison made by a friend of Henry Clay, whom the Whigs had passed over for the presidential nomination. Doing Clay no favors, the friend said of Harrison, "Give him a barrel of hard cider" and a pension, and Harrison would "sit out the remainder of his days in a log cabin."[6] The blue in Harrison's blood humor was instantly lightened by hard cider and hard times. Thus was born a principal manner: Harrison as the hard-cider, log-cabin candidate.

The image-makers didn't stop there. Harrison had a fairly undistinguished military career. Not to worry. As governor of the Indiana Territory he had led forces that defeated the Shawnee chief, Tecumseh, at Tippecanoe. Here was a mannerism, albeit not spectacular, to widely publicize and promote into an appealing manner: "Hero of Tippecanoe." Harrison's blue blood balanced with black bile thus made for a dynamic, decisive, choleric humor. With John Tyler on the ticket, the ditty "Tippecanoe and Tyler Too" was the lath for smacking Martin Van Buren.

As the Whig campaigners transfused Harrison's humors with those of the people, they also exploited Van Buren's alleged mannerisms to make him the snit of the contest. In a three-day congressional harangue Congressman Charles Ogle of Pennsylvania accused Van Buren of converting the White House into a royal court rivaling the most ostentatious of any emperor in history. Ogle poked fun at the Van Burens' household furnishings, golden goblets, silverware, fancy bedsheets, lace handkerchiefs, filet gloves, rubies adorning the neck, diamonds on the fingers—an endless rendition of mid-nineteenth century one-liners comparable to unleashing Jay Leno or David Letterman on a sitting president. Ogle's charge that Van Buren had the manner of an aristocratic snob, however, hit home hard, coming as it did only three years after a severe economic crisis, the Panic of 1837. Whigs jumped on the snobbish manner: Van Buren lounging in the lap of luxury while The People suffered. Had there been a televised presidential debate perhaps Ogle would have, in Carole Simpson's objective journalese, confronted Van Buren with, "I know people who cannot afford to pay the mortgage on their homes, their car payment. But how has it affected *you*, and if you have no experience in it, how can you help *us*, if you don't know what *we're* feeling?"

But there were no debates. In fact, heretofore tradition had dictated that presidential candidates made no speeches appealing directly to the populace for votes. Given the piebald makeup of the tenuous Whig coalition (nationalists *and* states righters, protectionists *and* free-traders, pro-central financial planning *and* anti-planning interests), Harrison's managers wanted tradition to prevail. The last thing the Whigs wanted was a Harrison gaffe that would split the fragile party. Such a blunder was as real a possibility for Harrison as it was to prove to be over a century and a half later for Dan Quayle. Said Harrison to a friend, "I suffer from the numerous (and as to the larger portion) most ridiculous [*sic*] applications for opinions on every subject."[7]

Campaign manager Nicholas Biddle, recognizing that the Whigs had a loose cannon, decreed that Harrison should "say not one single word about his principles or his creed," should "say nothing, promise nothing," should allow no one to "extract from him a single word about what he thinks now and will do hereafter." Moreover, urged Biddle, "Let the use of pen and ink be wholly forbidden as if he were a mad poet in Bedlam."[8] But like many a current-day candidate, Harrison ignored the advice. He was the first presidential candidate to take to the stump. Still, he said nothing to jeopardize his appeal to the voters; like Ronald Reagan repeatedly urging Republicans to win one for the Gipper, Harrison never tired of describing himself as just an "old soldier and a farmer." Reagan was not the Gipper, but he played one in films; Harrison was an undistinguished soldier and not much of a farmer, but he played one in 1840. The closing lines of a Whig campaign ditty capture the comedy of farce and humours that was 1840:

> For Tippecanoe and Tyler Too. Tippecanoe and Tyler Too.
> And with them we'll beat the little Van, Van, Van;
> Van is a used up man,
> And with them we'll beat little Van.

So they did. Election campaigns, especially presidential campaigns, since 1840 have not always proved so boisterous. That has not been for want of trying. Through the years campaigns of farcical humors have become commonplace. Indeed, one could argue that the major thrust of the burgeoning specialization in the roles of campaigners, particularly since the 1950s, has been to afford campaigners a growing sophistication in comedic artistry. Campaigners exploit their crafty cunning to (1) obscure plot and character development; (2) create subtle and not-so-subtle sticks to slap opponents with; and (3) caricature candidates and voters by contriving and taking advantage of unbalanced humors.

Campaign Consultants: Glutinous Maximus?

Throughout the twentieth century electoral reform has changed the face of campaigning. The expanded use of direct primaries at local, state, and federal levels not only gave the populace a voice in selecting nominees for public office, it enlarged the pool of candidates competing for those nominations. Moreover, at local and state levels initiatives, referenda, and recall elections increased the likelihood that political interests would take their appeals to voters in order to achieve their special goals. The tragicomic fiasco known as Watergate during the 1972 presidential election provoked an outcry about dirty politics and campaigning that spawned reforms in campaign finance, presidential primaries and caucuses, and, indirectly, news media coverage of elections. As with earlier electoral reforms, those added to the electoral script following Watergate enlarged the sentimental role assigned the Good Citizen in politics.

With more and more candidates running, more and more elections held, and more and more opportunities to hold candidates accountable, electoral politics was, in theory, becoming more popular. In fact, it was unpopular. Levels of voter turnout failed to nudge upward and, in presidential elections, declined. This, however, did not deter candidates from seeking office. Yet, it did deter them from pursuing their ambitions via electoral dramas with clear-cut plot lines. With so few voters flocking to the show, why bother to talk about specifics? Moreover, it became clear to many candidates that, regardless of their boasts to the contrary, most of the social problems that cried out for electoral debate were intractable. Hence, as dramatic characters they could do little to control plot development even if they wanted to.

Here, then, was the candidate's reasoning—sometimes explicit, sometimes implicit: I am one of many running for the office. If I address specific social ills with specific solutions, and no other candidate is doing the same, no one will listen. Voters are indifferent. If I do address specifics, and so do my opponents, the few voters who listen will figure out that *none* of our proposed specifics will solve the insoluble. Thereby, there is an imperative for all candidates who befuddle electoral plot lines that threaten to get specific: *all* candidates avoid character developments that might pin *any* down to promises of clear-cut achievements rather than ambiguous personal qualities. Hence, there entered the first ingredient of classic farce: excite laughter not through plot or character; turn elsewhere.

The elsewhere candidates turned to was exaggerated, improbable situations, gross incongruities, coarse wit, and horseplay. To stage the slapstick they turned to media consultants, speech writers, advertising specialists, and pollsters. As members of the candidate's performance team, these twentieth century Nicholas Biddles substituted stand-up one-liners for plots, caricature for character.

The art of the one-liner, first perfected for popular audiences in America in the persona of the vaudeville and nightclub stand-up comic, is crucial to successful farce. A machine-gun-like firing of one-liners can put an audience in such a mirthful mood that the absence of plot or character can easily be forgiven. Contemporary cases in point: *Airplane* and the *Naked Gun* movies. In electoral politics the one-liner is called the sound bite, relabeled to conform with TV's imperative to redesignate everything. The list of "spontaneous" but meticulously orchestrated one-liners in electoral politics is so protracted as to seem endless. However, the last four presidential elections offer typical examples of not so thought provoking one-liners: Ronald Reagan chiding Jimmy Carter in 1980, "There you go again, Mr. President"; Walter Mondale asking Gary Hart in 1984, "Where's the beef?"; George Bush's meta–one-liner in 1988 as he asked Michael Dukakis, "Is it time for us to trot out our one-liners?"; and Ross Perot claiming it's time to shovel out the barn and clean out the manure.

The one-liner or sound bite is a weapon; it constitutes one of the sticks that define slapstick. As a switch for exciting laughter through exaggeration, however, the one-liner need not be verbal. A picture can substitute for plot and character just as well. A classic forerunner of the farcical fare that has come to dominate campaigning was an election held in 1946 in San Francisco to recall the city's mayor. The group behind the recall offered no candidate to replace the mayor. The mayor's advisers capitalized on that fact by inventing an opponent, "The Faceless Man." In a pre-TV age San Francisco was saturated with huge billboards. Appearing on each was a giant politician, but without a face, and the question, "Who's Behind the Recall?" The gimmick worked; the recall failed.[9]

Moving from the mammoth billboard of the 1940s to the thirty–second televised spot commercial of the 1990s may have diminished the size of the lash used to thump one's opponent, but the farcical intent remains the same—exaggerate a mannerism into a manner, a humor into a caricature. Aiding the media consultant, speech writer, and PR agent in this endeavor are pollsters working with advertising specialists. The pollster's contribution is to discover the humors of the voters, both the humors they seek most in their elected officials and the humors that motivate them to applaud one candidate over another in a drama lacking both plot and character development. The advertising specialist then uses the pollster's findings to turn the sow's ear into a silk purse.

The contribution of TV spots to the campaign's comedy of farcical humors began in the 1950s. With each passing decade there has been a shift in the dominant ways ad specialists have caricatured major candidates and the electoral times. For example, stilted and trite though they appear today, the spots made for Dwight Eisenhower's campaign in 1952 painted a candidate with acceptable bloodlines, a sanguine leader: beneficent (he would bring down taxes, go to Korea, and wipe out corruption), joyful (always smiling), and amorous ("I Like Ike, You Like Ike, Everybody Likes Ike" was a ditty for one ad). Contrast that campaign with, say, 1964. Both parties' candidates, Democratic Lyndon Johnson/Republican Barry Goldwater, appeared in spots as choleric: angry over what the federal government could do to alleviate/cause injustice; impatient with the too slow/too fast course of events; obstinate; and vengeful (e.g., Democratic spots portraying Goldwater as wanting to saw off the East Coast and let it float out to sea).

The presidential campaigns of the 1970s stressed, by contrast, a phlegmatic humor: cowardly (Richard Nixon's cover-up of Watergate, Gerald Ford's pardon of the defrocked Nixon); colorless (George McGovern); muted, subdued (Jimmy Carter, who would never lie to the American people). Campaigns were back to an aggressive bile in the 1980s with Ronald Reagan confronting the Evil Empire, Walter Mondale promising to raise taxes. Finally, there is the melancholic humor of the 1990s: both Bill Clinton and Ross Perot painting the Reagan-Bush years as gluttonous, backward, unenterprising, languid, and, like black bile, cold, dry, and lacking compassion.

And what of the spectators to the stand-up and sit-down one-liners and sound bites; what of the voters who voted for caricature rather than character?

THE DEMOCRATIC VOTER:
HEALTHY HUMORS OR VENTED SPLEENS?

In late July of the 1992 presidential campaign Democrat Bill Clinton led incumbent George Bush by a whopping twenty-two points in the polls. Clinton's handlers took comfort in that, yet knew it meant little. The Republicans had yet to hold their national party convention. If the past meant anything, just the convening of that love fest and the publicity surrounding it would narrow Clinton's lead substantially. Moreover, the nitty-gritty of the campaign had scarcely started; Republicans had yet to unleash a blitzkrieg of negative propaganda on the Democratic challenger. In this context Clinton's strategists regarded it as essential to maintain the lead. To that end they used a series of focus groups to test the effects of the likely attacks the Bush entourage would launch. What types of humors did voters perceive in Clinton?

One finding alarmed Clinton's mesmerizers. Potential attacks denouncing Clinton as too liberal for average Americans proved very effective. One segment of swing voters (those on the fence but who had supported Bush in 1988) responded to charges that Clinton was just another tax-and-spend Democrat by fleeing to Bush. In effect, they found Clinton melancholic:

gluttonous in taxing, indifferent to middle-class needs. Another segment flocked to Bush when mock ads attacked Clinton as a draft dodger during the Vietnam War, who now wanted to lop huge sums from defense spending. Here, then, was a phlegmatic Clinton—dull, pale, cowardly.

To neutralize these biles and their potentially threatening temperaments, Clinton's aides created sound bites to counter any such possible attacks by Bush's camp. Their polls and focus group research indicated that such countering bites would win approval from six of every ten voters. Clinton should simply respond, "This is more of the same old 'read my lips,' " that George Bush was slinging mud "instead of doing anything about the real problems facing this country, like the economy and health care."[10] Adding those lines to Clinton's script helped his consultants to snatch their candidate back from the unbalanced torrents of a liberal Slick Willy image to be reborn as a sanguine populist—beneficent, joyful, and amorous.

In seeking to learn what humors stamped Bill Clinton's temperament, or image, in the eyes of voters in 1992, the candidate's lackeys were undertaking an age-old inquiry of politicians and political scientists. Namely, they sought to identify the humors that move voters. Not surprisingly, researchers have found that the biles that flow through the electoral body offer a potent mix of many hues, some healthy and many more that are bled and purged through the act of voting itself.

If voters were the unspoiled and natural Good Citizens depicted in democracy's romantic comedies, then they would, to a person, be creatures of healthy humor and temperament. With all liquids in balance they would match the requirements of the Voter as Rational, being the Good Citizen of democracy's romantic comedy. This does not mean that healthy, or rational, is a synonym for altruistic. The democratic electorate is not comprised of a mass of musketeers crying "All for one and one for all." Rational action, like one's health, is more individualistic than that. It consists of calculating appropriate means to achieve desired ends. Whether the goals of action are altruistic or selfish is not the issue; means of achieving them are. So characterized, a rational voter can, first, always make a choice when confronted with alternatives; second, the rational voter ranks those alternatives so that each is preferred to that below it in the ranking, inferior to those ranked higher, or it is a matter of indifference between two options (there are ties); third, it follows that if a voter prefers A to B and B to C, A also gets the nod over C; fourth, the rational voter selects the choice with the highest preference ranking; and, finally, acts consistently to repeat the same choice when faced with the same options.[11]

As we hinted in discussing democracy's comedy of romantic love, the healthy balance of humors that constitutes rational citizenship may lead rational voters not to vote at all. For example, suppose a voter looks at two candidates (or three, or four, or more). The examination discloses no discernible difference in the competitors. So, the voter might say, "Since it makes no difference who wins as far as my benefits are concerned, and since it does cost me time, energy, and money to vote, the rational thing to do is cut my costs and abstain."

Candidates obviously have a vested interest in stamping out that kind of healthy rationality whenever they find it. Oh, to be sure, each candidate may be a clone of every other one running in, say, the primary election. But no campaigner will admit to that any more than the corner Fill and Save Store will confess that its brand of gasoline, coming as it does from the same refinery and transported in the same tanker as the brand sold at Save and Fill, is just another gasoline. No, Fill and Save hawks extra mileage, Save and Fill that the customer can pay by credit card! Hence, like Clinton (or Bush, or Perot) in 1992, or the Whigs in 1840, democratic candidates must give voters a tune they can whistle, or in the physiology of humors, a bile they can purge. Will Rogers expressed it with his usual aplomb:

The average citizen knows only too well that it makes no difference to him which side wins. He realizes that the Republican elephant and the Democratic donkey have come to resemble each other so closely that it is practically impossible to tell them apart; both of them make the same braying noise, and neither of them ever says anything. The only perceptible difference is that the elephant is somewhat the larger of the two.[12]

Fortunately for candidates, but as an insult to voters, politicians and political scientists find healthy members of the democratic electorate to be as rare as physicians find acceptable levels of cholesterol among their patients. Citizens, political research informs us, don't vote as they do—or choose to abstain instead—because they are rational. No, it is a faulty condition of humors that moves the American voter. For example, one school of thought argues that whereas healthy, rational voters act on their own initiative and volition, most voters are passive, choosing among political alternatives as a reflex triggered by dominant traits in each voter's makeup. Enter the Voter as Fool.

The foolish voter, more than other members of the electorate, is a farcical caricature. Here is a comic actor with the chilled bearing of the ancient physiognoists' cold elements, water and earth. Here is a voter passive to the point of melancholic indifference, politically reactive to the point of dull predictability. At least that is how researchers, using numbers to paint the portrait, delineate the picture. Responding as they do to election appeals in mindless, conditioned ways, these farcical voters are foils for any critic eager to place the blame for the alleged ills of democracy on the populace rather than its leaders. The reflexive voter takes a good deal of whacking from both politicians and political scientists.

The theory of reflexive, foolish voting argues that the melancholic and phlegmatic temperaments of the members of a democratic electorate flow from the black bile and phlegm of upbringings. In research these biles are labeled as sociopolitical categories—occupation, education, and income; age, sex, religion, residence, marital status; political party affiliation and ideological leanings. Since these factors—akin to the fluids of a comedy of humors—influence how people vote, the basic tactic of a campaigner is, first, to identify which potential voters fall into each category; second, to employ the Mesmer-like magnets of promises and images to attract the voters most likely to vote for one's candidacy; and, third, to neutralize opposing humors by bleeding them into neutrality or purging them on the opposition. Since voters are melancholic or phlegmatic, they don't really *think* about the appeals candidates make, they just react to the push and pull of the magnetic forces.

Almost a half-century of research into the character of the voters in U.S. presidential elections establishes a constancy in some humors and fickle-ness in others. For instance, in the last five presidential elections (1976–1992) well over half of black and Hispanic voters reacted favorably to the Demo-cratic contender; a majority of those earning less than $12,000 a year have done the same; so also have a majority of members of labor unions, those who call themselves liberal, and, of course, Democrats. There is constancy on the Republican side as well: voters earning more than $20,000 a year, men, residents of the West, conservatives, and those who identify them-selves as Republican or independent have been far more likely to vote for elephants in recent elections. There are also fickle humors: a majority of self-proclaimed moderates voted for Jimmy Carter in 1976 and Michael Dukakis in 1988, but did not go Democratic in the other elections; with Ross Perot's 1992 candidacy, whites failed to give Republicans a majority of their votes for the first time in recent elections; and the Republican Midwest of 1976–1988 yielded plurality support for Bill Clinton in 1992.[13]

Yet, this fickleness does nothing to diminish the caricature of the reflexive voter held by many politicians, "even successful politicians, who act as though they regarded the people as manageable fools."[14] And it is not just the politician's conventional wisdom that demeans the intelligence of the reflexive voter. The farcical caricature also emerges from scholarly research:

Nor does a heroic conception of the voter emerge from the . . . analysis of electoral behavior. They can be added up to a conception of voting not as a civic decision but as an almost purely deterministic act. Given knowledge of certain characteristics of the voter—his occupation, his residence, his religion, his national origin, and perhaps certain of his attitudes—one can predict with a high probability the direction of his vote. The actions of persons are made to appear to be only predict-able and automatic responses to campaign stimuli.[15]

Humorist Will Rogers was more scathing in his depiction. The American voter "has been fooled all his life and he will always be fooled," Rogers wrote sixteen presidential elections ago, in 1928. "The oldest form of Bunk in the world is to say how 'Well informed the voters are and that they can't be missled [*sic*] by our opponents.' " Nonsense, he intoned. "I doubt if at any time during the history of the world were we as ever as downright *Dumb* as we are today."[16] If Rogers left anything out in damning politicians' hoodwinking of foolish voters, perhaps he could have found it in H. L. Mencken's stinging 1921 assessment: "The average democratic politician, of whatever party, is a scoundrel and a swine," and "the average citizen of a democracy is a goose-stepping ignoramus and poltroon."[17]

The melancholic, phlegmatic oaf taken for granted by politicians, researchers, Rogers, and Mencken is scarcely a flattering caricature. The voter as fool lacks the romance of the voter as Good Citizen as much as the voter as rational person lacks the realism of how most voters decide. So both politicians and researchers have searched for a middle ground, a caricature less foolish and less reasoned than other stereotypes. They have made a "perverse and unorthodox argument," namely, "that voters are not fools."[18] Here the voter as Clever Fox walks on stage. Still, the fox as depicted in humorous fables and animated cartoons too can be a farcical character of unbalanced humors.

The foolish voter responds to campaigners' urgings in ways determined by long-term categorical affiliations and loyalties; the fool is a Pavlovian canine. By contrast, the fox stalks prey using short-term scents, craft, and cunning; so too does the vulpine voter. Foxy voters shift their partisan loyalties from election to election; they respond to specific issues and appraise candidates on the basis of a "what have you done for me lately" criterion that transcends social, doctrinal, and party devotions. Foxlike voters respond to the here-and-now; this is not an "electorate straightjacketed by social determinants or moved by subconscious urges triggered by devilishly skillful propagandists." Instead, it is "an electorate moved by concern about central and relevant questions of public policy, of governmental performance, and of executive personality."[19]

The voter of craft and cunning, however, differs from the rational voter who, like a racetrack handicapper, uses a carefully devised formula that compares strong and weak points, pluses and minuses, costs and benefits to pick a trifecta as if ranking Horse (Candidate) A over B, B over C, and so on. Nor is this crafty citizen, whom some scholars label "the responsive voter,"[20] so foolish as to place bets because of the jockey's looks (candidate's image) or colors (candidate's party). Nor is the foxy bettor tricked by the horse's name ("I'm a Ford, not a Lincoln," said the thirty-eighth president of the United States).

For example, when Senator Ted Kennedy of Massachusetts first ran for that office in 1962, his primary opponent was Edward McCormack. In a televised debate between the two candidates, McCormack urged voters not to be seduced by the magic of Kennedy's name. "If his name was Edward Moore, with his qualifications . . . your [*sic*] candidacy would be a joke, but nobody's laughing because his name is not Edward Moore. It's Edward

Moore Kennedy."[21] What McCormack did not say was that he too was from a well-known political family and that he was the nephew of the Speaker of the U.S. House of Representatives, John McCormack. As so often in the farcical comedy of campaigning, we have the pot calling the kettle black.

No, acting like a fox, the responsive voter does what Will Rogers said: "Every guy just looks in his own pocket and then votes." And "the funny part of it is that it's the last year of an administration that counts." A president "can have three bad ones and then wind up with everybody having money in the fourth, and the incumbent will win so far he needn't even stay up to hear the returns." Ergo, "conditions win elections, not speeches."[22]

Political scientists have exploited Rogers' insight, but true to their calling, have stamped out the humor and called this type of foxy behavior "retrospective evaluation."[23] Simply stated, the vulpine voter evaluates conditions, like a fox familiar with the territory sniffing out a rabbit, on the basis of accumulated experience. A fox knows the most likely place to flush out the quarry. A voter knows what the past performance of parties and their elected candidates has been while in office. It is in the light of that past performance that the retrospective voter evaluates current claims: What did each party's candidate promise before? What actually happened? As Rogers asked, is the stomach, dinner pail, or pocket full or empty?

The fox is an obstinate creature. Whether acting as the pursuer of the rabbit, or being pursued by the hounds in a fox hunt, the canny little beast "keeps on going, and going, and going," ironically more the Energizer Bunny than a fox. And as portrayed in children's cartoons, the fox is also impatient and vengeful. Outwitted by Bugs Bunny, the predatory fox plots revenge on the furry-tailed, carrot-chewing, hopping hare. In short, the fox possesses the characteristics of Volpone in Ben Jonson's comedy of humors of the same name. The fox suffers from an overbalance of yellow bile, hence is prone to the choleric temperament—angry, impatient, obstinate, and vengeful.

We all know that creatures with these characteristics, in spite of their craftiness and cunning, can be tricked just as fools can. After all, hopping hares do get away, foxes do get treed. And so it is with the foxy voter. Campaigners know about retrospective evaluation. They exploit it—just as they exploit a voter's social characteristics, credit rating, or stargazing at celebrities, be they rock singers, Hollywood starlets, or politicos. Ronald Reagan in his only televised debate with Jimmy Carter in 1980 invited retrospection by, in Will Rogers fashion, urging voters to look at their pocketbooks: "Are you better off today than you were four years ago?" he asked voters to ask themselves. Reagan outfoxed the foxy voter.

As foxes, voters of the choleric humor share vulpine qualities of that four-legged canine. They check their stomachs and, if times are bad, they grow impatient with the "ins"; the standings in the polls of the "outs" rise in a predictable fashion. If conditions do not improve, they not only display foxlike impatience, they grow angry. It is time to throw the rascals out of office, to punish the scoundrels with vengeance. Yet, as Will Rogers said, let them run their quarry to ground in the last year of a presidential administration and their wrath shifts from the ins to the outs—although not for long.

Voters as rational are of healthy humors, as fools they are melancholic and phlegmatic, as clever foxes they are choleric. Are they ever sanguine? Yes, they are. For research offers another caricature of the American voter, the Voter as Lovable Drunk—beneficent, joyful, amorous. The lovable drunk was a fixture of many early Hollywood films and, later, TV programming. Comic actors became famous in roles of lovable drunks: W. C. Fields, Leon Earle, Charlie Chase in movies, and Red Skelton, Jackie Gleason, and Ernie Kovacks on TV are but a few. And now, it seems, the lovable drunk populates the electorate. How so?

We hasten to add that "drunk" as a voter stereotype refers not to a state of continuing inebriation; the blood humor is not ninety proof. Rather it refers to a process voters use to reach decisions, one called the "drunkard's search." Comics tell a joke about a gentleman of means who spends an evening imbibing on the town. Sadly, he drinks too much and becomes tipsy. After "one more for the road," he walks (he does not drive and drink) back toward his apartment. Presently another gentleman comes along and finds our wobbly friend on hands and knees under a street lamp. "What are you doing?" "Looking for my apartment key," says Mr. Nonsobriety. "Did you lose it here?" "No," says the man of means, "I dropped it somewhere back there." Asked why he doesn't look where he dropped it, he responds, "The light is better here!"[24]

As jokes go, this one is not side-splitting. But it makes a point. Often when we try to find things, search for answers to puzzling questions, and try to reach decisions, we look for help in unlikely places simply because it is easier to do so. It saves wear and tear on our mental and physical capacities. It is this tendency that is the "drunkard's search." One polling consultant, political adviser, and political scientist, Samuel Popkin, uses that principle to describe how voters make choices.[25] His account provides a profile of the voter as a lovable drunk.

In campaign politics there is a proliferation of symbols, symbols inflated by hype, hyperbole, redundancy, euphemism, jargon, and the abuse of negative campaigning. So much information and misinformation cloud the political skies that the voters are shrouded in darkness; they don't try to deal with all of it, but instead try to penetrate the gloom with pinpoints of light. Voters find these lighted points not only from standard campaign sources, such as the candidates and the news media, but from their daily-life experiences.

Popkin argues that by using informational shortcuts, voters "go without data." For example, they focus on the current claims of the political parties, unlike the foxy voter, who focuses on past performance; theirs is a concern for the personal morality of candidates rather than institutional morality, as with the rational voter; perceived competence is uppermost on their minds, rather than a detailed inventory of official achievements. Voters also "go beyond data" by using representative heuristics, that is, simple cues and rules-of-thumb to judge if candidates will do the right thing.

The result, at least in Popkin's analysis, is that voters make choices through a drunkard's search, a search "among obvious differences."[26] Like the happy, sanguine inebriate searching under a street lamp for a lost key, voters look in unlikely places for clues as to how to choose between obvious differences because the light is better there. Rather than the "no pain, no gain" philosophy of the healthy, rational voter, our amorous drunk's sanguine humor produces a more joyful, beneficent attitude: "Why sweat it?"

There is ample opportunity for finding humor in the humor of our voter as a lovable drunk. For example, in democratic primary elections voters have vast amounts of information to sort out. The drunkard's search serves in an ironic way not to tell voters what each candidate *is* but what that candidate *isn't*. Under these conditions, "when there is a well-known trait by which the other candidates distinguish themselves from the front-runner, the communications of the lesser-known candidates become easier." The reason for this paradox, namely, that unknown candidates have an easier time getting known than known candidates, is that "they can communicate by negatives, telling voters what they are not, and letting voters fill in the rest." Thus, it was easier for voters to decide that George Bush was *not* "voodoo economist or bomb thrower," that Jimmy Carter was *not* a politician, that Jerry Brown was *not* a southern fundamentalist, and that Gary Hart was *not* a tool of unions or blacks.[27]

A CANDIDATE WHO "CHEWS TO RUN"

If we take seriously comic Will Rogers, dubbed by *Life* magazine "the only politician who is funny intentionally,"[28] we may locate "bunk" as the central temperament of democracy's electoral comedies of farce and humor. Bunk goes by other names. For instance, H. L. Mencken wrote of the American political campaign in a book he titled *A Carnival of Buncombe*.[29] Buncombe, like bunk, is insincerity in language—nonsense, baloney, humbug, bull. (The word "buncombe" derives from a speech made in the Sixteenth Congress by a representative from Buncombe County in North Carolina.)

Will Rogers thought all campaigning was bunk. To prove the point he mounted a fanciful campaign in 1928 for the presidency. His only vehicle was the pages of *Life*, at that time a weekly humor magazine. Rogers ran as the "bunkless candidate" of the Anti-Bunk Party. His only campaign promise was that, if elected, he would resign. Every week, from Memorial Day through Election Day, Rogers caricatured the farcical humors of grave campaign politics. The following sampling parodies the progress of Rogers' campaign (for that matter, the "progress" of any democratic campaign): What issue-oriented humor would motivate voters? Prohibition: "What's on your hip is bound to be on your mind" (July 26). Should there be presidential debates? Yes: "Joint debate—in any joint you name" (August 9). How about appeals to the common man? Easy: "You can't make any commoner appeal than I can" (August 16). What about the needs of the farmer? Obvious: "He needs a punch in the jaw if he believes that either of the parties cares a damn about him after the election" (August 23). Can voters be fooled? Darn tootin': "Of all the bunk handed out during a campaign the biggest one of all is to try and compliment the knowledge of the voter" (September 21). What about a candidate's image? Ballyhoo: "I hope there is some sane people who will appreciate dignity and not show-manship in their choice for the presidency" (October 5). What of negative campaign rumors? Don't worry: "The things they whisper aren't as bad as what they say out loud" (October 12). What of the religious issue? We have no religion: "So the Anti-Bunk Party has no opposition and no support" (October 19). Election prospects? Gloomy, very gloomy: "The trouble with us is we're too far ahead of our time with a platform of no bunk" (November 2).

On November 9 *Life* telegraphed Rogers that the Great Silent Vote had elected him president, even though the official tally elected Herbert Hoover. *Life* asked Rogers if he wanted a recount, or just to forget the whole thing. Rogers replied that since he had won the Great Silent Vote, that was good enough for him and he would do as promised—resign. "We went into this campaign to drive the Bunk out of politics. But our experiment while noble in motive was a failure."[30] Given the comedies of campaigning, nothing else could be expected.

NOTES

1. Oscar G. Brockett, *The Theatre: An Introduction* (New York: Holt, Rinehart and Winston, 1964), p. 111.

2. Readers familiar with political science treatises on why Americans vote as they do will find methodological parallels between theories of voting and theories of humors. The theory of humors was two-dimensional: hot vs. cold, wet vs. dry. This permits a fourfold classification: hot-wet, cold-wet, hot-dry, cold-dry. Compare this to Democrats vs. Republicans, women vs. men: Democrat-woman, Republican-woman, Democrat-man, Republican-man. Unfortunately for humors theorists, however, they were limited to two-by-two tables and cross-tabulations. One wonders how lasting their contributions might have been were they packaged with beta weights, multidimensional scales, and probit measures.

3. Kenneth Burke, *Attitudes Toward History* (Berkeley: University of California Press, 1937), p. 55.

4. Steven K. Gragert, ed., *He Chews to Run: Will Rogers; Life Magazine Articles, 1928* (Stillwater, OK: Oklahoma State University Press, 1982), p. 100.

5. Paul E. Boller, Jr., *Presidential Campaigns* (New York: Oxford University Press, 1984), p. 65.

6. Ibid., p. 66.

7. Robert Grey Gunderson, *The Log-Cabin Campaign* (Lexington: University of Kentucky Press, 1957, p. 222.

8. Boller, *Presidential Campaigns*, p. 70. Clearly our forefathers voiced views in politically incorrect ways. Biddle's closing today should read "as if he were an emotionally different poet in a rehabilitation center for the developmentally challenged."

9. Stanley Kelley, Jr., *Professional Public Relations and Political Power* (Baltimore: Johns Hopkins University Press, 1956).

10. Howard Fineman, "The Torch Passes," *Newsweek*, Special Edition (November/December 1992): 78–79.

11. Anthony Downs, *An Economic Theory of Democracy*, (New York: Harper and Row, 1957).

12. Gragert, *He Chews to Run*, p. 1.

13. "What Voters Said Election Day," *Public Perspective* 4 (January/February 1993): 90–91.

14. V. O. Key, Jr., *The Responsible Electorate*, (Cambridge, MA: Harvard University Press, 1966), p. 5.

15. Ibid.

16. Gragert, *He Chews to Run*, pp. 77–78. Emphasis in original.

17. H. L. Mencken, *A Carnival of Buncombe* (Chicago: University of Chicago Press, 1956), p. 47.

18. Key, *Responsible Electorate*, p. 7.

19. Ibid., pp. 7–8.

20. Gerald Pomper, *The People's Choice* (New York: Dodd, Mead, 1975).

21. Murray B. Levin, *Kennedy Campaigning* (Boston: Beacon Press, 1966), p. 182.

22. Bryan B. Sterling and Frances N. Sterling, *Will Rogers' World* (New York: M. Evans and Co., 1989), p. 84.

23. Morris P. Fiorina, *Retrospective Voting in American National Elections* (New Haven: Yale University Press, 1981), pp. 65–83.

24. Abraham Kaplan, *The Conduct of Inquiry* (San Francisco: Chandler, 1962), p. 11.

25. Samuel L. Popkin, *The Reasoning Voter* (Chicago: University of Chicago Press, 1991). Popkin's analysis of American voting rests on assumptions and findings derived from cognitive psychology. Hence, he couches his views in the concepts of schema, low-information rationality, frames, etc. His use of the drunkard's search serves as a summarizing device.

26. Ibid., p. 92.

27. Ibid., p. 130.

28. Gragert, *He Chews to Run*, p. viii.

29. Mencken, *Carnival of Buncombe*.

30. Gragert, *He Chews to Run*, p. 110.

CHAPTER 3

Voices of Public Opinion:
Comedies of Wit

Of all of William Shakespeare's historic, tragic, and comic characters, few are more lovable than Sir John Falstaff. Famous in literature simply as Falstaff, he is the jolly, jocular companion of Prince Hal in Shakespeare's *Henry IV*. He is also the rollicking lead character of the bard's *Merry Wives of Windsor*. By all assessments Falstaff was a wit if ever a wit there was, or if ever a wit was portrayed in fiction. 'Tis a pity we do not have the jovial, rotund fellow with us today to liven up our political life as he did Prince Hal's.

There is, some would argue, a pale imitation. Says Falstaff to his page:

Men of all sorts take a pride to gird at me; the brain of this foolish-compounded clay, man, is not able to invent any thing that tends to laughter, more than I invent or is invented on me: I am not only witty in myself, but the cause that wit is in other men. (*Henry IV, Part II*, Act 1, Scene 2, 6–10)

It is too much to say that Rush Limbaugh, radio and TV talk show guru possessed with unfathomable popularity, might be justified in treating Falstaff's words as his own; yet it is not beyond imagination to say that Limbaugh would claim that Sir John's self-assessment applies as well to himself. Certainly, Limbaugh judges himself as witty. Moreover, judging by the barbs directed at rotund Rush by other wits, from comic David Letterman to cartoonist Gary Trudeau, Limbaugh is the "cause that wit is in other men."

In several respects Limbaugh represents many of the modern-day wits that play roles in America's comedy of democracy. They are, as the poet John Dryden (1631–1700) wrote in *The Hind and the Panther* (Part 3, line 1), political commentators in whom "much malice is mingled with a little wit." Be they talk show celebrities like Limbaugh, Larry King, Phil Donahue, Oprah Winfrey, Montel Williams, Jenny Jones, or Ricki Lake; journalists cum TV chatterers like David Broder, George Will, Jack Germond, John McLaughlin, Sam Donaldson, or Cokie Roberts; or the legion of other reporters, academics, and entertainers telling Americans what to think about and what to think about it, they are the Falstaffs citizens welcome into their homes.

Sometimes the comic performances get ribald and appear to have nothing to do with politics. For example, take TV talk show gurus. Sooner or later, no matter how tangential the topic, the question comes up, "What should government, the law, the police, etc., do about this?" How tangential? Among the talk show topics on a single day, November 4, 1994 (incidentally, the sixteenth anniversary of the seizure of American embassy personnel in Teheran and the beginning of the "Iranian hostage crisis"), were the following. None, of course, dealt with the former crisis but dealt instead with other "crises": *Donahue*, "Sex Survey"; *Oprah Winfrey*, "Dreams Come True"; *Jenny Jones*, "Cheating Boyfriends"; *Gordon Elliott*, "Marital Sex"; *Susan Powter*, "Obesity"; *Rolanda*, "Simpson Home Videos"; *Ricki Lake*, "Sex After Breakups"; *Geraldo*, "Lives Caught on Videotape"; *Maury Povich*, "Black Sheep of the Family"; *Sally Jessy Raphael*, "Cheating Newlyweds"; *Leeza*, "Compulsive Disorders"; and *Montel Williams*, "Bodybuilders."

Whether the latter-day purveyors of ribald wit are, as some of them would have us believe, like the Lord in Psalms (107: 14, 27), who is come to bring us "out of darkness and the shadow of death," or, instead, simply babblers who leave us "to reel to and fro and stagger like a drunken man" at "wit's end," only time will tell. In either case they and the other new Falstaffs raise questions worthy of concern to the citizen-actors of the comedy of American democracy.

COMEDIES OF WIT

Comedies of wit share certain characteristics with comedies of manners. Both mock the incongruities that occur when people follow artificial codes of behavior rather than the dictates of natural desires and responses; both strive to warn against the self-delusion that arises out of slavish etiquette; and both feature characters who display charm and guile. What sets comedies of wit off is a reversal of a Burkian ratio. Comedies of manners stress sophisticated agents (the characters) who use sparkling dialogue (agency) to attack sham, that is, an agent-agency ratio. Traits a person brings to a situation influence how one behaves in it. Comedies of wit, by contrast, stress clever expression (agency). Pointing out unexpected connections between seemingly unrelated ideas is the essence of witty expression, remarks that surprise and delight *both* those who utter and those that hear them (agents). The ratio is one of agency-act: a person's facile talk governs behavior.

Witty expression abounds in skillful phraseology, puns, surprising contrasts, paradoxes, epigrams. Falstaff's verbal fencing, punning, and verbal sleights-of-hand served as dramatic agencies to extricate Shakespeare's character from tricky wickets, thus allowing Sir John to save face. To be sure, the character of Falstaff is ludicrous, blustery, and bluffing. He, typically perhaps, laughs at himself as much as at everything else. Yet, as with all true wits, Falstaff is open and not duplicitous, jocular and not bitter, and, in Dryden's words, a model of "propriety of thought and words."[1]

However, propriety is not always characteristic of political wits. Witty utterance is rapid repartee, razorlike in its incisiveness and often lethal, as in the case of a humiliating put-down. Political actors—politicians, journalists, spokespersons for various causes—often use wit as invective, striving for a stinging, vindictive outcome. There was more than a little invective in 1988 when syndicated columnist George Will, a self-styled wit, referred to Vice President George Bush's role in the administration of President Ronald Reagan as that of a "political lapdog." Thus did Will capture the essence of Dryden's phrase, "much malice . . . mingled with little wit."

There is an apocryphal story of Great Britain's World War II prime minister, Winston Churchill. Churchill, who had a fondness for brandy, encountered a woman at a party. "You, sir, are drunk," announced the woman. "And you, madam, are ugly," retorted Churchill, who then with inspired wit continued, "In the morning I shall be sober, but you, madam, shall still be ugly." Today the prime minister, should such a story reach the tabloids, would be pilloried for his insensitivity, chauvinism, and political incorrectness. At the very least Churchill should have said "cosmetically different," not "ugly."[2]

Regardless of whether or not they act out of malice, "the wit of politicians flourishes in a democratic society, but not in a tyranny."[3] Shakespeare calls brevity the soul of wit," but brevity alone is not the soul. Openness counts too. Wit is the open expression of incongruities between arbitrary ideas, an openness frowned on by tyrants. No wonder, then, that a democratic culture nurtures comedies of wit, while tyrannies use potent pesticides to rid the ground of such noxious weeds.

In America's democracy the comedies of wit that play themselves out surround efforts to identify and account for the role of the most venerated of our comedy of democracy's characters. In fact, it is the lead character we encountered in discussing both comedies of romance and of manners, and a major player in the comedies of farce and humors. It is The People. Few catch phrases so evoke the spirit that democracy is alleged to possess as the cherished words uttered by Abraham Lincoln at Gettysburg, "government of the people, by the people, for the people." As rephrased by today's politicians, the expression is condensed: "democracy is government by public opinion." The question is, however, Who speaks for public opinion and, moreover, in what voice?

SNOW WHITE AND THE SEVEN DWARFS
OF PUBLIC OPINION

"The public be damned," said railroad tycoon William Vanderbilt as his train steamed into Chicago in 1882.[4] If his sentiment were widely shared today, then the unemployment rate would jump precipitously. For trying to define, influence, cater to, court, seduce, and obey public opinion constitutes the livelihood of countless politicians, journalists, pollsters, entertainers, merchandisers, public relations specialists, academics, and sundry freelance flacks. Everybody, it seems, wants to speak for public opinion—and be paid for doing so.

Given the glut of contestants vying to be The Voice of Public Opinion, each rival—if one is to be taken seriously—must be positioned in a unique way relative to the competition. Otherwise one is not The Voice, just another whisper or, worse yet, a tree toppling in a deserted forest with no one to hear the sound. It is a little like the Seven Dwarfs in the romantic fairy tale, *Snow White*: Happy, Sleepy, Sneezy, Doc, Dopey, Bashful, and Grumpy. Each stands in line for a kiss, a reward for serving the lovely and pure of heart princess of the forest. As some dwarfs were embraced more than others, so some voices are heard more often.

Given the soberness of our times, however, we had best be cautious. It is more politically correct to employ the redesignation for *Snow White* coined by the witty cartoonist, Buddy Hickerson of "The Quigmans." Hickerson retitles the fairy tale "Repressive Celibate and the Seven Politically Height-Challenged." Hence, there are Self-Actualized (Happy), Chemically Dependent (Sleepy), Nasally-Challenged (Sneezy), Control Freak (Doc), Deep Denial (Dopey), Passive-Aggressive (Bashful), and Realistic (Grumpy).[5]

Walt Disney's classic adaptation of the Grimms' fairy tale about a satanic queen using an apple to rob a beautiful maiden of her virginity was filmed in animation in 1937 and released the following year. Coincidentally, that same year a noted public opinion analyst published a seminal essay exploring the "fictions and blind alleys" in defining and speaking for public opinion.[6] In the maiden issue of a scholarly journal, *Public Opinion Quarterly*, the analyst, Floyd Allport, sought to strip away virginity; unlike the Queen taking aim at Snow White, however, Allport's target was the conventional, fairy tale notions of public opinion of the time.

There is a remarkable similarity between each of Allport's fictions of public opinion and each fictional character in Disney's venerable animation. What could have been a witty comparison almost a half century ago had anyone sought to make it, remains so today. For, like the dwarfs mining for diamonds, public opinion researchers mine for the wealth underlying any reading of the public mind. Hence, in the words of the dwarfs' song (Hi ho, hi ho, It's off to work we go) let us examine the resemblance.

Were a contestant for the accolade of The Voice of Public Opinion to approach the rivalry positioned as the self-actualized Happy, we would expect a bouncy, optimistic expression. Happy would reflect the scholar's fiction identified as the *personification* of public opinion. Personification is the practice of converting all things, animate or inanimate, into persons. Indeed, even to speak of public opinion as possessing a voice is to personalize the phenomenon, much like saying "Wall Street responded today to inflation jitters," or "Congress gave a cold shoulder to the president's proposals for reform of the savings and loan industry." Wall Street personifies economic trends, or Congress personifies opposition to the president, in the way Falstaff personifies wit.

Of course, to speak of streets or institutions as persons is nonsense. It bears as much semblance to reality as talking about "Mother Nature" and "Father Time." Yet, we do it without reservation every day. And so it is with The Voice of Public Opinion. Like the ever-smiling Happy, delighted by a good meal one evening and just as pleased by a bad dinner the next, in personifying public opinion we endorse the fiction that public opinion is a person who expresses one view at one time and another view at another time, yet is always the opinion of John Q. Public. For instance, from the 1930s through the 1960s, the voice of public opinion sanctioned cigarette smoking, then in the 1980s and 1990s condemned it. Connecting the two expressions is some underlying soul or personality, "public opinion." As does Happy's perpetually bright countenance, public opinion remains undaunted, albeit inconsistent.

Actually, there is a double confusion in the personification of public opinion. One lies in what we just described, namely, the assumption that there is a single voice, fickle though its utterances be, speaking for the collective soul of opinion. The other lies in the tendency to think of "the Public" as a super-organic being "turning its gaze, now this way, now that."[7] The super-organic personification of the public does not take the form of Happy, so much as it resembles Snow White's wicked stepmother's looking glass. The mean, vain Queen, so in love with her image, seeks truth from her super-organic mirror. Acting in the fashion of an aspirant for the U.S. presidency, Snow White's stepmother asks, "Magic mirror on the wall, who's the fairest one of all?" In the fairy tale the mirror of public opinion is something of a ubiquitous espionage agent, gazing left and right, then delivering the bad news to the Queen that Snow White is the fairest in the land. In the real life tale of Democrat Bill Clinton's quest for the presidency, when he asked the question of his mirror of public opinion in 1992, the reply he received carried more punch: "It's the economy, stupid!

A little reflection, either mental or mirrored, reminds us that looking glass images are distorted; neither wicked queens nor ambitious politicians should rely too much on magic personifications. Neither "the Voice" nor "the People" exists. Instead politicians find sets of individuals agreeing at one time on specific matters, disagreeing at another. The voice is actually a gaggle of conflicting expressions, and the people are a rebellious lot. Yet, some of the world's finest minds have insisted on making public opinion a transcendental being. "The public is a fool," cried Alexander Pope in his *First Epistle of the Second Book of Horace*; Voltaire also was not kind. "The public is a ferocious beast; one must either chain it up or flee from it," he wrote. Nicolas Chamfort caught the spirit in another way: "The public! The public! How many fools are needed to make a public?"[8]

As wits have dissected the voice, the public, and the voice of public opinion, they have generated another fiction, namely, the *group fallacy* of public opinion. There is a drowsiness about this fallacy akin to *Snow White*'s somnambulant Sleepy struggling to keep his eyes open even as his co-workers and beloved princess remind him he should wake up. Politicians wed to the group fallacy pride themselves on understanding full well that "the public" is comprised of individuals rather than a single entity. However, like Sleepy, having awakened momentarily to that realization, they soon slumber off again. Their snoozing reveals itself in tendencies to utter such phrases as "the public wants a tax hike," or "the public demands health care reform," or "the public seeks a war on crime." Whatever the policy fad of the day, the alleged public cries out for it.

Journalists too succumb to the group fiction, for example, awakening from slumber to report, as they did in 1994, that congressional election returns mean that "the country rejected incumbents." Still, we should not be too hard on journalists; sometimes their dozing sharpens their senses when they finally do wake up. Remember, it was Sleepy who was the first of the dwarfs to realize, when the creatures of the forest sounded the alarm, that the wicked queen had captured Snow White. Similarly, members of the press doggedly fought off their drowsiness to report the mendacity of Watergate.

Happy and Sleepy, wonderful fictions that they are, remain simply that: fictions. So too do the personifications and group fallacies of public opinion that the two characters resemble. Both depict public opinion as totally inclusive, the expression of a single public or group. A third appraisal of public opinion attacks the problem from an opposite view, namely, claiming that the public is "made up, not of entire individuals but of an abstraction of a single interest (or set of interests) common to a certain number in the population." Those sharing "such a common interest are said to constitute a *'public.'* "[9] This appraisal too is a fiction, that of *partial inclusion*.

To what, we might ask, is poor Sneezy, our nasally challenged fairy tale friend, allergic? Given his watery eyes, sniffles, and need for a lifetime supply of Kleenex, one might say "everything." Indeed, when the allergic dwarf sneezes, no matter how hard he tries not to (for when you gotta, you gotta), his exhalation blows everything away—dishes, chairs, tables, forest creatures, even the other dwarfs. Sneezy's plight of being allergic to all things is as totally inclusive as the fictions of personification and the group. While such a global diagnosis makes Sneezy's allergist rich, it does not help Sneezy. Being allergic to everything, he is allergic to breathing, hence, to life itself.

It would be more comforting to Sneezy to identify specific allergens that cause his discomfort. Maybe the whole, Sneezy's misery, is attributable to only a portion of the environment, not to total inclusion of all allergens but to partial inclusion of a few. In the same vein imagine that individuals making up *a* public (specific, shared interest) are not at the same time members of some other partially inclusive public. (It is as if Sneezy's nasally challenged condition is attributable to only one set of pollens and no others.) And assume that one public does not overlap with another, just as a wisp of fungus in the air does not increase or decrease with the presence of mold, or ragweed, or dust. With each public independent of any other, then each public consists of the number of people pursuing a unique interest and holding an opinion concerning it. If that be the case, as with Sneezy's nasal challenges, public opinion consists solely of the opinions of members of distinctive publics.

Unfortunately, there is a hitch. Dust does carry pollen, mold, and fungi; so too are people members of overlapping publics. Suppose that an individual member of Public A, an interest favoring a national lottery to finance the costs of national health care, is also a member of Public B, an interest seeking federal financial assistance in fighting gambling addiction. Here is a very un-Happy-like, but very Sneezy-like, dilemma. Two interests contradict one another—one encourages gambling via lottery, a lottery to raise money to finance gambling addiction! The difficulty lies in the fact that, like Sneezy's allergies, "opinions are reactions of individuals; they cannot be allocated to publics without becoming ambiguous and unintelligible."[10] Telling people not to contradict themselves by joining groups with conflicting aims is about as feasible as telling Sneezy that the only way to get relief from postnasal drip is to avoid all pollen by not breathing. He accounts for, and wards off, each and every individual micrograin of offending pollen; yet, the cure of "terminal inconvenience" (death) for Sneezy would prove worse than the malady.[11]

If public opinion is a conflicting gaggle of individual opinions, then how does any politician actually divine it, beyond, of course, claiming that public opinion is "what I say it is"? That puzzle has vexed both philosophers and politicians since the term "public opinion" came into vogue during the Enlightenment. One principal way of solving it is simply to deny the puzzle's existence. That is Dopey's approach. Dopey is not as happy-go-lucky and optimistic as Happy, as somnambulant as Sleepy, or as set upon by miseries as Sneezy. The mute Dopey, who doesn't know if he can speak because he has never tried, is simply affectionately oblivious to problems. In that respect he behaves as do students of public opinion who engage in the fiction of *ideational entity*.

Many who speak of democracy as "government by public opinion" simply deny that public opinion itself is the opinion of the multitude. It is instead a kind of Platonic essence, an "anonymous and impersonal tribunal" that is external to the everyday political world, unified in content rather than divided, infallible rather than inconsistent or contradictory.[12] Such a view, that public opinion in a democracy transcends the individual opinions of democracy's citizens, reflecting instead an abstract common good rather than a compromise of individual interests, has persisted throughout U.S. political history. In fact, we find this Dopey-like denial of conflicting individual opinions in one of the nation's most sacred documents, the Declaration of Independence. References to "one People," "the Opinions of Mankind," and "Truths" that are "self-evident" reek of the ideational character of public opinion. Almost two centuries after the Declaration, the noted journalist Walter Lippmann, who understood the news media's comedy of manners as well as anyone (see Chapter 3), gave his own support to the ideational fallacy: "When we speak of popular sovereignty, we must know whether we are talking about The People, as voters, or about *The People*, as a community of the entire living population, with their predecessors and successors."[13]

A strong challenge to the ideational view of public opinion stems from scholars who deny that public opinion must imply *either* total or partial inclusion. They turn away from mystical sources where public opinion might reside to the processes, and outcomes of those processes. By emphasizing the means politicians employ to create and control public opinion, these scholars redefine democracy as government *of* public opinion rather than *by* public opinion. In the fashion of another of *Snow White*'s characters, Doc, politicians are control freaks seeking to manage public opinion and not merely to respond to it. They are, as academic and bureaucratic jargon puts it, proactive rather than reactive. This fiction of public opinion as a *group product* holds that public opinion emerges from the give-and-take of group discussion. Doc-like politicians may, like the cartoon character, get their words mixed up and practice obfuscation, yet they are so eager to please that they forge a group consensus as a product of their skills.

Views that personify public opinion, or that make of it an ideational entity, fortify politicians with weapons they can use to guide public discussion. Politicians claim that they are "above politics," "nonpartisan," even "nonpolitical." To hear them tell it, politicians never mess with narrow concerns at the expense of the public interest; they pursue altruism rather than self-interest, and are invulnerable to the demands of pressure groups. Politicians illustrate Kenneth Burke's notion of comic irony through "didactic" forms of drama:

In the bourgeois body politic, even *politicians* damn an opponent's motive by calling it *political*; and professional partisans like to advocate their measures as *transcending* factional antitheses. Candidates for office say, in effect: "Vote for our faction, which is more able to *mediate between the factions.*"

Thus, says Burke, the delegation of authority by people to a politician in a democracy is "the popular selection of a puppet to act as a public convenience." Citizens vote politicians "an identity, a dramatic role in regulating the traffic of the state." The problem is that, in the end, the puppets are still but puppets.[14]

Since puppets do not control themselves, savvy politicians work to create the illusion that they, not their electors, are in control. By claiming that public opinion emerges from discussions in groups that they lead, politicians also claim control of opinion itself. Here too, however, lies an irony. By claiming that public opinion is the product of group discussion, politicians convert a manner (discussion) into a mannerism (public opinion). Public opinion is nothing more than a burlesque, continuous talk for talk's sake rather than talk to achieve consummation of policy. Policy is made not through open, public discussion, but behind the scenes in the trading and jousting of politicians who may or may not take into account the expressed interests of constituents. In drawing the parallel between politicians and Doc in *Snow White* as control freaks, one recalls the Algren Precept: "Never play cards with a man named Doc."[15] For what you see, or hear, is not what you get.

The group-product fiction gives rise to yet another fallacious view of public opinion. It is one that politicians, and journalists, frequently exploit. Ideally, through its free exchange of views public discussion permits the discovery and correction of errors, the creation and perfection of enlightenment. The emergent product will thus not only be *more* than the sum of its individual products, it will be *better*. Hence arises a *eulogistic* fiction.

In a classic Hollywood film, *Casablanca*, a Nazi colonel tries to intimidate a resistance leader endeavoring to flee to Lisbon with his wife. The resistance leader expresses a desire to speak to a man (Urgarte) who has been taken into police custody. The prisoner might have information that would aid the leader's escape. "May I speak to him now?" the resistance leader asks. Replies the Nazi colonel, wryly, "You would find the conversation a trifle one-sided. Signor Urgarte is dead."[16] Group discussions do not, of course, involve the terminally inconvenienced, however they too are usually a trifle one-sided. We all know that in group discussion it is not the group that thinks, talks, and expresses opinions; individuals do that. We also know that, more likely than not, a few individuals talk, others listen. There are far more citizens who are like Bashful in *Snow White* than there are Docs. They suffer from what communication scholars call "communication apprehension,"[17] turning red with embarrassment at the thought of speaking out.

What makes the eulogistic fiction so appealing to politicians is not that public opinion arises out of group discussion. Rather, it is precisely the opposite. Public opinion is the opinion of political leaders whose views are unfettered by the silence of the Bashfuls. Like Bashful, who wanted Snow White to tell the dwarfs a love story, silent citizens want to be lulled by the fantasies of public opinion recounted by their leaders.

In fact, research into the phenomenon of public opinion suggests that it is the silent Bashfuls who contribute to the tendencies of democratic politicians frequently to misread public views on controversial matters. When there is a problem that divides opinions, people naturally look around them and assess how well their own views match those of other people. The Docs of the world who believe their views are, and will be, the dominant ones, even if they are not dominant at the moment, are eager to speak out in public. But those who feel that their opinions are losing ground, and are in the minority or soon will be so, fear speaking up; they are the Bashfuls. Mark Twain caught the essence of the phenomenon when he said to a lady friend with whom he was arguing:

I explained that what I meant by that phrase "public opinions" was *published* opinions, opinions spread in print. I said I was in the common habit, in private conversation with friends, of revealing every private opinion I possessed relating to religion, politics and men, but that I should never dream of *printing* one of them, because they are individually and collectively at war with almost everybody's public opinion while at the same time they are in happy agreement with almost everybody's private opinion.[18]

The irony in all this is that, even though, as Twain urged, the private views of the Bashfuls may in fact be in the majority and those of the Docs in the minority, so long as the Docs keep speaking out and the Bashfuls keep quiet, there is "a spiraling process" where the minority view comes to dominate the scene and the majority view disappears "from public awareness as its adherents [become] mute. This is a process that can be called a 'Spiral of Silence.' "[19]

In *Snow White* Bashful's shyness allows his co-workers occasionally to take advantage. One who takes advantage in an irritating way is Grumpy. His tart tongue and sour demeanor lead him to express views that Bashful would never dare utter. Grumpy does so in a way reminiscent of Richard Brinsley Sheridan's *The School for Scandal* (1777): "There's no possibility of being witty without a little ill-nature; the malice of a good thing is the barb that makes it stick." It is Grumpy who says that trouble is "a brewin'" when Snow White shows up at the dwarfs' doorstep, who speaks against the "wicked wiles" of women (even though he has no idea what a wicked wile is), and who vehemently denounces the princess' suggestion that dwarfs should wash their hands before dining.

There is a bafflement over the character of public opinion closely allied with the ill-natured Grumpys of the world. It confuses public opinion with how the phenomenon is presented. This *journalistic* fiction takes seriously what for Mark Twain was a facetious view, namely, it equates "public" opinion with "published" opinions (now "broadcast" opinions as well). Journalists have a vested interest in sustaining the avowal that public opinion and published opinions are identical. The claim has cash value in prestige for themselves and their craft. The fiction is an old one, extending back at least to the eighteenth century, when Joseph Addison and Richard Steele were publishing their spontaneous and witty prose in *The Spectator*.

In the United States generations of newspapers professed to speak for public opinion on their editorial pages. In the 1920s and 1930s journalists David Lawrence, Walter Lippmann, and their imitators added independent columns of political opinion to newspapers, eventually giving rise to the contemporary op-ed page. A whole new source of published opinions, the views of columnists soon competed as voices of *public* opinion. Following the advent of broadcast journalism, radio networks allotted fifteen-minute segments to "news commentators."

It was not until television journalism pushed radio aside after World War II that commentators such as Gabriel Heater, Fulton Lewis, Jr., Edward P. Morgan, and Edward R. Murrow vanished from the airways. That did not mean, however, that news commentary and analysis, a euphemism for claiming to speak for public opinion, vanished with them. TV journalism continued radio's tradition of news commentary, but in preciously allotted ninety-second segments rather than the extravagance of a quarter of an hour. There Eric Sevareid, Bill Moyers, John Chancellor, and others read the tea leaves of public sentiment. As America entered the closing decade of the twentieth century, the clamor of journalistic voices claiming to represent public opinion moved to new venues—radio and television talk shows, TV news magazines, network and syndicated morning "wake you up and get you on your way" programming, and late afternoon television tabloids.

With so many journalistic outlets for opinion expression in newspapers, news magazines, tabloids, radio talk shows, and televised public affairs programs, the journalistic fiction has taken on new forms. In an earlier era the fiction paralleled that of personification in claiming public opinion as an entity of total inclusion. Editorials spoke as *the* voice of public opinion and reminded politicians of *the* public conscience. Today published opinions emanate from so many Towers of Babel that virtually anyone's opinion on any political matter finds its way into print or onto the airwaves. The oft-repeated aphorism that in the TV age everyone can be famous for fifteen minutes takes on new meaning: now any opinion can be famous for fifteen seconds.

Moreover, opinion expression is now Big Business, namely, the entertainment business. This is so not only for avowed entertainment programming, such as *Donahue* or *Oprah*, but also for *Today* or *Good Morning America*, or *Jay Leno* and *David Letterman*. But as every channel surfer knows, the TV ratings game catches even the innocent Snow Whites of public affairs programming up in the entertainment imperative—the Sunday sermonettes like *Meet the Press* and *This Week with David Brinkley*, the insomniacs' palliative, *Nightline*, or even the sainted *MacNeil/Lehrer Report*. To be sure, the wits who populate these offerings differ widely in their styles. For example, Ted Koppel grills his guests with an urbane, droll staccato. David Brinkley and his friends (columnist George Will, TV pest Sam Donaldson, and news starlet Cokie Roberts) interview and comment with sophisticated charm and guile (sophisticated as in sophistry). The resident pundits at CNN's *Crossfire* engage in a slapstick of "let's-you-and-him-fight" by exploiting the pie-in-the-face technique. Jay Leno and David Letterman offer political witticisms as stand-up comics who sit down. William Buckley, virtually the grand old man of televised political punditry, smiles and flashes his stiletto-like barbs. Yet others bring outrage (Geraldo Rivera), an "aw, shucks" homeyness (Phil Donahue), or sheer sensationalism—virtually any studio talk show.

Although many might think so privately, rarely do any of the voices of the people heard in print or broadcast journalism claim that their public views are certifiable as *the* public opinion. Instead, their claim is usually a little more modest. They avow that no grumpy journalists, no Snow Whites, none of the other dwarfs, and certainly no politicians know precisely what the public thinks. There is, however, one notable exception, radio and TV talk show host, author, columnist, and self-proclaimed raconteur Rush Limbaugh. It is the same Rush who combines Grumpy's voice with a Falstaffian image. Setting aside his self-avowed conservative views, Limbaugh's style is not one of outrage, it is outrageous.

Consider the remarks that peppered one of Limbaugh's syndicated columns, one in which he strictly disavowed any interest in seeking the presidency of the United States ("I am not running for anything"). Like Falstaff, who, having served Prince Hal, then Henry IV, feels qualified to lead, Limbaugh writes, "Thirty years after Ronald Reagan's brilliant enunciation of conservative ideals at the end of Barry Goldwater's campaign, the torch has passed to me." Liberals, he says, quake at the thought. Why? Because of Limbaugh's public following: 659 radio stations nationwide and on shortwave throughout the world, 250 TV stations in the United States. Far from being a "hatemonger and a blowhard," Limbaugh claims to "provide information and analysis the media refuse to disseminate—information and analysis the public craves." He goes on, "I validate the convictions of ordinary people. . . . I champion the extraordinary accomplishments of ordinary people." That, he concludes, "is why liberals are terrified of me. As well they should be."[20] Limbaugh epitomizes the journalistic fiction of public opinion: "Vanity of vanities, saith the Preacher, vanity of vanities; all is vanity" (Ecclesiastes 1:2).

Falstaff was not pure. Rush Limbaugh, however, claims to be like the Ivory soap bar, ninety-nine and forty-four one hundredths percent pure. The claim parallels a final fiction regarding public opinion propagated by another set of political wits. Those wits assert Snow White's purity and chastity, or at least confidence at the 95 percent "level of significance." They, like Snow White, are kissed by entranced princely politicians with whom they ride off into the sunset, leaving the seven dwarfs of public opinion behind in the dust. Those wits consist of the pollsters who define public opinion as what public opinion polls measure.

Public opinion polling is an industry that ties together politicians, journalists, academics, product marketers, public relations specialists, and image makers of all stripes. The industry gives rise to, and has a vested interest in preserving, the *measurement* fiction.

Even people whose parents had not been born at the time the photographer snapped the picture have seen one of the most memorable photos in the history of U.S. politics. There stands President Harry Truman, triumphantly holding aloft a copy of the *Chicago Daily Tribune* with its banner headline, "Dewey Defeats Truman." The Trib had been a trifle premature, and Truman wanted everyone to know that polls, pollsters, pundits, and prognosticators aside, Thomas Dewey had *not* won the 1948 presidential election. (Don't try asking a representative sample of Americans about that today; Dewey might come out the winner!)

The Trib was not the only organization with egg on its personified face. The nation's leading polling firms also had missed the call. The results of the 1948 presidential contest literally sent pollsters scurrying back to their drawing boards to find out how they had erred. In the eleven presidential and hundreds of other elections since 1948, pollsters have worked as diligently to clean up their act as Snow White did to keep the seven dwarfs' small cottage neat and tidy with the aid of her representative sample of forest creatures—bluebirds, robins, squirrels, rabbits, beavers, chipmunks, deer, a tortoise, even a skunk.

Pollsters have redesigned their sampling procedures, tested and retested the wording of their questions to ferret out bias, improved their interviewing techniques, and tried to distance themselves from clients who insist that the magic of polls declare them the fairest in the land. Professional pollsters have adopted codes of conduct urging guidelines and safeguards pertaining to how the news media should report poll results. Surely by now their righteous efforts have made polls and polling as pure as the driven snow.

Not necessarily. Certainly the overall accuracy in measuring Americans' views on a multitude of matters has increased: on political candidates, concerns, causes, and crises; on entertainment celebrities, fads, preferences, and fantasies; on marketed goods, products, services, and nostrums; on sexual habits, hallucinations, hangouts, and hangups; and on social practices, problems, prejudices, and manners.[21]

But in defining public opinion the accuracy of measurement of individual opinions may not always reflect *public opinion* at all. For one thing, to equate public opinion with the aggregate of responses to questions asked in nationally representative samples, no matter how accurate the findings, creates as much of an illusion of public opinion as it does a flawless photo of it. Until citizens are asked about matters, indeed, when they are asked, there is no assurance that they have any opinions at all about, say, health care reform, gun control, sexual harassment in the workplace, restrictions on immigration, or sundry other items on which they are queried. Yet when aggregate responses are tallied, polling wits assure audiences that, for example, only one-third of Americans believe that "most elected officials care what people like me think"; or slightly over one-third opine that "school boards ought to have the right to fire teachers who are known homosexuals"; and whopping majorities believe it's "time for Washington politicians to step aside and make room for new leaders," or "we should restrict and control people coming into our country more than we do now" (79 and 82 percent, respectively). And in the spirit of "doing as I say, not as I do," two-thirds "completely agree" with the view that "it is my duty as a citizen to always vote."[22]

One has no reason to doubt the fidelity of such a profile of Americans' responses any more than one could believe that Snow White was feckless. However, think about snow. A white blanket of snow is smooth, untarnished, and unsullied—all of the symbolism conjured up by "white" in C. Clement Moore's "The Night Before Christmas" ("the moon, on the breast of the new-fallen snow") or Irving Berlin's popular song, "White Christmas." It is not until a rabbit hops across, or a garbage truck defaces, or factory soot despoils, that there is any mark, any modulation on the whiteness. And so it is with popular opinions; frequently, not until roused by interviewers' telephonic interruptions (often during the dining hour at night) does the blank face of public opinion yield any expression at all—an expression prompted by intrusion. Herman Melville's saga *Moby Dick* tells of a Great White Whale of pristine beauty until it is pocked by the harpoons of whalers, not all well intentioned, yet, like pollsters, certainly bent on making a living.

Let us, however, suppose that Americans do hold views about a host of politically relevant matters, abstract and ambiguous sentiments not precisely formed but nonetheless constituting the fuzzy images of subjective understanding.[23] Political scientist V. O. Key, Jr., called these views "latent opinion," views that might or might not become politically important: "So long as it remains latent, it cannot well be inspected," hence measured by polls, surveys, and other devices. "Yet," wrote Key, "in the practice of politics and government latent opinion is really about the only type of opinion that generates much anxiety."[24]

Thus does Key, in his own witty fashion, put into striking focus the irony of what polling wits are about. They are less like Snow White, virginal and chaste, than like "The Snowstorm" of Ralph Waldo Emerson's poem, "the frolic architecture of the snow." To the degree that they estimate what citizens' opinions politicians should adjust to, pollsters frolic to measure the unmeasurable. For latent opinion "cannot well be inspected." Moreover, "if activated," even by pollsters' methods, "it has ceased to be latent." The frolic of the pollsters' snow, or snow job, having activated latency, then serves a purpose quite different from the impartial, accurate measure of public opinion. Poll results (derived from politicians' "tracking polls," TV stations' "bullet polls," and marketing firms' "consumer surveys") are puffery. Their principal use is as publicity tools to promote candidates, causes, products, news and public affairs programming, personalities, celebrities, and entertainment programs.

Key's key (pun intended) problem with public opinion was its illusory nature—a phenomenon more spoken of in fictional ways than as what truly exists. He wrote, "To speak with precision of public opinion is a task not unlike coming to grips with the Holy Ghost."[25] No matter what fiction of total or partial inclusion, no matter whether symbolized by Happy, Sleepy, or Sneezy, by Doc, Dopey, or Bashful, or even by Grumpy journalists and Snow White pollsters, public opinion is but a *witty invention*: "a sort of secular idol . . . 'god-term' to which citizens, scientists, and office-holders alike pay allegiance, partly as an act of faith, partly as a matter of observation, partly as a condition of sanity."[26] Ah, sanity! Are we sane, or merely at our wit's end?

AT WIT'S END

In the comedy of democracy political analysts who grasp for jocose insights into public opinion are, in the words of the Book of Psalms (107: 27), likely "to reel to and fro . . . at their wit's end." The source of the problem lies not in the stagger of the drunken, but in the unique quality of American democracy as "government by publicity," a "force uniquely indispensable to the American system in which 'public opinion' is called on daily," in which "publicity affects not only men and policies but the fundamental balances of government itself."[27] It is government by publicity that harnesses in parallel the selective processes of news and public opinion, the parallel comedies of manners and wit.

In their habitual newsmaking practices of converting manners into mannerisms (recall Chapter 3), journalists are selective. At any given moment, be it in a small village or the global village, innumerable things happen simultaneously. In the selective process of newsmaking only a few become events, fewer still of those are newsworthy, and even fewer become news items, let alone news stories. In the words of St. Matthew (23: 14), "Many are called, but few are chosen." In accordance with journalistic values, the chosen few happenings become stories of contests, conquests, crime, crisis, celebration, and so on.

Running along beside the newsmaking practices of journalists, like two stallions pulling the chariot of democracy, are the opinion-making practices of politicians. At any given moment, virtually anywhere, conflicts occur— over well-being, wealth, status, morals, love, learning, and control.[28] Like happenings, most such conflicts go unnoticed. Nobody but the parties personally involved in the conflict care. Still, sometimes outside parties do care. Perhaps it is because the people who are bickering with one another appeal to others for support in an effort to get the upper hand in the contest. Or it may be because, like children watching their parents fight, outside parties sense that struggle is going to affect their own interests. For whatever reason, outsiders get drawn in.

Just as a few of many happenings come to the attention of people and thus become events, so too do a few of many conflicts draw outsiders into the fray. It is at this point, wrote philosopher John Dewey, that publics are born. The consequences of human acts, said Dewey, either "affect the persons directly engaged in the transaction" or "affect others beyond those immediately concerned." In this "we find the germ of the distinction between the private and the public." When the consequences of conflicts "do not extend beyond A and B, the activity lies between them; it is private." Yet, if the consequences "extend beyond the two directly concerned . . . the act acquires a public capacity, whether the conversation be carried on by a king and his prime minister or by Cataline and a fellow conspirator or by merchants planning to monopolize a market."[29]

Not all events are newsworthy to journalists, and not all public conflicts catch the eye of politicians. Following Key's imperative that public opinion consists of opinions that "governments find it prudent to heed,"[30] then the public conflicts politicians find it prudent to heed give rise to political issues. Typically they are issues that the politician can exploit to advantage; or they may be issues that will not go away, that simply can't be ignored. In any event, just as journalists convert some events into newsworthy events, then a fewer number into stories, so too do politicians convert some conflicts into political issues, then heed as "public opinion" views expressed on issues selected for their strategic value, or forced upon them as inescapable.

Thus, public opinion, when viewed as a comedy of wit, shares common reins with news viewed as a comedy of manners. Neither news nor public opinion exists in fact. They are both hit-or-miss *labels*, constructions that fallible journalists and/or politicians driving the chariot affix to a relatively small number of potential happenings and conflicts. Those "Made in America" labels signal what journalists and politicians want to pay attention to in the world, what they want to privilege at the expense of what they choose to ignore, and what they select to legitimize their own jobs. When journalists and politicians publicize the same happenings-as-conflicts, government by publicity is a harmonious blend of voices; but when the two sets of wits disagree over what conflicts should count most in the scheme of things, government by publicity gets contentious, rancorous, sometimes petty.

To say that neither news nor public opinion exists apart from the actions of journalists and politicians who exploit happenings and conflicts for their own purposes is, of course, to express the heretical view that neither, as Holy Ghosts, should be taken seriously. Heretical though it may be, however, it is also the witty view. It looks the ghost squarely in the eye, much as Scrooge looked at the ghost of Jacob Marley in Charles Dickens' *A Christmas Carol*, and intones that there is "more gravy than grave about you." Wits have expressed it many times. Most notable was Walter Lippmann, full-time journalist, part-time politician. He did not back away from the heresy: "I hold that this public is a mere phantom."[31] It is no more to be taken seriously than people who go to the theater because the reviews say it is the place to be. They "arrive in the middle of the third act and will leave before the last curtain, having stayed just long enough perhaps to decide who is the hero and who is the villain of the piece."[32] Hence, the "enduring popularity of public men does not come from trying to guess what the people will applaud," for "it is no comfort whatever" for a politician to know that one "is a good judge of public opinion;" citizens trust a politician, concluded Lippmann, "only if they have some evidence" that the politician "is a good judge of the public interest"[33] no matter what "news" or "public opinion" says.

NOTES

1. Quoted in William Flint Thrall, Addison Hibbard, and C. Hugh Holman, *A Handbook to Literature* (New York: Odyssey Press, 1960), p. 509.

2. Henry Beard and Christopher Cerf, *The Official Politically Correct Dictionary and Handbook* (New York: Villard Books, 1992), p. 90.

3. Leon A. Harris, *The Fine Art of Political Wit* (New York: E. P. Dutton, 1966), p. 18.

4. H. L. Mencken, *A New Dictionary of Quotations* (New York: Alfred A. Knopf, 1991), p. 991.

5. Buddy Hickerson, "The Quigmans." *Dallas Morning News*, June 25, 1993, p. 7C.

6. Floyd H. Allport, "Toward a Science of Public Opinion," *Public Opinion Quarterly* 1 (Winter 1937): 7–23.

7. Ibid., p. 8.

8. Mencken includes the words of Pope, Voltaire, and Chamfort in his *New Dictionary of Quotations*, p. 991.

9. Allport, "Science of Public Opinion," p. 9. Emphasis in original.

10. Ibid., p. 10.

11. Beard and Cerf, *Official Politically Correct Dictionary*, p. 74.

12. M. Ozouf, " 'Public Opinion' at the End of the Old Regime," *Journal of Modern History* 60 (1988): S11–S12.

13. Walter Lippmann, *The Public Philosophy* (New York: Little, Brown, 1955), p. 32. Emphasis in original.

14. Kenneth Burke, *Attitudes Toward History*, 3rd ed. (Berkeley: University of California Press, 1989), p. 78. Emphasis in original.

15. From Nelson Algren's essay, "What Every Young Man Should Know,": "Never eat at a place called Mom's. Never play cards with a man named Doc. And never lie down with a woman who's got more troubles than you." In Paul Dickson, *The Official Rules* (New York: Dell 1978), p. 39.

16. Howard Koch, ed., *Casablanca: Script and Legend* (Woodstock, NY: Overlook Press, 1992), p. 135.

17. James C. McCroskey, "Oral Communication Apprehension: A Summary of Recent Theory and Research," *Human Communication Research* 4 (Fall 1977): 78–96.

18. Mark Twain, *The Autobiography of Mark Twain*. ed. Charles S. Neider (New York: Harper and Row, 1959), p. 356.

19. Elisabeth Noelle-Neumann, *The Spiral of Silence* (Chicago: University of Chicago Press, 1984), p. 5.

20. Rush Limbaugh, "Liberals Fear Me Because I Am Effective," *Dallas Morning News*, October 13, 1994, p. 25A.

21. "Accuracy" here refers to a reduction of sampling error. In 1992, for example, six political polling organizations predicted the outcome of the presidential election. On average, not weighted for each poll's sample size, the six polls overestimated Bill Clinton's share of the vote by three percentage points (46 percent predicted; he received 43 percent), underestimated Ross Perot's by three points (16 percent predicted; he received 19 percent), and hit George Bush, as did the campaign, right on the head (38 percent predicted and received). See Robert M. Worcester, "A View from Britain: You Can Do It Better," *Public Perspective* 4 (November/December 1992): 17–18.

22. These findings are reported in a wire service news story headlined "Poll Finds Americans discouraged. Cynicism on Rise; Compassion Down." *Dallas Morning News*, September 21, 1994, 1A, 13A. The poll was conducted by the Times-Mirror Center for the People and the Press. The survey included 3,800 adults interviewed September 9–11, 1994, and had a margin of error of plus or minus 3 percentage points "meaning any response could vary by that amount in either direction" (p. 13A). One must assume that is any aggregate response, not any individual's response!

23. Kenneth E. Boulding, *The Image* (Ann Arbor, MI: University of Michigan Press, 1968).

24. V. O. Key, Jr., *Public Opinion and American Democracy* (New York: Alfred A. Knopf, 1961), p. 263.

25. Ibid., p. 8. See also the critical analysis of public opinion studies by John Zaller, "Positive Constructs of Public Opinion," *Critical Studies in Mass Communication* (September 1994): 276–287.

26. Avery Leiserson, "Notes on the Theory of Opinion Formation," *American Political Science Review* 47 (March 1953): 171.

27. Douglas Cater, *The Fourth Branch of Government* (Boston, MA: Houghton Mifflin, 1959), pp. 10–11.

28. Harold D. Lasswell and Abraham Kaplan, *Power and Society* (New Haven: Yale University Press, 1950).

29. John Dewey, *The Public and Its Problems* (Denver, CO: Alan Swallow, 1927), pp. 12–13.

30. Key, *Public Opinion*, p. 14.

31. Walter Lippmann, *The Phantom Public* (New York: Macmillan, 1925), p. 77.

32. Ibid., p. 65.

33. Walter Lippmann, "The Bogey of Public Opinion," *Vanity Fair* 37 (December 1931): 51.

CHAPTER 4

Politics and the News Media: A Comedy of Manners

If the world were as ideal as romantic theorists of democracy would have it, citizens would gather information about what is going on in politics from only the most impeccable of sources, say, the reference room of the public library, political science texts, the pages of the *New York Times*, and PBS' *Mac-Neil/Lehrer Report*. However, having learned in Chapter 1 that in the romantic comedy of democratic citizenship Americans are more interested in the peccadillos of politicians than the intricacies of health care reform, it is no surprise that citizens use less prestigious sources of political intelligence.

In the last decade of "America's Century,"[1] popular, glitzy news sources challenged, and for many people supplanted, the tried-and-true media that Americans once scanned for news about politics. No longer do nightly TV news programs, metropolitan dailies, and *Time*, *Newsweek*, and *U.S. News & World Report* provide Americans with allegedly trustworthy and reliable political reports; new kids on the block challenge for that informational task. On TV, for example, CNN had the audacity to make cable TV a twenty-four-hour source of political news. Then there were, first, the morning cereals (*Today*, *Good Morning America*, *CBS This Morning*) that expanded their audiences with soothing patter and information. Soon, serial talkers killed conventional news formats: *Donahue*, *Oprah*, *Sally Jessy*, *Geraldo*, and a cast of thousands. And afternoon TV spawned the serial killers—for example, *Hard*

Copy, Inside Edition, and *A Current Affair*—of TV programming in the tradition of tabloid journalism. Moreover, in 1982 *USA Today*'s sprightly, colorful style introduced a truly national daily newspaper. Finally, the weekly newsmagazines too met their match as publications such as *People* offered upbrow pablum for those too embarrassed to stuff the *National Inquirer* or *National Star* into their carts in supermarket checkout lines.

This diversification of news sources underscores what long has been the dramatic form contributed by the news media to the comedy of American democracy. Like comedies of romance, farce, and humor, the comedic form of news springs from ancient roots. It is the comedy of manners.

NOT A MISS, BUT A COMEDY OF, MANNERS

Machiavelli, as we saw in the Introduction, fully appreciated the comic qualities of politics. He also understood that politics is often brutal as well. Old Nick had scarcely been in his grave a century when English politics entered an especially nasty period. The reigning kings, first James I (1603–1625), then Charles I (1625–1649), were locked in a bitter dispute with Parliament. The monarchs insisted that as rulers they possessed a divine right to govern; Parliament thought otherwise, insisting that legal rights restrained kingly prerogatives. Added to the row was a monumental religious conflict. Anglican forces supported the monarchy; reformist and Puritan elements sided with Parliament. After civil wars, numerous military campaigns, and countless beheadings and other forms of bloodshed—including Charles losing his head for treason in 1649—the monarchy fell. After a brief period of a quasi-democratic Puritan Commonwealth, Oliver Cromwell instituted a Protectorate, with himself as hereditary protector.

But in politics, a father-god like the ancient Greeks' Zeus does not impose, enforce, and punish transgressions of morals forever. As Aristophanes said, "Whirl is King, having driven out Zeus."[2] Cromwell's death in 1658 unleashed whirl-like forces in English politics; after a couple of years of tumultuous reaction to Puritan rule, the English monarchy was restored with the accession of Charles II to the throne. The ensuing period (1660–1688), known as the Restoration, witnessed a persecution of Quakers and a return of militant Anglicanism.

During the Restoration a bubble, bubble of toil and trouble percolated new forms of drama. One was the *comedy of manners*. It was a style not suited to appeal to the tastes of the Puritan elements that had dominated politics in Cromwell's Protectorate. Comedies of manners viewed humans as corruptible creatures, a viewpoint shared by Puritans. But whereas the Puritans reacted to corruption with moral indignation and outrage, Restoration playwrights taught that moral corruption should be viewed with sophistication and tolerance. Their comedies did not imply, however, that anything goes, that any form of behavior is acceptable no matter how heinous. Rather, comedies of manners were satires that taught a Socratic lesson, namely, "Know thyself." It is up to people to learn their failings and fallibilities via comic instruction, then correct them.

The targets of a comedy of manners, then, are the *self-deceived*, people who con themselves, then con others—the fops, know-it-alls, holier-than-thous, pretentious big shots, and, yes, self-righteous politicians. And the standard against which to measure the foolish manners of the self-deceived is the standard of those "who are truly witty and sophisticated, who see others and themselves clearly, and who act accordingly," those "who accept everything with a worldly air."[3] Beyond mocking the conventions of members of an artificial, pseudo-sophisticated society, comedies of manners possess other distinguishing characteristics. For one, these dramas subordinate plot to criticism, generally through clever, brilliant dialogue. As on the *Late Show with David Letterman*, a sparkling and scintillating repartee substitutes for analytic probes. Style dominates content, that is, *how* something is said masks *what* is said.

Moreover, in comedies of manners the principal characters are seldom distinct personalities. More commonly they are types, even stereotypes. For example, consider the characters in Richard Brinsley Sheridan's *School for Scandal*, one of several of his plays that revived aspects of Restoration comedy a century after it had become passé. The "school" is a contemporary social setting consisting of shallow, superficial people who fail to know themselves or to recognize the depth of individuality and distinct qualities in others. Hence, a leading character in the play, Charles Surface, is a stereotype of an immature young man—open and honest, yet rash and unthinking. Joseph Surface is a hypocrite, pretending to be mature but actually ludicrous. Sir Peter struts the decorum of a man of advanced age, yet marries a young woman. Collectively, Sheridan's characters are *caricatures* of members of a narcissistic leisure class. One need not search hard for analogous news media depictions of politicians—young John Kennedy, new Richard Nixon, and seasoned Ronald Reagan—in the political school for scandal of the past four decades.

Finally, in comedies of manners "scandal" is a word with more generic meaning than that applied by Sheridan alone. A distinguishing feature of comedies of manners is the presence of an illicit love duel between at least one pair of amoral lovers, and often more.[4] Unlike the well-intentioned but bumbling escapades of lovers in romantic comedies, or of their accomplices in comedies of farce and humors, the lovers in comedies of manners are truly shameful and shocking. A political rule that the end justifies the means prevails. For instance, an oft-used plot sees a young lover advising his sweetheart to wed a rich suitor, contrive to divorce him, extract a fortune from the settlement, then return to the amoral boyfriend. America's great political scandals (the XYZ Affair in John Adams' administration, Crédit Mobilier during that of Ulysses S. Grant, Teapot Dome with Warren Harding, Watergate with Richard Nixon, IranContra surrounding Ronald Reagan, and Whitewatergate for Bill Clinton) were more complex than a comedy of manners; yet news stories told a tale of political love duels of intrigue and deception anyway.

Thus, comedies of manners are dramas that subordinate plot to style, that criticize the self-deceptive scandals of stereotyped categories of people (but not the nuances of unique characters), and that apply standards of comparison defined by the "truly" witty, sophisticated characters with a worldly bearing. The political comedies of manners that appear in newspapers and magazines and on TV each day bear these identical characteristics. For instance, the style of the "good" news story typically sensationalizes events while masking the actual facts of what took place. But so be it. News is not what actually happened but an appealing account of what might have happened: "This is the West. When the legend becomes fact, print the legend!"[5] Moreover, the pettiness and foibles of scandalous candidates and officeholders stereotyped as "politicians" are the focus of news accounts, not the everyday political accomplishments of public officials. Finally, the witty, sophisticated judges with a worldly bearing are the members of the news media, the collective Miss Manners of politics sitting in judgment of political propriety. Alexis de Tocqueville might have had the members of the press in mind when he wrote, "Nothing does democracy more harm than its outward forms of behavior; many who could tolerate its vices cannot put up with its manners."[6]

NEWS MANNERS AND MANNERISMS

For weeks seemingly without end in 1994–95 America's TV viewers were riveted to an unfolding drama—a real-life courtroom tale of violence, murder, accusation, incarceration, and denial so fascinating that it bumped from network TV the staples for fictional presentations of escapist entertainment, the soap operas. The burning question: Did football idol O. J. Simpson murder his ex-wife and a male acquaintance? During the televised preliminary hearing on July 7 at 5:57 EDT, ABC-TV news anchor Peter Jennings, with sophisticated, worldly demeanor, shared a secret with his audience: TV, he said, was not a neutral medium; televising an event changes it. In fact, "the Law proceeds . . . differently in real life than it does on television as a rule."

In a single remark Jennings captured the essence of the comedy of manners that is news coverage of *all* politics. For TV news, along with all other popular news media that mimic TV's style and format (including newspapers and newsmagazines), is not real. *News is burlesque.* It is a comedy of manners that "converts a manner into a mannerism," one that is "partial not only in the sense of *partisan*, but also in the sense of incompleteness."[7]

A century ago, in 1896, Adolph Ochs purchased what was to become one of the world's greatest newspapers, the *New York Times*. He adapted as the paper's motto "All the news that's fit to print." It is a deceptively simple phrase. It suggests, first, that there is news; then, news fit to print; the *Times* publishes only the latter. It is as if famed fan dancer Sally Rand had said, "All the flesh that's fit to display": there is skin, then skin deserving of public display; the dancer exhibits only the latter. Like a fan dancer's stylized gyrations, journalists deciding what's news—let alone what is fit to report—is more tease and titillation than evidence and enlightenment.

An essential quality that makes for burlesque's conversion of manners into mannerisms is a discrepancy between subject matter and style.[8] Burlesque may use a dignified style to portray nonsensical matter, as did Miguel de Cervantes (1547–1616) in his *Don Quixote*. Or a nonsensical style may ridicule a serious subject, as did the films of the Bowery Boys burlesquing problems of teenagers in the big cities of a Depression-ridden America. A similar discrepancy of subject matter and style typifies the distinction between news and news "fit to print" (or televise). That incongruity yields the penchant of journalists to convert manners into mannerisms, news into comedy.

One of the foremost figures in American journalism was Walter Lippmann (1889–1974). Although far better known for his sagelike pronouncements than his displays of comic wit, his insights into the nature of news summarize succinctly the qualities of burlesque inherent in journalism. Writing in the 1920s, coincidentally the decade when the striptease was the main feature of burlesque as a comic form, Lippmann described what news is all about. We have, wrote Lippmann, "circumstances in all their sprawling complexity, the overt act which signalizes them, the stereotyped bulletin which publishes the signal, and the meaning that the reader [today add viewer] injects."[9]

Hence, news is the result of a highly selective process; it "is not a first hand report of the raw material" but "a report of that material after it has been stylized."[10] Thus news resembles the striptease: far more circumstances may lie behind the fans than the stylistic gyrations (stereotyped bulletins) that signal them (what is fit to print). In sum, journalists convert manners into mannerisms by generating events from happenings, newsworthy events from events, and news from what is newsworthy.

Ralph Waldo Emerson once complained that newspapers do their best "to make every square acre of land and sea give an account of itself at your breakfast-table."[11] Actually, all manner of things happen in the world at large and in our own private worlds of which we are scarcely aware. People are born, people die; some gorge themselves on fast food, others starve; families live in harmony, others squabble all of the time. Unless some outlandish event occurs, we ignore it all. However, if Lippmann's "overt act . . . signalizes circumstances in all their sprawling complexity," we sit up and take notice. And if it is sufficiently outlandish, journalists too take notice. The event becomes newsworthy; a stereotyped bulletin, or news flash, signals it across the land.

THE NEWSMAKING MANNER: THE SOPHISTICATED VALUES OF JOURNALISTS

And what constitutes that overt act, that event that becomes newsworthy? Something extravagant. Modern burlesque in America patterned itself after a highly popular extravaganza, *The Black Crook* (1866). What made the stage production so popular was a chorus line of female dancers who, at least for the time, were scantily dressed. The extravagant promise that there was far more to be revealed than had ever been dreamed of in earlier productions is the same promise that drives journalism—an ever more extravagant lode of what is fit to print and view.

Extravaganzas that define newsworthiness, however, are not limited to scantily clad dancers. No, there are a host of other provocative factors, labeled *news values* in the trade, that dictate what events make the printed page or TV broadcast. In effect, each value—like the exposed cleavage of the burlesque dancer—is a manner moving toward being a mannerism. For example, one such value is timeliness. Something that happened since the publication or broadcast of the last news account, preferably in the last twenty-four hours, qualifies as a timely event. An adage of the craft is that nothing is so old as yesterday's news.

Converted into a mannerism, the timely manner, like the dancer's fans, masks several realities of news coverage. One is that breaking news takes priority over accounts of a protracted nature. As an example consider the lead stories in a six-week period extending from mid-July through the end of August in 1994. First, news coverage focused all eyes on a crisis in Serbia, only to ignore the unresolved crisis to replace it with another—a refugee crisis in Rwanda. That too remain unresolved, nonetheless, we must assume it was, for it vanished from headlines to be replaced by a threat of U.S. military invasion of Haiti. That threat did not subside, but news coverage did as a crisis of Cuban refugees fleeing to the United States became the happening of the moment. Then the United States president went on vacation, and Americans ended the dog days of summer in relative peace and quiet—nothing spectacular happened in the news. But he returned, threatened a Haitian invasion, and the news whirl began anew.

A second, and ironic, aspect of the timely manner is that it frequently does not "just happen." Frequently it is carefully programmed. For instance, it is common practice for local TV news outlets to hold production staff meetings early each morning to project the "timely" stories that will air on their 5 P.M. and 10 P.M. newscasts. This puts a premium on projecting routine, predictable features, but airing them as "hard" news. In effect, yesterday's old news, despite the old adage, becomes today's timely news.

Politicians readily adapt to the timely manner. Recognizing that the news media portray the mannerisms of world events as unusual and unpredictable, yet in their production planning struggle for the routine and down-to-the-second or column-inch predictability, politicians take advantage. If, say, a president faces an intractable problem, or even one the administration wants to dodge, there is a way out of the dilemma. "If you have nothing to say," goes an old advertising rule, "sing it!"[12] Confronting a chronic, insoluble situation, a politician presents the news media with a decoy, or what historian Daniel Boorstin labeled a *pseudo-event*.[13] Stage an event—a press conference, an overseas trip, a ceremony to honor the Super Bowl champs, or maybe the liberation of Grenada or Haiti. Announce a "bold new initiative." Designed as they are for news coverage, they provide the unpredictable predictability (or predicably unpredictable) on which the press thrives. Ronald Reagan's handlers were masters of the pseudo-event. In the absence of an education program, Reagan instead visited primary schools, there to be videotaped smiling and clowning with six-year-olds. And since in politics perceptions are everything, on TV news, at least, the President cared about education.

Another manner that shapes all the news fit to print is proximity. A happening's newsworthiness varies directly in proportion to its closeness to home. To a resident of Lebanon, Virginia, a murder in Fairbanks, Alaska, is a murder in Fairbanks, but a murder down the block on Boyd Lane is a crime wave. By the same token, the imprisonment of a former prime minister in Italy gets a polite nod on the evening's news; if the same happens to former President Gerald Ford, the news coverage portrays the republic in the throes of a crisis of trust. The proximate manner of the news media's political burlesque yields a mannerism of politics as intimate, neighborly, and having a vast impact on everyone's everyday life. Small wonder that repeated surveys of the American electorate show that citizens think Congress as a whole does only a poor to fair job, but give high marks to their own congressional representative: Congress be damned, I love my congressman.

Another manner cum mannerism in the striptease of political news coverage is the news value placed on a happening's dramatic conflict. If, for example, surveys of TV news editors are to be believed, the "let's you and him fight" factor is a key element in selecting what stories to air, what not.[14] Journalism textbooks emphasize that conflict is a key quality in news.[15] Conflict is the bump and grind of dramatic burlesque. Its presence solves a puzzle of political news coverage, namely, how to provide continuity and unity to unique, seemingly unrelated happenings. On one level each specific news report of a dispute can be packaged as a single brawl with beginning, middle, and end—just as the removal of each garment provides a unique performance.

But a single performance does not make a continuing burlesque production that keeps voyeurs in the theater, nor does a single reported political
quarrel make a continuing story that keeps readers buying newspapers and
viewers tuning in. Hence, individual stage performances and individual
political conflicts combine in a dramatic narrative: presidential candidates
vie with one another in Iowa, then New Hampshire, and on, and on; a
Supreme Court nominee fends off questions from members of the U.S.
Senate, then from lobbyists for sundry groups, then charges of sexual
harassment; a crime bill squeaks through a House committee, breezes by
the House, gets revised in the Senate, then is filibustered; or a scandal
surfaces, suddenly famous and suspect officials are implicated, and the
dark question is asked, "What did the president know and when did he
know it?"

As a manner of press coverage of politics, dramatic conflict provides a
burlesqued mannerism of politics as an intense, fervent, passionate, and
compelling drama. The mannerism ignores what makes the republic work
on a daily basis, namely, the hundreds of thousands of happenings engaged
in by officials, lobbyists, and subalterns buried in the subterranean depths
of federal, state, and local bureaucracies largely ignored by the news media.
Like the noise of one hand clapping at the last show at the Kit Kat Klub,
they make no sound.

Celebrities—people famous for being famous[16]—do make sounds,
sounds audible enough to attract the attention of even the most aurally
challenged political reporter. It is the manner of political reporting to
personalize the news by focusing the drama on the principal actors involved. Once established, the spotlighted persona readily translates into
the mannerism of celebrity. The translation occurs in a couple of ways. In
the first the news account extracts from all the happenings involving people
those that concern famous personages. For instance, a trivial but nonetheless illustrative case of news burlesque took place on January 25, 1993. A
twelve-year-old girl arrived for her first day at school in Washington, D.C.,
scarcely a newsworthy happening. On February 5 she suffered from a
headache and went to the school nurse, again hardly something to stop the
presses. She asked for an aspirin. Checking her records, the nurse discovered that the girl's parents had not signed a standard release form permitting her to give medication to the student. So the nurse said it would be
necessary to contact the parents. "My mom's away; you better call my dad,"
replied the girl. How often such happenings arose elsewhere on February
5 no one knows. But everyone quickly learned the story of the twelve-year-
old, for it was Chelsea, daughter of Bill and Hillary Clinton.

The burlesque of news celebrity does not necessarily contribute to news
accuracy, a value much written of in journalism texts but not a manner often
practiced by the press. Of twenty major newspapers, radio accounts, and
news service reports of the "Chelsea and the Nurse" bedtime story, not *one*

got it right. Although citing sources such as a "highly placed friend in Washington," "a well-connected Democrat," "my Washington source," "insiders," and "Hill tongues," each report gave the story a spin that implied Hillary Clinton was too fraught with political ambition to care about her daughter. Remember, Chelsea had said "My mom's away"; yet every account reported that she had said, "My mom is too busy," "She's very busy," or "Mom's rather busy." (Incidentally, four of the twenty accounts reported that Chelsea went to the nurse with a rash.) Moreover, talk-show guru Rush Limbaugh reported that the story was a joke, one that he had started on his radio show![17]

Plautus, whom we met in the Prologue, wrote in *Mercator* (c. 200 B.C.) that "manners go on deteriorating."[18] When it comes to the news media's comedies of manners, he was correct. Shakespeare gives Hamlet the telling lines, "I am native here, / And to the manner born."[19] Long after Hamlet the phrase acquired the connotation of a person able to rise to the heights of political success because of having been born into riches and breeding, like Franklin D. Roosevelt or John F. Kennedy. It can now be replaced by "to the mannerism born," or, perhaps more aptly, to celebrity born.

Hence the news emphasis on persons of political fame and fortune. However, not every political drama involves celebrities. When the ingredient of fame is missing, the news media personalize stories in another fashion by emphasizing "human interest." For example, news accounts of complex policy issues such as health care reform have little appeal if they are but recitations of drab statistics, intricate legal ramifications, and analyses of costs and benefits of contending proposals. To jazz the subject up reporters focus on a previously unknown person, say an unemployed, single mother of five suffering from a catastrophic illness. The mother may not become queen for a day, but for ninety seconds on ABC's *World News Tonight* she is a celebrity.

Thus, despite the passage of over seven decades and the advent of radio, TV, satellites, cellular phones, virtual reality, and all manner of news communication wizardry, the burlesque of events via news personalization described by Walter Lippmann in 1922 persists. Using as his example novelist Sinclair Lewis' "Miss Sherwin of Gopher Prairie," Lippmann's description of her quandary during World War I remains valid: "Miss Sherwin has no access to the order of battle maps, and so if she is to think about the war, she fastens upon [French General] Joffre and the [German] Kaiser as if they were engaged in a perpetual dual."[20]

Advances in communication technology have, however, contributed to a heightened interest in a final manner, or news value, of political coverage. It has never really been sufficient for news organizations to simply tell a story; they like to *show* it. The visual manner of news presentation consisted first of newspaper sketches, then cartoons. Then came still photography, newsreels, and television. As 1 Corinthians 15:33 warns us, however, "Be not deceived: evil communications corrupt good manners." In this instance the corruption is via visuals that create a mannerism that all of politics must be vivid, showy, lively, vigorous, even picturesque. The costs for that corruption of visuals into vividness are multiple. One is to ignore happenings as not newsworthy if there are no pictures to sustain them. For instance, rampant hunger and starvation have been a fact of life in Eastern Africa for generations—in Abyssinia, Ethiopia, Somalia. Yet the chronic crisis was largely ignored by news media until TV pictures provided the visual that made the suffering newsworthy. A second cost is that many events are considered newsworthy simply because visuals are readily available. Politicians know this and stage pseudo-events in vivid ways even though nothing of substance happens in such settings—be they ribbon-cuttings, a president coptering over a flooded plain, or a secretary of transportation trudging through the debris at the site of a disastrous air crash.

Finally, where evil communications indeed corrupt good manners is at the point where the imperative to provide visuals for a news account results in fakery. It happened during the Civil War when still photographers enhanced the vividness of bloody battlefields by dragging in extra corpses to create fields of death. (And it still does happen: in 1994 *Time* "enhanced" its cover portrait of O. J. Simpson.)[21] It happened routinely with newsreel photography; one scholar argues that apparently every newsreel producer between 1894 and 1900 routinely faked news film as a matter of practice.[22] And it has happened with TV news coverage: in 1989, for its *World News Tonight* report on espionage, ABC "simulated" a transaction between a U.S. diplomat and an agent from another country. The corruption of the visual manner into a vividness mannerism is, as CNN's Ed Turner says, "part of this mad search for pictures, pictures, pictures."[23]

Thus, in the comedy of manners newsworthy politics possess mannerisms of the extravagant: unpredictability, intimacy, intensity, celebrity, and vividness. That these mannerisms curtain off a wizardry that is actually far more programmed, remote, mundane, obscure, and pale—leaving little room for citizens' maneuvering is the underlying irony.

THE MANNER OF JOURNALISTS AS SOPHISTICATES

Aristotle did not have journalists in mind when he wrote of putting on airs, but he was close to the mark: "It is not ill-bred to adopt a high manner with the great and powerful, but it is vulgar to lord it over humble people."[24] If the great and powerful in our democracy consist of corporate tycoons, chief executive officers, holders of key political offices, and the like, America's working journalists are, for the most part, not among them. For every news anchor like Dan Rather of CBS who holds celebrity status and commands riches and wealth, or for every political columnist like George Will who flirts with purchasing a major league baseball franchise, there are thousands of political journalists who do not lead the lifestyles of the rich and famous. Still, they are not your humble working stiff either. They are white (95 percent), male (seven of ten), and well-educated (nine out of ten are college graduates; over half have had postgraduate study); they are better paid than the plebeian, reside in the Northeast, and are politically liberal.[25]

Political journalists exploit their middling position of being not so well off as the powerful, but better off than the humble. They assume the posture of the guardians of the humble, not petitioning the great and powerful on behalf of readers and viewers, but adopting a high manner toward their betters. Thus, in democracy's comedy of manners political journalists direct barbs against the fops, the pretenders at wit and sophistication. The fop in the news media burlesque of politics is, of course, the politician. The actions of the fop politician merit ridicule because they simply do not measure up to the standards set by true sophisticates. For the true sophisticates in democracy's comedy of manners are the journalists. Just ask them. Unlike politicians, journalists are uninhibited in expression, yet objective, and thereby fair-minded and ethical. Just ask them.

As guardians of the humble against fop politicians, news media sophisticates claim a privileged place in American life. In the 1951 science fiction film *The Thing*, Scotty, a crusty, battle-worn, and witty reporter, pleads with a military commander. Scotty asks permission to report to the world an indestructible alien monster uncovered in the Arctic. The commander claims he needs air force authority. "You've got your authority and it's the Constitution of the United States!" retorts Scotty. This claim of journalistic privilege goes beyond science fiction. Journalists routinely appeal to the First Amendment to the Constitution: "Congress shall make no law . . . abridging the freedom of speech, or of the press" assures more than an unfettered manner symbolized as freedom of the press. The claim constitutes a mannerism, that is, news sophisticates as the guardians of "the people's right to know." That guardianship implies in journalists' eyes uninhibited expression, including no pre-publication or pre-broadcast censorship, immunity from libel, and journalistic determination of what is fair and unfair reporting.

The guardian role also implies the right to privileged access to news sources as well as the right to protect sources from public disclosure when necessary and to delve into the private lives of the great and powerful and even the humble to protect the people's right to know. In exchange for a privileged position, news sophisticates promise to hold public officials and politicians to a high standard so that neither great and powerful nor humble citizens will fall into self-deception. Thus journalists as guardians of the people's right to know become guardians of objectivity.

Recall that Kenneth Burke stressed that the method of burlesque is caricature, that is, to convert a manner into a mannerism is "partial" in part because it is "partisan."[26] Certainly a true sophisticate must be complete, not partial, and unbiased, not partisan. This is particularly important for the political journalists acting as sophisticates, because what sets off the politician from other mortals is a partisan manner. To avoid charges of political partisanship, news organizations urge news sophisticates to be "objective." But there is an underlying irony in the objective manner of the journalists: journalistic objectivity does not inhibit partisanship, it masks it.

As practiced, journalistic objectivity is a form of comedy dating back to very early times, to the commedia dell'arte, later called masked comedy. As in that comedic form, journalists play conventional figures such as "news anchor," "investigative reporter," "White House correspondent," and so on. Each is akin to the standardized roles of masked comedy's harlequin, pantaloon, or buffoon. In the comedy of manners journalistic objectivity is a *ritual* practice, a routine with little bearing on removing partiality or partisanship from reporting.[27]

Journalistic sophisticates employ a variety of devices to construct the impression that they are impartial even as politicians are partial. One is to present in news accounts conflicting possibilities. This is particularly useful when reporters have few, or no, actual facts to report, only their own speculations. Will, for example, the president of the United States order an invasion of a tiny republic in the Caribbean whose regime is contemptuous of human rights? A White House correspondent does not know and is scarcely privy to the president's deliberations. But facts or no facts, the red light on the TV camera on the White House lawn alerts the correspondent that it is airtime. Succinctly, the correspondent reports speculation of an invasion, then quotes a "highly placed source" in the State Department that invasion is unlikely, followed by a quote from "a reliable source" in the Department of Defense—invasion is inevitable. The White House correspondent concludes, with more sophistry than sophistication, "Invasion or not, governing officials must first get their respective acts together." The red light flicks off; the correspondent trudges off in search of other conflicting possibilities.

A second device is to present evidence in a news story that may not actually support the reporter's account, but seems to do so. "Gubernatorial candidate Walter David," writes the campaign reporter for the *Daily Guardian*, "brings to the contest a mastery of administrative procedures." The *Guardian* copy editor asks the basis of the reporter's claim. "Read on," says the reporter. The editor finds a reference to the fact that candidate David served three years as assistant provost of an academic institution, a "fact" thus justifying the reporter's claim of mastery.

Another veil masking partiality the way heavy makeup shrouds a stripper's varicose veins is the judicious use of quotation marks. A congressional reporter may want to claim that a U.S. senator is an inept committee chair. To make the claim, however, would be partisan. So the reporter quotes one or more committee members, preferably both Democratic and Republican, that the chair is inept. A partisan point is objectified.

There are other illusions of objective reporting, for example, presenting "both sides of the story" but giving greater weight to a preferred account; staging a TV reporter's standup account in an objective setting, say, on the steps of the Supreme Court; labeling portions of a newscast as "analysis" or "commentary," thus leading viewers to assume that any report not so labeled is objective; labeling sources as "experts" or "authorities," thus equating objectivity with specialized knowledge; and, of course, making grandiose claims that news is objective because it is comprehensive, not selective—the *New York Times'* "all the news that's fit to print," a local radio station's promise of "more news *when it happens*," or a TV news department's claim to be "Eyewitness News." Whatever the devices, the avowals that they are sophisticated ways that journalists, in Aristotle's words, adopt a "high manner with the great and powerful," conceal the fact that they are actually *"strategies through which newsmen protect themselves from critics and lay professional claim to objectivity."*[28]

THE SOPHISTICATED STYLES OF NEWS:
THE MANNER IS THE MATTER

As the statesman Lord Chesterfield put it, "In everything the manner is fully as important as the matter."[29] Marshall McLuhan coined a different aphorism for a similar thought, namely, "The medium is the message."[30] In political news coverage the medium is less the technique of transmission—print, radio, TV, and so on—than the news story itself. And in shaping the news the manner of the story is fully as important as its message content or matter. In the comedy of democracy the news media have developed several standardized formulae for packaging news stories. Each convention enhances the illusion of objectivity and cloaks partiality and selectivity. In Walter Lippmann's phrase, each stylizes the raw material of circumstances in all their sprawling complexity. For each Miss Sherwin of Gopher Prairie, the stylized manner portrays a complexity of simplified mannerisms.

SPRING FORWARD! FALL BACK! On the first Sunday of every April and the last Sunday of every October Americans get a lecture on the front pages of newspapers and from the final words of every newscast to set their clocks one hour ahead (in April) and one hour back (in October). The news is as predictable as the swallows coming back to Capistrano, the last minute rush of Christmas shoppers, or the Chicago Cubs each year failing to make it to the World Series. In politics accounts of such a routine nature include the federal government's monthly release of unemployment rates, interest rates, and changes in the consumer price index; the quadrennial arrival of the Iowa caucuses and the New Hampshire primaries; or claims by the incumbent presidential administration that everything is coming up roses while the congressional opposition sees nothing but a bed of thorns.

Any drama, argued rhetorical critic Kenneth Burke, be it tragic or comic, involves five elements, or questions: "what was done (act), when or where it was done (scene), who did it (agent), how he did it (agency), and why (purpose)."[31] Coincidentally, generations of journalism students have sat through the catechism, repeating solemnly, that the elements of any news story are the five Ws and an H: who (agent), what (act), where (scene), when (also scene), why (purpose), and how (agency). Burke goes one step further by arguing that in any drama a pairing (or "ratio") of key elements packages the situation. Lady Macbeth, for example, as agent works to salve her guilty conscience, a guilt derived from her provoking her husband to his bloody deeds; she compulsively washes her hands (act) again and again: "Out, damned spot! Out, I say!" (Act 5, Scene 1, 39). This is an agent-act ratio, the act's rationale contained in the nature of the character of the agent, a strong-willed lady.

The manner of a *customary* news story, such as that surrounding daylight saving time or that contained in the headline "Cost of Living Index on the Rise, Experts Say," is of the type described in a book of etiquette. That is, a certain obligatory manner (act) is demanded at certain times and places, for example, using the dinner, not the salad, fork to chase your peas around on the plate at a formal setting. SPRING FORWARD! FALL BACK! has become so ingrained a news manner that it speaks less of a purpose (setting of the clock to be "on time") than an obligatory ritual or series of mindless acts. Everyone knows it's coming, just as everyone knows the president will deliver a State of the Union address. The customary manner emphasizes act-scene ratios, conforming to the news mannerism of a packaged story where content, or message, is incidental to the routine itself.

Contrast a customary story with one of *contest*. A contest, be it a Wheel of Fortune or Family Feud, the World Cup or the Super Bowl, the New Hampshire primary or Super Tuesday, is about winners and losers. The dramatization is what means (agencies) winners use to win, losers lose. Even a casual reading of news accounts or monitoring of TV news coverage of an electoral contest, for example, reveals an agent-agency mannerism: Did George Bush (agent) defeat Michael Dukakis in 1988 by labeling (agency) the Democratic candidate as soft on crime? Did Bill Clinton (agent) defeat George Bush in 1992 by keeping the eye on the donut, not the hole, that is, by the challenger repeating (agency) to himself, "It's the economy, stupid!"? Will Bill Clinton (agent) fail at reelection in 1996 because his administration has a vacillating foreign policy (agency)?

Customary news, like obligatory manners, contains cues that are so widely taken for granted (such as spring forward, fall back) that few people need additional details to know how to react. Hence the stories are typically brief, factual, scheduled well in advance of the event they purport to be about, and rely on "experts" or "authorities" as news sources (for example, "Communication analyst Dub L. Kade prophesied that the upcoming electoral campaign would introduce a new round of negative televised political ads"). News coverage of contests, however, is of long duration, involving an extensive buildup, protracted conflict, and the winners and losers as sources. For example, the contest between President Clinton and congressional opponents over health care reform received news coverage well before he was inaugurated and continued for two years; it was a soap opera of policy ups and downs of a president, his wife, Senate minority leader Bob Dole, and a host of contending special interests.

News stories of *conquest* also feature agents, namely, who is doing the conquering, but the emphasis is less on how the conquest occurs than why, that is, an agent-purpose pairing. In 1969 when U.S. astronauts landed and walked on the surface of the moon, news coverage trumpeted a successful conquest of space ("One small step for man, one giant leap for mankind," said Neil Armstrong.) By the twenty-fifth anniversary of that feat news coverage had shifted. It was still a story in the manner of conquest, but a failed conquest: men walked on the moon but had failed at the colonization of space because economic costs were too high; Americans no longer would pay any price or bear any burden.

The agents in conquest stories are heroes and/or villains, the purposes good or evil. Thus, valorous Americans conquered evil fascism in World War II, and evil Saddam Hussein in the Gulf War of 1991. And dedicated scientists conquered the crippler of children, infantile paralysis, in the 1950s, but villainous AIDS marches on in spite of dedicated efforts to conquer it in the 1990s. As with stories of contest, those of conquest are enduring, continuing accounts featuring the deeds of news sources who are brave and courageous (especially as victims), valiant and gallant (in purpose), and stouthearted (as vanquishers).

In the manners of news coverage, successful contests and conquests evoke stories of *celebration*. And given the commanding tendency to personalize events, it is not surprising that celebrations focus on the celebrants. The pairing is one of how the party takes place and who gets invited, an agency-agent manner. Basic to all celebration stories, be they of electoral victories, a president's signing of legislation after a hard fought congressional skirmish, the return of conquering heroes after the Gulf War, a visit of Super Bowl victors to the Oval Office, America's Bicentennial, or Liberty Weekend '86, there is one collective agent that proper manners demand always be invited to the celebration. That agent is The People.

The consistent celebration plot line is that wars are fought, elections won, space conquered, mountains climbed, new beers brewed, tartar fighters and fluorides added, fiber optics installed, and the Super Bowl played for benefit of The People. But just as because Miss Sherwin couldn't imagine divisions fighting World War I, let alone armies, news coverage featured a

duel between General Joffre and the Kaiser, celebration manners dictate that
The People as news source appear as a child waving a flag at a parade, a
bubbly campaign worker at the candidate's victory rally, the local bar-
tender, or the butcher behind the meat counter. Their fame, like a story of
celebration, is brief—here today, gone tomorrow. Reporters, however, per-
sist endlessly.

Not every newsworthy event is a cause for celebration. Accidents happen
and often give rise to coverage of *chaos*; also, people rape, murder, rob,
plunder, and commit other heinous acts, so news organizations offer stories
of *crime*; finally, things happen that, although not accidental, are unforeseen,
producing news depictions of suffering and sacrifice in coverage of *crises*.
"Fifty Car Pileup on the Ryan Expressway, Dozens Die. Details at Ten." Thus
we have sprawling complexity, the stereotyped bulletin that signalizes the
event. However, in the case of chaos coverage, the complexity is increased
by the intervention of fortune, at least initially. The where and the what, the
scene-act take the spotlight. That does not last long, however, for a search
for "why" follows quickly. Hence, a conversion to a purpose-act manner—
the pileup happened because of ice on the roads, faulty brakes, drunk
driving, and so on.

On September 13, 1994, a light plane with only the pilot aboard crashed
on the lawn of the White House. The pilot was killed. The president and his
family were not in residence. There were no other casualties. An accident?
Perhaps. But news manners dictate that reporters are simply not doing their
job if they chalk things up to nothing but chance. Conspirators, not chance,
are the authors of chaos. Hence, the search for the why of the crash began.
Was it an attempted act of terrorism that had breached inadequate security?
If so, then we have a story of crime, in fact, dual crimes involving criminal
terrorists and a criminally lax security force. Or was the crash the product
of a vainglorious suicide on the pilot's part, perhaps a crime of another sort?
Again, was it a crisis? Did the pilot suffer a heart attack; was there a
mechanical failure; did he run out of gas? Did the pilot die heroically trying
to avoid crashing into the White House? Or, heaven forbid, did the crash
result from a failed prank, a slapstick act gone awry?

News coverage of the crash on the White House lawn included all of the
above possibilities. It illustrates that all the news fit to print implies a
reporting manner that searches for a fitting mannerism of the moment; the
details of the reported event are secondary. Typically chaos yields to stories
of crime or crisis; chance takes a holiday. It also illustrates something about
the penchant for highlighting the accidental in human happenings.
Whereas customary, contest, conquest, and celebration stories frequently,
indeed usually, are about happenings promoted into events by authorities,
contestants, combatants, and party animals involved, accident reports are
unintended happenings promoted for media coverage not by those involved but by journalists seeking the cause of the chaos.[32] It was not Senator

Ted Kennedy who promoted accounts of a 1969 automobile accident that killed Mary Jo Kopechne. No, it was journalists asking "Why?" who had a vested interest in promoting the story.

There is thus a tendency for news manners to evolve, especially when an event first labeled accidental or coincidental shifts, for instance, to a crime scenario. The agents are the guilty, the victims, and/or the innocent; agencies are corruption, scandal, conspiracy, and the perversity of human beings. Once the crime label adheres, chance no longer is in the picture. When chaos evolves in the direction of crisis, reporters focus on agents as victims dependent upon authorities responsible for coping with rare, nonroutine, unexpected events. Unlike the manner of crime stories, however, in crisis accounts political authorities are rarely the *causes* of the problem. An exception occurred in 1992 when the postmaster of the U.S. House of Representatives resigned for irregularities—illegal cash payments to two unidentified legislators. Here was a scandal whose "causes" were public officials. By contrast, in 1993 floods ravaged the Midwest; news headlines read "Destruction awes Clinton; he plans $2.5 billion in aid."[33] This manner of crisis stories features authorities tempering events, calling for salvation either by sacrifice or by throwing money at the problem.

In some cases chaos manners may evolve into multiple mannerisms. For instance, when in 1986 the *Challenger* space shuttle exploded shortly after takeoff, killing all crew members, reporters first stressed a story line of chaos. Then, however, came crisis—a failed conquest of space and a crucial decision point for the U.S. space program facing funding authorities. Another plot quickly ensued, a scandal via revelations that the shuttle was launched under conditions program officials deemed dangerous. Whatever the direction of evolution, when accidents happen they rarely remain only accidents.

THE CONTINUOUS COMEDY OF POLITICS VS. THE STOP-ACTION TRAGEDY OF NEWS MANNERS

The predominant manner of political news is tragic. Aside from the "Happy Talk" sideshow of many TV newscasts, journalists package news events as routine and customary, as contests, and as conquests, often followed by celebration; if accidents happen, repackaging yields crime and crisis. All the news that's fit to print is populated by experts and authorities, victors and vanquished, heroes and villains, criminals, victims, and The People as portrayed by the Average Joe and Josephine. There is little to laugh at, even in celebration.

One must wonder why that is, why news packages so few events as comic. For, as we saw in the Prologue, comedy and politics share overlapping characteristics. Unlike tragedy, comedy is frequently improvised. Things happen, but scarcely in the structured way so characteristic of serious drama. Tragic drama features stop-action breaks that punctuate shifts from the introduction, to rising action, falling action, and denouement. Comic performances, by contrast, sometimes pop up out of nowhere, and at unpredictable times and places. Whereas the pace of serious drama is precisely punctuated, interrupted by pauses so that audience members can catch their breath, relax, and prepare for the next buildup, this is not so with comedy. Comedy is continuous; laughs rarely cease. To be sure, there is the seasonal character of comedy—the birth, growth, decay, and death of spring, summer, fall, and winter. Yet the transitions are hardly noticeable; there is continuity of action and expression of thought.

Moreover, resolutions of problems in serious drama are final, sometimes by death, sometimes by transcendence, sometimes by living happily ever after—but final. Even when Rhett walks out on Scarlett in *Gone with the Wind* and she vows to rise above it all, there is an air of finality. But when Charlie Chaplin struts away as *The Tramp*, viewers are not at all certain it is really "The End." For comedy adds an element to its cycle of seasons not characteristic of more tragic forms, namely, rebirth and regeneration. Comedy adds a caveat to Yogi Berra's famous phrase, "It ain't over 'til it's over," namely, "and that ain't ever likely."

Finally, serious drama portrays heroes and villains, winners and losers, criminals and victims, patriarchs and sufferers, The Lionheart and The People. Comedies tell of the continuous antics, foibles, and innocence of fools and The Folk. Comedy, in short, is common, maybe even coarse and crude; it is about community.

And what of the character of politics? Politics too is far more improvised than plotted, continuous than punctuated, seasonal than structured drama, and coarse, common, and crude. Niccolo Machiavelli, as we have seen, warned princes never to let down their guard: *politics never ends*. Problems are intractable, conflict breeds conflict, change brings change, and everything is in flux. There is no finality of resolution, only the rebirth of politics as usual. The only rules of politics are not dramatic but cyclical. As we noted, Machiavelli taught that politics is necessary because *fortune* (accidents), play the key role in the lives of fallible human beings. Moreover, he taught that the first law of politics is that those same foolish beings are prone to boredom. It is the task of the politician, also a foolish and fallible creature, to anticipate cycles of popular interest and boredom, and to intervene *before* the seasonal shift occurs—often by stirring up trouble when there is none, temporizing when there is; agitating for war during peace, for peace during war; and, demanding sacrifice when there is abundance, providing bread and circuses when times are tough. In short, the politician must *exploit incongruities in human affairs* just as does the comic.

There are reasons for the absence of a comic approach to news. One is that politicians long ago learned the manner and mannerisms of journalism and adjusted themselves accordingly. Regardless of how mundane, bumbling, nonheroic, pedestrian, and foolish the actual manner of their governing, politicians grasp the necessity to promote some things they are doing while keeping others behind the scenes. They recognize the selective ways journalists decide what is fit to print or air, and hence dress up what they want to promote in suitably solemn and majestic ways.

Politicians spin their accounts, emphasizing the appropriate dramatic pairings to camouflage an event as routine, contest, conquest, celebration, crime, or crisis. Candidates for the presidency no longer run in mere contests for office, they run "crusades." In office they do not merely propose legislation, they mount "wars" to "conquer" poverty, unemployment, disease, illiteracy, sexism, and child abuse, as well as trade, budget, and all manner of deficits. Faced with popular skepticism, they discover a "crisis of confidence," "crisis of the spirit," or "crisis of fulfillment." And if there is scandalous conduct among subordinates, they turn to the customary: Watergate as a third rate burglary, Irangate as not being in the loop, or Whitewatergate as a routine real estate transaction. Comic stances are infrequent. The comic sense displayed by John F. Kennedy and Ronald Reagan was refreshing for each president accomplished a rarity, namely, admitting foibles and foolishness.

More important, however, by its very nature the news *story* is a reconstruction obeying the imperatives of narrative, not those of catch-as-catch-can political life in action. The news story possesses a dramatic logic: beginning, middle, end; punctuated pacing; final resolutions of conflict. That logic, so admirably suited to depicting the tragic in human affairs, is ill-equipped to explore and *appreciate* the chaos, improvisations, incongruities, contradictions, fallibility, and sheer foolishness that define the very nature of political life.

News sophisticates, in their unceasing efforts to mock the conventions of members of what they regard as an artificial, pseudo-sophisticated society (namely, the politicians), and thus stamp out self-deception, ironically end up being deceived themselves. For, by using conventions of newsmaking that are in themselves artificial and largely inappropriate to the continuous comedy of democratic politics, news sophisticates do not stand apart from the manners they decry, they misread them. And in the misreading they entangle themselves in precisely the comedy of manners they seek to warn us against. Small wonder, then, that the Donahues, Geraldos, Oprahs, and Sally Jessys of "new" news formats serve up a comedy of wit perhaps more in keeping with democratic voices of public opinion.

NOTES

1. The term is applied by Ronald Steel to describe U.S. world dominance in the twentieth century. See his *Walter Lippmann and the American Century* (Boston: Little, Brown, 1980).

2. Walter Lippmann, *A Preface to Morals* (Boston: Beacon Press, 1929), p. xv.

3. Oscar G. Brockett, *The Theatre: An Introduction* (New York: Holt, Rinehart and Winston, 1964), p. 197.

4. William Flint Thrall, Addison Hibbard, and C. Hugh Holman, *A Handbook to Literature* (New York: Odyssey Press, 1960).

5. The insight derives from Dutton Peabody, fictional editor of the local newspaper in the fictional town of Shinbone in the fictional American West in the 1962 Paramount film *The Man Who Shot Liberty Valance*. Tony Thomas, *A Wonderful Life: The Films and Career of James Stewart* (Secaucus, NJ: Citadel Press, 1988), p. 207.

6. Alexis de Toqueville, *Democracy in America*, ed. J. P. Mayer (New York: Anchor Books, 1969), p. 607.

7. Kenneth Burke, *Attitudes Toward History* 3rd ed. (Berkeley: University of California Press, 1989), p. 55. Emphasis in original.

8. Thrall et al., *Handbook to Literature*, p. 66.

9. Walter Lippmann, *Public Opinion*. (New York: Macmillan, 1922, reprint 1960), p. 349.

10. Ibid., p. 347.

11. Ralph Waldo Emerson, *Society and Solitude* (New York: Houghton Mifflin, 1870), p. 163.

12. Anthony Pratkanis and Elliot Aronson, *Age of Propaganda* (New York: W. H. Freeman, 1991), p. 139.

13. Daniel Boorstin, *The Image* (New York: Atheneum, 1972), p. 11.

14. James Buckalew, "News Elements and Selection by Television News Editors," *Journal of Broadcasting* 14 (Winter 1968–70): 47–54.

15. See, for example, Melvin Mencher, *News Reporting and Writing* (Dubuque, IA: William C. Brown, 1981).

16. Boorstin, *Image*.

17. Chip Rowe, "Chelsea Goes to the Nurse . . . ," *American Journalism Review* 15 (June 1993): 37–39.

18. H. L. Mencken, *A New Dictionary of Quotations* (New York: Alfred A. Knopf, 1991), p. 752.

19. William Shakespeare, *Hamlet*, Act 1, Scene 4, 14–15.

20. Lippmann, *Public Opinion*, p. 13.

21. Richard B. Stolley, "People Pictures," *Columbia Journalism Review* 23 (September/October 1994): 41–44.

22. Raymond Fielding, *The American Newsreel* (Norman: University of Oklahoma Press, 1972).

23. Quoted in Bill Carter, "ABC News Divided on Simulated Events," *New York Times*, July 27, 1989, p. C20.

24. Richard McKeon, "Nicomachean Ethics," in *Introduction to Aristotle* (New York: Modern Library, 1947), p. 386.

25. See Robert Lichter, Stanley Rothman, and Linda S. Lichter, *The Media Elite* (New York: Hastings House, 1990); C. Cleveland Wilhoit and David H. Weaver, *The American Journalist*, 2nd ed. (Bloomington: Indiana University Press, 1991); and John W. C. Johnstone, Edward J. Slawkski, and William W. Bowman, *The News People* (Urbana: University of Illinois Press, 1976).

26. Burke, *Attitudes*, p. 55.

27. Gaye Tuchman, *Making News* (New York: The Free Press, 1978).

28. Gaye Tuchman, "Objectivity as Strategic Ritual," *American Journal of Sociology* 77 (July 1972): 676. Emphasis in original.

29. Lord Chesterfield (Philip Dormer Stanhope) in a letter to his son, November 19, 1750. Quoted in Mencken, *New Dictionary of Quotations*, p. 752.

30. Marshall McLuhan, *Understanding Media* (New York: Signet, 1964).

31. Kenneth Burke, *A Grammar of Motives* (Berkeley: University of California Press, 1945), p. xv.

32. Harvey Molotch and Marilyn Lester, "News as Purposive Behavior: On the Strategic Use of Routine Events, Accounts, and Scandals." *American Sociological Review* 39 (February 1974): 101–112.

33. Calvin Stovall, Dick Mallary, and Ashley Weissenberger, eds. *Best of Gannett* (Arlington, VA: Gannett Co., 1993), p. 6.

PART II

The Political Comedies
of Policy Makers

CHAPTER 5

Hell to the Chief:
Comedies of Character

When John F. Kennedy was president-elect in the winter of 1960, awaiting the departure of the Eisenhowers and the advent of the "New Frontier," he read a new book by Harvard political scientist and special consultant to his transition team, Richard Neustadt, entitled *Presidential Power*. When Jimmy Carter was president-elect in 1976, he read a new book by a Duke political scientist named James David Barber entitled *Presidential Character*. The change is significant, not only because of the differing personalities of the two presidents. In the late twentieth century, voters, journalists, and scholars increasingly focus on presidential character rather than presidential actions. It is as though presidential success and failure emanate from personal character rather than executive skill. Hence, in our mass-mediated political culture the president is not only head of state but also the head celebrity. In a popular culture of voyeurism, "inquiring minds want to know," as the tabloid slogan goes, not only what presidents *do* but more fundamentally *who* they are—private lives and past lives. In the "new news" of political reporting (Chapter 3), coverage of the president consists of character analysis.

This major shift in the public evaluation of, and reporting on, the presidency is fraught with wondrous comic aspects. In the conventional comic form, that is, a comedy of character, public emphasis is on the eccentricities of the protagonist, in this case the president; in Jean Molière's (1722–1773) phrase, it is on his, perhaps someday her, hypochondria, miserliness, and hypocrisy.[1]

COMIC CHARACTER IN THE WHITE HOUSE

The shift to character appraisals featured in presidential comedy has transformed journalists into character analysts, part psychologists, part moralists. The reporting of the presidency has taken a subjective turn of narrative, that is, what is key is not the objective actions and consequences of a presidential protagonist but rather the psychic state that motivated the character's actions. The "new journalism" of the 1960s first delved into the character of political actors, searching for psychic clues to explain political behavior. By the 1990s, the press corps simply accepted the premise that presidential character is the essential subject of their reporting task. The hidden forces and private motives that comprise the presidential character, perhaps even presidential pathology, are increasingly *the* story of the presidency.

A leading media president watcher describes the White House press corps as "the world's most elaborate personality cult"; journalists "believe that nothing a politician does in public can be taken at face value, but that everything he does is a metaphor for something he is hiding." The current generation of political journalists take for granted their own omnipotence in unmasking and deconstructing hidden realities; "they believe in the power of what they have created, in the subjectivity of reality and the reality of perceptions, in image." Their job is not objective reporting of actions but subjective interpretation of mental states, of the presidential psyche on the one hand and the public perceptions the president manipulates on the other. For today's political journalist, politics is "not about objective reality, but virtual reality."[2]

For contemporary journalists presidential power is less a world of Niccolo Machiavelli's precepts about princely maneuvering than one of Marshall McLuhan's aphorisms about electronic images, not the "outputs" or achievements of the exercise of power as much as the fleeting perceptions and imaginative postures of the presidential docudrama. The press evaluation of presidential performance has moved from *politics* (the constitutional success of proposals and programs, the ability to administer and build coalitions) to *histrionics* (the theatrical success of a press conference, the staging of a "town meeting," conducting a summit). Audiences see less of doing presidential things, more of acting presidential.

Since Richard Nixon and the Watergate intrigue (see Chapter 7) the press has pointedly undertaken dramatic criticism of presidential performance. This general shift away from political reporting to literary criticism has witnessed the attribution of heroic achievement to the unmasking critic and villainous or foolish intent to the presidential protagonist. The heroic reporter/pundit of contemporary Washington labors to discover the "metaphoric event that presumes to cut through the theater to show the true man."[3] Journalists seek the hidden, secret, occult incidents or telling remarks that disclose a president's public image as but a mask he uses to fool citizens.

These flashes of insight into a characterological "backstage" by journalists take on a life of their own, not as mere journalists' subjective perceptions, but rather as the objective "reality" of the presidency. Not privy to the secret councils of government, and knowing that much of what they observe is public dramaturgy, opportunistic correspondents probe even the smallest of details that depict the genuine horror beneath the emperor's new clothes. In fact, what is truly real about presidential politics may not be palpable at all, merely a faddish journalistic perception of the man behind the purple mantle of the presidential role. No matter. The perception still provides a trendy subject for pontificating about the president's past (real or imagined), associations (political or social), private remarks (real or attributed), emotions (genuine or faked), personal habits (charming or gross), and peccadillos (actual and alleged).

The cult of personality that underscores contemporary coverage of the president does not venerate, but rather dissects, the person, perhaps even destroying the credibility of both the incumbent and the office. For critiques of presidential character direct the press corps to discovering, or inventing, metaphors to explain the president's "true" self and motives. This is the stuff of "take" journalism, the substance behind news talk shows and op-ed columns. A journalist's take on presidential behavior is his or her *perception about perceptions*, rhetorical explanations that draw attention to each journalist's success in the "perception competition" of Washington. In the immediate "context of no context" of newstalk, takes are about right *now*. Once voiced, the rhetorical display of the pundit's acumen quickly passes into the media void. The "competition among pundits to see whose view prevails depends less on the inherent validity of the position than on the rhetorical skill with which it is put forward."[4]

As it has developed, take journalism depicting the presidency has grown hypercritical, condemnatory, and apocalyptic. Although marvelously nonpartisan, from the viewpoint of presidents and their advisers, it resembles rituals of the ancient priests who tore the Fisher King to pieces once they deemed him no longer competent to rule. After the fall of Richard Nixon in 1974, journalistic attacks on the president, then presidential character, became commonplace. News audiences seemed willing to believe the worst; competing news analysts obliged, compiling the worst they could find or invent. "Take" analysis correlated with the newly legitimated practice of *lateral attribution*, the practice of raising an issue or story, no matter how unsubstantiated, gossipy, dubious, or hostile in origin so long as it was deemed newsworthy (e.g., "people are talking about . . ."; "questions are being raised . . ."; "the perception exists . . .").

All this is part of a larger communication pattern and process called the paranoid style of explanation. In that style everything and everybody plays roles in an expansive and sordid drama. Singular events and persons possess no integrity; they have meaning only as intertwined in the overall plot. The style is remarkably close to that of comedies of character in Moliere's time. For example, those comedies often featured masked balls where everyone knew everyone else's identity, yet pretended not to by hiding behind masks. What made the comedies funny was that anyone unmasking an "impostor" then postured as being very perceptive indeed for having done so; yet, audience members saw the pretense for what it was, a simpleton's trick.

The assumption of today's journalistic simpletons (called analysts) is that "the truth is hidden beneath the surface of events," and the "prizes . . . now go to people who can claim, however absurdly, to have detected the real complexion of events behind a mask of particulars that are mere cosmetics." Fashioning this new reality out of perceptions includes the paranoid habit of disclosing a "pattern" of transgressions, perhaps committed long in the past, that serves as metaphor for what "they are up to now"—experimenting with marijuana as a youth, an alleged racial slur, a chauvinistic comment, and so on. After all, "the truth can be found only in disguise, behind the scenes."[5] To the degree that the press shares, and feeds, popular paranoia about politicians, it is facile to interpret every presidential act as part of a conspiracy.

The particular take on the president is that he is up to no good, and perhaps is no good. In any case, he is not what he seems to be, and certainly is lying, for hidden reasons of his own. In style, the Washington press corps increasingly acts in larger popular culture of bio-porn, where biographers describe in detail how wretched the great and powerful really are behind the scenes (e.g., Kitty Kelly on Nancy Reagan). Or the selfsame great and powerful themselves proclaim how dreadful they are (e.g., Prince Charles), or how wrong they *really* were when they once had claimed to be so right (Robert MacNamara).

In their effort to discover presidential villainy and misconduct, journalists since Watergate have succeeded merely in making presidents look foolish. Their microscopic look at presidential life has scarcely discovered immense and evil misconduct, just ordinary and comical missteps. *Rather than a heroic, or a tragic figure, the president has been transformed into a comic figure.* The press once enhanced the popular view of the president as a heroic figure until proven otherwise; now the story line is that the president is hapless, inadequate, incompetent, and a bungler. Presidential news is comic in tone, reported by a news media whose members self-cast themselves as morally and intellectually superior to an alter-cast president exposed as laughably not up to the job.

In the modern, yet all too primitive, style of a priesthood that kills kings, political journalists view each president not as a figure of strength but rather of weakness, an executive marked by blundering and foolhardiness rather than skill and foresight. Indeed, no matter what the incumbent does, he should have done, or be doing, something else: a bold action shows his recklessness, a cautious action his timidity; a quick decision demonstrates hipshooting, a slow one indecisiveness; reflection is brooding, speaking out as overreacting; attention to detail is silly as micromanaging, but a hands-off approach is seen as bored and inattentive. No longer hero, no longer villain, the mediated president is a fool.

THE PRESIDENT AS FOOL

It is noteworthy that editorial cartooning before Watergate caricatured politicians not so much as fools as bloated plutocrats, scheming villains, and other serious types; since Watergate the dominant motif draws politicians, especially presidents, as foolish—dopey, out of it, befuddled, without a clue, and often reduced to a childlike or buffoon's state. The first president to receive sustained comic treatment as a criterion of evaluation was Gerald Ford. Ford, a man of considerable political experience and personal warmth who was eminently qualified to be president, became the first president to be victimized by the new comic dispensation.

The conventional wisdom was that Ford was an accidental president and not up to the job. Proof allegedly resided in widely publicized missteps that served as visual metaphors of what a stumblebum he was. Ford was probably the best athlete to be president, but videotaped public spills—stumbling off *Air Force One* or tripping on a stair—plus several verbal misstatements ("freeing Poland" in a debate with Jimmy Carter) gave the impression of a lack of physical and mental coordination.

Ford was too nice a man (especially in contrast to his predecessor) to characterize as evil or villainous; since it was no longer appropriate to "take" any president as heroic, the only alternative left was to portray Ford as a fool. In consequence, the spread of such a reputation became a self-fulfilling prophecy: the more he tried, the more he floundered; the less seriously he was taken, the more comic his efforts seemed. Comic Chevy Chase, on *Saturday Night Live*, merely pretended to fall down à la Ford and brought enthusiastic guffaws.

It is, perhaps, no accident that presidential impressionists such as David Frye and Rich Little flourished during the Watergate and post-Watergate periods. Stand-up verbal and gestural caricatures of a president had once made audiences uncomfortable. Jimmy Cagney's mocking of President Franklin Roosevelt in the film *Yankee Doodle Dandy* seemed out of place to many citizens in World War II. But beginning with Vaughn Meader's satire of the Kennedys, *The First Family*, presidents became fair game for increasingly savage and telling mimicry. Comedians built careers on mimicking one president well, such as Dana Carvey's George Bush or Al Franken's Bill Clinton.

The demand for evidence that presidents are indeed fools now sends many "take" journalists in search of obscure or dubious factoids, apocryphal tidbits, true or false, that demonstrate presidential foolishness. David Gergen, communication adviser to presidents, cites one variety, namely, "a naked moment in politics" that "tells" the press and public that the man who would be king is more appropriately a court jester. An otherwise innocuous or innocent event or presidential remark acquires the status of metaphorical truth that reveals the president as a pretender to heroism, an idol with feet of quicksand.

Jimmy Carter's widely reported encounter with a "killer rabbit" was a case in point. On a fishing trip Carter had to fight off a ferocious rabbit with a paddle. Editorial cartoonists portrayed his famous smile as the grin of an imbecile and sketched him with the small stature of a child. By the last year of his presidency, the rabbit incident and similar gaffes (offending Mexicans with his talk of a bout with Montezuma's revenge; becoming short-winded jogging on an incline—the photo was captioned "Can't Get Up the Hill") heightened press contempt. Presidential habits or utterances once viewed as too minor to report were representative anecdotes that disclosed the comic foolishness of the man. Obscure events and important ones collapsed together in the mosaic of the new presidential image of foolish incompetence: how can you expect a man who can't deal with a killer rabbit to cope with the Ayatollah Khomeini and the Iranian revolutionaries?

Similar incidents have beset more recent politicians. In the election of 1992, both George Bush and Dan Quayle opened themselves up to journalists' ridicule with embarrassing naked moments. In Bush's case, he apparently encountered his first checkout scanner while grocery shopping as a photo opportunity (Barbara Bush claimed it was not)—irrefutable proof of a president "out of touch." Dan Quayle ran into difficulty over the spelling of "potato." And as many "take" reporters would have it, fast food restaurants expose Bill Clinton's character not as one of self-sacrifice but of overconsumption. Taking the take journalists seriously, comic David Letterman joked, "What does Clinton like to hear all the time? Would you like fries with that?" That quip prompted a sober-sided Vice President Al Gore to retort to Letterman, "That's the President of the United States you're talking about, pinhead."

In all cases, the "naked moment" serves as a journalist's metaphor for the foolishness, and thus the foolhardiness, of the comic protagonist. Such moments have the potential to linger, accumulate, and fashion a "character pattern" that reveals the true man is but a phony. Too, the president, vice president, and presidential candidates go through comic diminishment when journalists allege that occult or obscure habits or incidents suggest a suspicious pattern of behavior. A claim to heroism, for instance, can be challenged. George Bush's record as a decorated navy pilot came into question (it is often not clear who is responsible when questions are being raised) in 1992; a veteran challenged Bush's, and the official, version of a World War II combat mission. Although never substantiated, the challenge implied that Bush had been a coward. Reporters in 1992 also sought assiduously and unsuccessfully to pin down rumors about Bush's "girl-friends" and mistresses, as well as crooked ties to Texas oil money.

Bush, however, is not the point. The assumption of tabloid journalism is that any president has skeletons in the closet to expose. In the tradition of lateral attribution, since reporters are looking for the closet, this is ample cause—proof is not necessary—to suspect culpability over something wicked or sinister. Presidential denial only raises suspicions of a cover-up of foolish ways in a foolish past.

No sooner had Bush been hooted off the presidential stage and Bill Clinton ushered onto it than the Clintons' investment in a retirement home at Whitewater in Arkansas became the subject of intense press scrutiny. Reporters such as Howard Fineman of *Newsweek* and Jeff Gerth of the *New York Times* wrote volumes from Little Rock about the alleged misdeeds that made Whitewater the functional equivalent of Watergate and Teapot Dome. Yet, if Arkansas reporter Gene Lyons is correct, all this intense reporting on Bill Clinton's past by the national press evokes an unrecognizable "carica-ture of either the man or his milieu in the national press." Gerth in particular, he notes, wrote stories "that combine a prosecutorial bias and the art of tactical omission to insinuate all manner of sin and skullduggery."

The journalistic rhetoric was revealing: Arkansas secrets, "seedy appear-ance," "the likely suspect," "snuggled up close to Arkansas oligarchs," "never quite escaped the orbit of the shadowy Stephens brothers," all evoking the image of a network of conspiratorial wheels within wheels in which the reformist president was enmeshed, obviously putting the lie to his claim to political competence. He tried to con us, such reportage says, but unmasking reveals Clinton as merely foolish for trying. Lyons quotes a typical backhanded press indictment from *Time*'s George Church: "The dealings in question are so complex that it is difficult even to summarize the suspicions they arouse, let alone cite the evidence supporting such suspicions. . . . Violations of law, if any, would be extremely difficult to prove."[6] The "take" is clear. Nothing can be substantiated, but that the president played the fool is certain.

Political news has always been viewed by segments of the press and public as bad news, but in the past it was muted and balanced by some measure of deference and respect for politicians and the political process and by the felt obligation to report good news that reinforces basic mythic messages, such as "democracy works," "the government is good," and "politicians are largely well-meaning." But those messages and the faith they supported have disappeared, and the burden of disproof has fallen on political figures. The assumption now is that the intentions of politicians are always bad, yet so thinly veiled that they are easily discoverable. Smirking comical analysis of press shamans will glean the occult and exorcise the demons of politics.

Political scientist Thomas E. Patterson discusses one example among many, a CBS "Reality Check" during the 1992 campaign by a master of the journalistic wink-n-nod, "know what I mean?" air, Eric Engberg. He scored Bill Clinton for not knowing every detail of the NAFTA agreement and suggested he was engaged in "statistical chicanery" and other deceptions that demonstrate bad intentions ("The candidate is in the middle and stalling . . . wants it both ways . . . is a conveniently slow learner"). All this, says Patterson, lets Engberg self-cast himself as "the truth-telling journalist combating the illusion-selling politician"; rather than an analysis of the wisdom of the NAFTA accord and the comparative positions of Bush and Clinton on it, "the economic issue was a pretext for an attack on Clinton's credibility."[7]

Engberg engaged in the common press practice of comic altercasting, using a political event and statement to shift to the meaning of what was happening; here the politician allegedly engages in deception, but he, Engberg, catches Clinton in the act. "Credibility" refers to a psychic rather than a political condition, something that can be inferred from a take on what Clinton said rather than an issue seriously discussed. By assuming and "proving" that he is engaged in an act of deception, the politician is then easily reduced to the status of an illusion-selling con artist who is insincere and slick, disingenuous and facile. Thank heavens for the political simpletons who are easily unmasked playing their charades!

JOURNALISTS AS COMIC CHARACTERS

Ironically, the very journalists raising character questions about politicians now face questions about their own characters; they too are unmasked at the ball. An enterprising media critic, Ken Auletta, asked fifty members of the "media elite" how much money they made on the lecture circuit. Sam Donaldson of *This Week with David Brinkley*, for example, had ridiculed President Clinton for not remembering that he had, several years earlier, loaned his mother $20,000; ironically, Donaldson couldn't even remember the groups he himself had spoken to for fees. Cokie Roberts of ABC and PBS earns $300,000 annually from speaking fees; she received $20,000 for speaking to the Group Health Association of America. She is the same correspondent who once declared that the single-payer health system, which the GHA group of health maintenance organizations opposes, "cost too much." She refused to allow C-SPAN to tape her remarks before the health group, then later donated her fee to charity. After recounting many other such examples, Auletta noted that "celebrity journalism and the appearance of conflict unavoidably erode journalism's claim to public trust," quoting Jay Rosen that "you're going to start having character stories about journalists."[8]

Criticism of journalistic ethics includes not only the influence of interested money that might affect their appraisal of politics and politicians, but their insider ties to politicians as well, for example, George F. Will coaching Ronald Reagan for a debate with Jimmy Carter, then writing a column declaring Reagan the winner, a "thoroughbred" of presidential stature, without mentioning his own nonjournalistic advisory role. Will, charges one critic, has moved from an "ethic of virtue" to an "ethic of self-interest" as he has developed ties with the mighty. Will pioneers an elite journalistic habit of shifting "the comparative status of elected or appointed officials and the journalists through whom their positions are mediated"; via a sniffy attitude toward politicians (including the rude practice of interrupting them), the journalist "habituates viewers to a treatment of public servants that ranges from benign dandyism to insolence."[9]

The decline in media manners is especially apparent among celebrity pundits (Will, Roberts, Donaldson, Ted Koppel, etc.). Presidents and other politicians are subject to media "outing," the unwilling exposure of their unworthiness. Television interviewing, for instance, not only involves interruptions but also innuendoes that the political guest is evasive, that what he or she is saying is not the truth, not to be taken at face value; the very political status that makes guests worth interviewing also makes them fair game for public humiliation. Interviews typically end on a snide note that suggests the guest didn't confess despite the host's best third-degree efforts to expose the truth. Politicians come and go, but the pundit class remains (Do we need term limits for pundits?) as arbiters of public virtue, as the inquisitors of a passing parade of hopelessly inadequate miscreants, or, perhaps, merely as the simpletons at the masked ball.

David Bromwich notes the "police-blotter slang" of contemporary literary criticism: "a work of art is *complicit* in crimes it does not confess; accordingly it must be not interpreted but *interrogated*."[10] In the same manner, political journalists treat the presidency as an artifice complicit in crimes the president and his retinue will not confess. Presidential acts, and indeed basic character, are not to be interpreted but rather interrogated. Just as a poem, novel, or text under the critic's interrogation is never a "realistic" rendering, only the appraisal of a "pessimistic" author, pundits find presidential work hopelessly flawed. And like a writer under the critic's gun, the president's work is flawed because he too is of unsound character, guilty of elitism, sexism, or other defects rendering one unworthy of public office or trust.

The take journalist's style of unmasking the character of politicians by fashioning a pattern of misconduct hidden in the past has been challenged. In an address in 1994 before the National Press Club, humorist Garrison Keillor (a Clinton supporter) argued that the Whitewater affair was a "shaggy-dog story" whose "point is its pointlessness." People are amused that they are still listening to "what apparently is a long, winding circumstantial joke that the teller keeps complicating by tossing in new unrelated elements." The difficulty is that such a story becomes "a story about itself," that is, a metastory. Even journalists begin to wonder, "Should we really spend so much time on this?" Such metastories acquire magnitude in an atmosphere of presidential mistrust, with an unrelenting search for "inconsistencies" in statements and possible secret deals and nefarious schemes cooked up long ago. But what if there is no smoking gun? "The American people," Keillor told the press elite, "are sitting on the bleachers waiting for the elephant to come out and all we see are the guys selling cotton candy. That's you."[11]

Keillor saw the humor in the political shaggy-dog story, but he didn't appreciate that comic condemnation does not now require the existence of an elephant, that people are quite satisfied with the tangled webs of sugary fluff that pass for presidential news. Cotton-candy news satisfies our hunger for, to use Popeye's term, "humilification." Since political celebrities are virtual figures, we are quite happy with virtual news about them. Indeed, it appears that the real point of nonstories such as Whitewater is precisely their pointlessness. A president spins in the delicious media sugar confection of scandal, confirming our expectations of scandalous politicians. The suspicious anecdote, no matter how apocryphal and virtual, confirms our suspicions: the elephant, although perhaps painted white by the purveyors of cotton-candy news, comes out for all to see.

BEING THERE, WITH RON AND NANCY

In 1970 Jerzy Kosinski published a short novel entitled *Being There*. This comic parable about politics in the television age centered on a character named Chance, a simpleminded gardener who lived a sheltered and secluded life inside the walls of a rich employer's mansion enclave. Chance's only link with the outside world, and the chief source of his social learning, was television. Chance discovered that with TV he could master the world's nature and create his own: "By changing the channel he could change himself. He could go through phases, as garden plants went through phases, but he could change as rapidly as he wished by twisting the dial backward and forward. . . . Thus he came to believe that it was he, Chance, and no one else, who made himself be."[12]

After Chance's employer dies, those responsible for the mansion discover that Chance has lived there since childhood and has had no contact with the world save TV; he cannot read or write, and has had minimal direct social encounters or emotional involvement with fellow humans. He is entirely a creature of the popular culture of television. Forced to leave the estate, he wanders through the streets. By accident a limousine hits and injures him. The wealthy woman who owns the limo errs in taking Chance's name, mistaking it for "Chauncey Gardiner." She whisks him to her own mansion for the type of treatment the rich and well-born deserve. Chance now has a new set of elite patrons who take the well-dressed and polite "Mr. Gardiner" to be one of them, a wealthy businessman. When Chance talks of wanting another garden to grow, they misinterpret his meaning, mistaking gardening as a metaphor for business: "A productive businessman is indeed a laborer in his own vineyard!"[13]

Mr. Gardiner's patron introduces him to the president. The chief also takes Chance to be part of the same economic elite that has taken the ex-gardener under their wing. The president asks him what he thinks of "the bad season on The Street," meaning Wall Street. Chance falls back on the only thing he really knows anything about, gardening. He offers a homily about the cycle of the seasons, and concludes that "as long as the roots are not severed, all is well and all will be well." The president is impressed with Mr. Gardiner's seemingly authoritative and insightful pronouncements. He judges Chance's erudite economic analysis "refreshing and optimistic" and wishes Gardiner's "good solid sense" was prevalent on Capitol Hill. The president later uses the four seasons metaphor in a speech, and credits Mr. Chauncey Gardiner.

The national news media, ever alert to an intriguing New Face, probe for newsworthy tidbits about the mysterious Mr. Gardiner. Reporters, however, are puzzled to find that they can uncover no past whatsoever about the New Face. Nonetheless, Chance's celebrity status earns him an invitation to appear on a television talk show. Again he muses about of the growth of "the garden." Quickly he becomes a national sensation for speaking so beautifully and optimistically of the inevitability of prosperity. The TV host hails Mr. Gardiner as a "financier, presidential adviser, and true statesman!" Pundits universally applaud the Gardiner style of "social confidence and financial security." The president and economic analysts regard Chance as a genius, foreign ambassadors court his favor, his wealthy patron's wife wants to be his mistress, and the country admires him as a beacon of hope.

In fact, everyone is beguiled by Chance's apparent lack of guile, his innocence and absence of a past, and the seemingly deep knowledge that permits him to overcome doubt and despair and believe in the American future. Chance's admirers take his simple and uninformed statements as the height of wisdom, at once popular and occult. Such straightforwardness is charmingly devoid of evasion; here is a man who speaks plainly from the heart and possesses oracular powers that let him see a bright and promising future. The inability of the investigative branches of government to discover any past for him is interpreted as evidence of his innate modesty and desire for privacy.

Not every observer of the new celebrity is of a positive mind. The U.S. and Soviet governments develop a paranoid fear that Chance is up to no good, possibly a leader of a group planning a coup d'état, or even a Soviet or CIA agent. Yet for most people, elite and mass, he is a vessel into which to pour their fears and hopes, since unbeknownst to them he is an empty shell of a man who can be all things to all people.

Finally, Kosinski imagines the inevitable: a candidate for president searches for a suitable vice presidential running mate; Gardiner's name surfaces. When there are objections from political analysts that Gardiner's background is unknown, politicos shrewdly conclude that it is a plus: all the other possible vice presidential candidates have too much background. But Gardiner

has no background! And so he's not and cannot be objectionable to anyone! He's personable, well-spoken, and he comes across well on TV! And, as far as his thinking goes, he appears to be one of us. That's all. It's clear what he isn't. Gardiner is our one chance.

Hence, from the point of view of kingmakers, Chauncy Gardiner is the perfect candidate. Kosinski concludes, "Not a thought lifted itself from Chance's brain. Peace filled his chest."[14]

There is clearly no end of humor in the idea of a *perfectly* stupid and innocent television personality becoming a national leader. There is also clear prescience. For the one exception to the recent fate of ridiculed U.S. presidents (in the non-Aristotelian sense of ridiculed in order to harm) is Ronald Reagan. He survived two terms of critical reviews. Kosinski's fantasy about the emergence of a holy innocent who embodies heroic qualities and enunciates wondrous platitudes and parables has, since 1980, reminded many readers of the career of Reagan. For Reagan *acted* like self-created Chance— comfortably at peace with himself and devoid of dark Nixonian hates and fears, or of Carteresque thoughtful, reflective pondering.

Reagan understood the popular thought and emotion of his times and was able to embody and articulate widespread, deeply experienced conventions while transforming them into political support. What he lacked in intellectual or even political knowledge he made up for in popular knowledge, in his ability to say, and actually to be, common American. Reagan unswervingly and unerringly styled himself as a citizen politician who was not "One of Them." When he first ran for public office, for governor of California in 1966, he sensed that the professional politician had no esteem in the eyes of the populace; hence, he ran as a citizen politician. Elected president in 1980, he came into and left presidential office damning the very government of which he was the chief executive, not as the solution to chronic problems but as The Problem.

As with Chauncey Gardiner, many of Reagan's admirers absorbed his homilies on religion, family, and the proper role of government as representing the great tradition of grass-roots democracy. Detractors viewed Reagan as less political savant than idiot. Gore Vidal, for example, remarked that Reagan "never stopped talking, even though he never had anything to say except what he had just read in the *Reader's Digest*, which he studied the way that Jefferson did Montesquieu."[15]

Unlike Ford or Bush, Reagan had no background in law, business, or politics; unlike Carter or Clinton, he had little grasp of the nuances and problems of governing a complex organizational structure and multitudinous nation-state. But he had something none of these other presidents possessed, namely, popular authority. Reagan was a celebrity from the magical kingdom of Hollywood, and was conversant with the national mythography created by the shamans of Warner Brothers. At a time when both charismatic authority (such as that possessed by John Kennedy) and legal-rational authority (such as resides in the bureaucracy of Washington) were suspect in the eyes of the populace, one who could represent the theater of popular national dreams was preferable. Reagan was a master of mythic politics, conjuring up our nostalgic yearnings in a postlapsarian age and relating a disillusioned present to a mysterious national continuity that would unite past and future in a remoralized and reordered world of American dominance.

Mythic politics let Reagan depoliticize himself, casting himself as a virtual nonpolitical figure who embodied and celebrated the wonder of our national rectitude. For some of his supporters and his detractors, his use of popular authority masked a draconian and "extreme" agenda—imposing an outdated conventional moral code, restoring a traditional order of class and status, relegating the poor to a life of deserved penury, and so on. Such an agenda openly presented would be "political" rather than mythic, and would mire Reagan as the shamanistic carrier of the myth in the quicksand of politics. Instead, the best way to advocate such values is to dramatize them in theatrical terms, as something all Americans should, and do, believe—without ardently trying to impose those values.

Critics viewed Reagan as "the acting president," playing the role of a lifetime, as if he didn't mean to do what he said. It was an act, a charade, a game of confidence that was not to be taken seriously. When his detractors said that he was a joke, *they said more than they knew*! For Reagan brought a lightheaded and relaxed tone to the presidency that reassured people at a subliminal level that *he didn't really mean it*. People couldn't quite take him seriously because he didn't mean to be taken seriously. He was too avuncular and Hollywood-like to pursue a draconian or punitive agenda, so he could say the meanest or most threatening things (propose prohibition of all abortions, bombing the Russians, etc.) without anybody really believing that he would try to realize the far right agenda. Critics could praise or condemn him, but everyone could be sure that the worst would not happen, simply because that would involve him in what he disliked the most, conflict.

Reagan thus survived while other presidents of the post-Nixon era were reviled and defeated, because he regarded the presidency as comedy. The ability of the "Teflon president" to remain relatively popular stemmed from his comic touch and tone, thus deflecting or mitigating criticism. Serious men have to take, and give, criticism seriously; nonserious men do not. Carter could talk about a national malaise, and Bush of the breakdown of family values; Reagan tolerantly smiled and laughed through the apocalypse, remaining ignorantly optimistic about national destiny in the face of brutal facts. He shrugged off the antics of his own dysfunctional family and indeed the national decline of family life. He was "the national host" as if he presided over a banquet as a comic master of ceremonies, able to make fun of himself at the national feast of fools that characterized the Reagan years.

Reagan responded to critics with quips. Everything, even nuclear war, could be joked about. Everyone was regaled with, and disarmed by, his inexhaustible supply of showbiz stories. Audiences loved his apocryphal anecdotes about big government (e.g., the bureaucrat at the Bureau of Indian Affairs who was forlorn because his Indian had died). Reagan even had a speech writer whose job was to write the joke or quip of the day, a ready and amusing response (when embittered aide Don Regan's tell-all book came out, Reagan on cue quipped, "I don't read fiction"). No one reads the speeches of Ronald Reagan the way they do those of, say, Thomas Jefferson or Woodrow Wilson. Few ever recall his pontification; instead, they remember his comic touch. No collection of his writings are of interest; yet a videotape of his funniest lines and tales does well in popular sales. He was our national good humor man, who, like the best comic actors, was in the happiness business. The serious grind of politics is made easy, and the psychic burden of the presidency lifted, if it is treated as comedy. In the Reagan era, power resided in the ability *not* to be taken seriously.

Reagan watchers, from the very beginning of his political career in 1966, often observed that his opponents always underestimated him. They could never understand that his self-deprecating lack of seriousness and his sustained cultivation of ignorance were assets. A comic figure does not need to display gravity or complexity, but rather "bearable lightness of being" and straightforward simplicity. The idea was to make the presidency look easy by taking it easy. Ease of manner negated any fears that Reagan was driven by Nixonian demons or Carteresque intelligence. He was the head of the very government he had made fun of for so long that it became easy to forget that he was now responsible for it. But rather than disestablish it, he simply set himself up as government's comic foil, as the head of the populace expressing comical contempt for the complicated operation of "the federal gummit." Reagan's political comedy made people feel superior to the established government and the political class of press, bureaucrats, and politicians.

For his admirers, Reagan was a comic authority who could point to the conduct of government as a big joke he discovered and shared with them. It could be argued that Reagan represented to many people that an ignorant person can go far without knowing anything, that know-nothingism works (in his speech to the 1988 Republican convention, he slipped and said, "Facts are stupid things"). Yet, that view is partial and incomplete: Reagan went far by expressing popular knowledge, a form of basic social thought that is based in grass-roots wisdom, that he, as a tribune and representation of the people, knows better than the professional elite in Washington. His air of bemusement at the alleged idiocies of government derived from mythic certainty of democratic common sense that somehow evaporates once people become politicians and cross the Potomac. Reagan could appeal to the common desire to believe that ordinary people, meaning those not connected to the government, knew better.

Ronald Reagan, then, was immunized against the disease of presidential character assassination. People were acutely sensitive to the comic character of Ronald Reagan; a frequent evaluation of him was "He's a real character," meaning that he was excluded from the kind of serious investigation that rendered the other presidents somehow unfit or unworthy. Reagan maintained his public character inside a charmed circle of celebrity status, leavening the most virulent attacks with his touch of humor. His opponents, and many in the press, thought him incurious at best, and stupid at worst. Yet his anti-intellectualism gave him a solid grounding in the popular wisdom that other elites so lacked. Like the Austrian emperor in *Amadeus*, Reagan the popular king simply said, "There's too many notes." Reagan shrewdly stuck to a simple tune of a few but recognizable cultural notes; he grasped totally the insight of the first rule of the theater of politics, "Give them a tune they can whistle."[16]

Like Chance, Reagan was a natural, a media creature of protean quality, whose simplistic metaphors and confident air of optimism charmed those many who willed to believe. He had Chance's refreshing and optimistic character and the good, solid sense so lacking in more complicated and driven souls in Washington. His past, in fact as tangled in money and women as those of other presidential figures, was made immune from devastating criticism by his association with the mythic dreamland of Hollywood.

Reagan's press reviews did not evaluate him in the same way as other political figures of the media age, all of whom had the burden of too much background. Reagan was of a mythic place, and of a comic authority, which made him virtually beyond criticism, certainly of the most politically damaging sort. Other presidents and presidential aspirants could only envy the power of comic rhetoric to invoke magical thinking and sustain an enchanted presence. Reagan was the characterological exception because he understood, either shrewdly or intuitively, that rhetorical rule in a political culture of hypercriticism is only possible through the good offices of amiable amusement, of playing a president of pleasant good humor took neither the role nor the political critics too seriously. Political wit is more powerful than political wisdom. Among the post-Nixon presidents of the late twentieth century, Reagan was the only one who got it right.

CARICATURED CHARACTERS

With the great turnover of presidents and presidential candidates, it is fair to ask if we are turning the presidency into a role of ritual degradation and martyrdom, elevating and then striking down kings in an endlessly recurrent cycle of characterological deprecation and rejection. Since journalists of the new news, and their fascinated audiences, view these recurrent falls from power and grace more out of glee than outrage, it is tempting to think that we are witnessing a manifestation of increasing cultural frivolity. We refuse to confer heroism or even good intentions on most politicians. Neither in nor, subsequently, out of office do they acquire villainous reputations. No, we regard them as mere simpletons devoid of virtue or skill, malice or will. Like the unmasked Wizard of Oz, they are not bad *people*, just bad *wizards*.

The only political strategy that seems to defend against being cast as a fool is for a president consciously to play a comic figure whose very foolishness is viewed as a popular virtue. The blood sport of presidential destruction can be avoided by becoming a comic antihero who is complicit in the cultural frivolity. This comic figure generates sincerity and authenticity, for the self-conscious comic president regards politics, including the presidential role with humility, that is, as something of a joke. Someone in public life who says, in effect, the joke's on me for getting involved in something so foolish and making a fool of myself, inspires confidence because he or she is without guile or intellect. "The joke's on me, not you," the president seems to say.

Our comic state of cultural frivolity relegates politics to the status of a flippant entertainment we do not wish to take seriously, and grants popularity to those who play the fool. On his deathbed, the great English actor Edmund Kean was asked if it was difficult to die. No, he replied, dying isn't difficult, "but comedy—*that* is difficult." Playing a presidential character in an era of press and public blood lust is difficult, but the only way to survive and prosper may be to master the difficult histrionic talents of the political comedy of character.

NOTES

1. Oscar G. Brockett, *The Theatre: An Introduction* (New York: Holt, Rinehart and Winston, 1964), p. 182.

2. Michael Kelly, "David Gergen, Master of the Game," *New York Times Magazine*, October 31, 1993, p. 63.

3. Ibid., p. 97.

4. John Taylor, "Take Journalism," *New York*, April 28, 1993, p. 10.

5. "Don't Mean Diddly," *The New Yorker*, July 10, 1994, pp. 4, 6.

6. Gene Lyons, "Fool for Scandal," *Harper's Magazine*, October 1994, pp. 55–63.

7. Thomas E. Patterson, *Out of Order* (New York: Alfred A. Knopf, 1993), p. 17.

8. "Fee Speech," *The New Yorker*, September 12, 1994, p. 47.

9. David Bromwich, *Politics by Other Means* (New York: Yale University Press, 1992), pp. 80–81.

10. Ibid., p. 112.

11. Garrison Keillor, Address to the National Press Club, Washington, DC, May 9, 1994.

12. Jerzy Kosinski, *Being There* (New York: Harcourt Brace Jovanovich, 1970), pp. 5–6.

13. Ibid., p. 43.

14. Ibid., pp. 147–148.

15. Gore Vidal, "Ronnie and Nancy: A Life in Pictures," in *At Home, 1982–1988* (New York: Vintage Books, 1990), p. 77.

16. Ferdinand Mount, *The Theatre of Politics* (New York: Schocken Books, 1973), pp. 224–231.

CHAPTER 6
Legislators Deliberate: Political Comedies of the Situation

When legendary Louisiana political boss Huey Long was asked what the state legislature would do with one of his proposals, he contemptuously replied, "Legislators! I shuffle 'em like a deck of cards and shuck 'em like a sack of corn." Legislators at the state and national level are not always pawns of political executives, yet many people have shared Long's contempt. "Congress," wrote Henry L. Mencken, "consists of one-third, more or less, scoundrels; two-thirds, more or less, idiots; and three-thirds, more or less, poltroons." Mark Twain also cited legislators' reputations for chicanery, low intellect, and cowardice: "It could probably be shown by facts and figures that there is no distinctly native American criminal class except Congress."

FROM HONEST GRAFT TO C-SPAN

There is nothing new, then, about the image of legislatures, and Congress in particular, as a comic drama of democracy. Long ago Henry Adams, a veteran observer of nineteenth century American politics, asked, "If a Congressman is a hog, then what is a Senator?" He answered as follows:

This innocent question, put in a candid spirit, petrified any executive officer that ever sat a week in his office. Even [Henry, the author] Adams admitted that Senators passed belief. The comic side of their egotism partly disguised its extravagance, but faction had gone so far under Andrew Johnson that at times the whole Senate seemed to catch hysterics of nervous bucking without apparent reason. Great leaders, like Sumner and Conkling, could not be burlesqued; they were more grotesque than ridicule could make them.[1]

During the height of the Gilded Age, the U.S. Senate was called "The Millionaire's Club." A British observer of American politics, Lord Bryce, noted that the driving force of such politicians was not so much power or glory as "the desire for office and for office as a means of gain." Senators were infamous for their shamelessly open pecuniary and political ties to special interests such as the railroads. One of their number, Senator Nelson Aldrich, the son-in-law of John D. Rockefeller, seriously proposed revamping representation in the Senate to allow senators to represent interests rather than states; thus a senator for oil, for cotton, steel, and so on. The corruption abounded throughout the United Steel, most notably in the big city machines such as New York's Tammany Ring and Chicago's party organization.

The ethic of office as a means of gain led a variety of people, well positioned like Aldrich, to prosper. A Tammany Hall functionary, ex-Senator George Washington Plunkitt, drew a moral distinction between honest graft and dishonest graft: the former included payoffs from, say, railroads in an honest exchange for favorable votes; the latter consisted of blatant bribes by bartenders and bawdy houses for political protection. Wits commented that this distinction, permitting "honest" graft, gave Americans the best legislators that money could buy! (The corollary to this principle is the view of an honest politician as one who, when once bought, *stays* bought.) As Plunkitt said of himself, "I seen my opportunities and I took 'em."

Since Plunkitt, legislatures have been full of politicians seeking opportunities for gain, not just monetary, but also to enhance reputations, connections, glory, privileges, and their standing in the political and social hierarchy. These individual ambitions and expansive egos associated with legislators contribute to the comedy of legislative deliberation, a setting where well-positioned and self-important people (largely middle-aged white male lawyers) proclaim commitment to benevolent government "for the people." The solon has acquired a comic reputation as a narcissistic blowhard, an image of a drunken and senile senator mocked by radio comic Fred Allen in the 1940s as Senator Claghorn: an overstuffed, cigar-chomping machine politico caucusing in smoke-filled rooms, a sweaty campaigner glad-handing and baby kissing at fairs to snow the rubes.

Occasionally (more so now than ever before) news accounts give away the game—a secret tape of a legislator taking briefcases of money from a surreptitious donor for favors; a mistress kept in an apartment on the public payroll by a committee chairman; Congressmen photographed at a posh resort while wined and dined by some powerful interest. Small wonder that many citizens view congressmen as comic figures unable to control or police themselves, and at our expense: writing themselves wondrous health care benefits but denying the same to the country, voting themselves pay increases in the middle of the night, and grousing about giving up their parking privileges.

Perhaps the biggest blow to the image of Congress has been close television scrutiny, especially with the televising of the House of Representatives and the Senate on C-SPAN. What precious little was left of the popular image of the Congress as a citadel of toga-clad Ciceros deliberating over great issues in eloquent tones worthy of Demosthenes is now gone. Consider the all too common C-SPAN video of congressmen addressing in indignant and alarmed voices the empty House chamber, as if speaking to an assembly of ghosts, or of senators wandering about the floor during a vote, like a bunch of fraternity alumni at a postgame football party. Here also sit bored old plutocrats, aping the manner of the nineteenth century French lawmakers of Daumier's painting *Le Ventre Legislative*.

Or TV viewers hear the rhetoric of the Senate, where Daniel Webster and Henry Clay once intoned, but where now Senator Alphonse D'Amato of New York sings an attack on a crime bill to the tune of *Old McDonald Had a Farm*: "President Clinton had a bill, eeiai, eeiai O; In that bill he has some pork, eeiai, eeiai O. Here pork, there pork, everywhere pork, pork . . ." The majesty of the eloquence boggles the imagination. Historian Edward Gibbon, in his classic study of the decline and fall of the Roman empire, noted that at one point in the descent of that once mighty power, the Roman Senate decided that "a law was thought necessary to discriminate the dress of comedians from that of senators." Perhaps the U.S. Senate needs a law to discriminate the *rhetoric* of senators from that of comedians. Like the Senate of the age of Twain and Adams, the contemporary Senate is its own burlesque.

Skeptical observers of the Congress and state legislatures might retort that rhetorical decline is the only way that these deliberative bodies have changed since the Gilded Age a century ago. The Congress is still awash in money, and the Senate is still a millionaire's club, except now the multimillionaires are challenging the mere millionaires. The spectacle of the extremely wealthy, belonging to the top .01 percent income bracket, writing laws supposed to benefit the rest of citizens strikes many Americans as laughable in itself—a senatorial billionaire's club acting as a plutocratic body preaching the dream of the success myth while eroding the benefits of the progressive income tax to the populace.

A plutocratic Senate would be the televised subject of *Lifestyles of the Rich and Famous* rather than *Washington Week in Review*. Here are senators who bill themselves as populists, yet without redistributing wealth. Such a plutocratic democracy might be preferable to a kleptocracy, a political class of politicians for sale. Hence, ironically, a superrich Senate could claim independence from special interests, that is, senators asserting freedom to act on "principle" since they are too wealthy to bribe! Better the manicured hands of a commercial plutocracy than the greased palms of the party hack. Like the priesthood that served European monarchs well because they were beyond worldly temptation, a Senate of plutocrats could rise above monetary temptation, without taking vows of celibacy or poverty.

Although the demography of the membership changes, Congress and state legislatures still legislate. In other words, they meet, talk to each other, make deals and push for what they want, hold hearings and obey rules and procedures, and even vote on bills that, if passed, become laws. Congressional officials like to think that what they do is important. Yet, many congressional measures are archaic or irrelevant, or even ignored by the public (e.g., the 55 mile an hour speed limit). The "dance of legislation," to use Woodrow Wilson's term, is often nothing more than a cosmetic minuet; acts and resolutions dramatize legislative "concern" or "commitment" but bestow no lasting benefits.

For the most part, what one sees on C-SPAN seems undirected and farcical—members milling about on the floor of the House and Senate, tedious committee hearings relieved only by partisan and procedural wrangling, and floor speeches and debates that demonstrate the low intellectual level and rhetorical crudity of the participants. C-SPAN has become a political variant of The Comedy Channel, revealing just how comic the legislative process actually is. On the Congressional Comedy Channel, one can watch stand-up comedy in the House well or Senate floor, with legislators making fiery and uncompromising speeches that no one heeds. Or one can view committees struggling to understand (at least those members who are awake) some arcane point of bureaucratic rulemaking, or the technology of the latest exquisite and pricey weapon.

For more hardy and persistent students of political comedy, there are the joys of the Senate filibuster, wherein a coterie of stubborn and indefatigable protectors of the republic prevent passage of popular measures favored by both the public and the majority in Congress. All in all, the comic spectacle of congressional deliberation leads us to conclude that it is not very deliberative, and impossible to take seriously. Oscar Wilde said that no person of feeling could read Dickens' account of the death of Little Nell without laughing; similarly, no person of minimal intellect can watch C-SPAN's coverage of the conduct of legislative activity in Congress without a similar guffaw. The world is tragic to those who feel, but it is a comedy for watchers of Congress.

THE COMEDY OF THE SITUATION

The comedy of Congress occurs in the ritual format of legislative conduct. Legislators represent very different interests and regions, and bring to their roles very different backgrounds and personalities. But they act within the ritualized framework of congressional traditions and rules, such as the constraints on what they can say to, and about, each other in public forums. They are not only actors in an institution, they are acting in a *comedy of the situation*. A comedy of the situation depicts the ludicrous consequences that derive from placing characters in ritualistic situations where they seem out of place—a middle-class housewife like Lucy Ricardo stomping in a barrel of grapes at a winery, or a rough-hewn Roseanne at the opera.

Situations might seem at first glance to be kaleidoscopic, with an infinite number of variations on human themes, but in fact they follow certain patterns. Both philosophers and psychologists understand the ritual patterns that human interactions assume at the personal level. These "games people play" comprise the context where people relate; the mix of the people who are doing the relating defines how the game is played and whether it is heavenly or hellish. The social context, and the definition of the situation within that context, imbue the relational pattern with its particular hue and thrust. The ritual patterns encompass the range of drama. A drama of courtship and marriage, for instance, may be tragic, pathetic, or comic; it may be high or low tragedy, happy or sad romance, sentimental or suspenseful melodrama, or romantic comedy, bedroom farce, a comedy of mistaken identity, and so on. When we ask "What's the situation?" we rely upon dramatic experience and expectations to give us a clue as to what's happening and what to expect.

Thus, *situational patterns are dramatic*, that is, stories with qualities and narratives stemming from our sense of drama. Situations possess a *ritual structure* that gives a story form and content audiences can follow and appreciate. The ritual structure of comedies of situation guides us in understanding comic dramas, staged or real. But what makes a situation comic? Think, for example, of the ordinary TV sitcom, the situation comedy in a familial setting. Beginning with *I Love Lucy* and *The Honeymooners*, TV has developed traditional formats for the domestic situation comedy. We have all seen the stories again and again, enjoying the predictable and familiar cultural tale of an ordinary family or group dealing with mundane but amusing problems that confront virtually everyone, except here the characters involved are more foolish than we. Lucy Ricardo, for instance, is no ordinary housewife; she gets herself involved in a variety of hilarious predicaments in her efforts to do something out of the ordinary (get into show business, glimpse a movie star), invariably getting into trouble with her husband. Similarly, Ralph Cramden is no ordinary bus driver, since he gets himself involved in situations wherein his foolish traits (vanity, temper) lead to some humiliation or quandary.

Although the major comic figures of TV sitcoms may seem typical— ranging from Robert Young of *Father Knows Best* to Mary Tyler Moore to Roseanne Barr and the Bart Simpson family—their power to make audiences laugh lies in their *clownish* quality; they are stereotypical personages whose chief characteristic is the ability to make fools of themselves because of common human faults and mistakes. Indeed, sitcoms are appealing because virtually all members of the ensemble of characters in the story are capable of becoming clown of the moment. In *All in the Family*, Archie Bunker, Edith, "Meathead," and Gloria at one point or another become the butt of the joke, much to their embarrassment. They are not circus clowns in a clown suit, nor are they funny because they are clowning around (à la Jerry Lewis); rather they are *everyday clowns*, funny because they appear foolish in ordinary situations at home or at work. In the situations of domestic comedy, one or more of the characters act the fool as the designated clown who is humiliated.

Situation comedy often includes a *degradation ritual*: someone, and sometimes everyone, is at some point degraded before his or her fellow actors and the audience. Thus, wisecracking in sitcoms involves rhetorical putdowns, the characters humiliating each other by reference to their behavior. Audiences can't and don't take such figures seriously: reduced to the humiliated lower status of a clown, characters are less than adults with dignity, and can be legitimately laughed at, like children or kittens clumsily at play.

Even if there is a "serious" theme in the sitcom, it is leavened by someone eating humble pie as comic relief. Television comedies and shows such as *Murphy Brown* and those created by Norman Lear deal with social issues in a comic frame, wherein the all-too-human actors bumble through their attempt to cope with familiar social ills—alcoholism, racism, sexism, AIDS, and so on. The character of Murphy Brown became a single mother, to great comic delight for her audience. Critics, however, such as then Vice President J. Danforth Quayle, condemned the show as contributing to the breakdown of morality and "family values" in America. It was difficult to know which was funnier, the shows charting the progress of Murphy's pregnancy or, following Quayle's remark, the political debate over the depiction of Murphy's out-of-wedlock baby as a symbol of an elitist media culture leading America's youth astray.

Political moralists, certainly the humorless ones, rarely regard popular TV as merely an entertainment medium. Quayle didn't "get it," that is, that Murphy Brown, like all sitcom characters, is a *social caricature*. A caricature is a comic distortion of a social type acting in a recognizable social setting. Caricature is humorous to us not by the accuracy of its social depiction, but rather by the ludicrous exaggeration or distortion of social personages or situations. Caricaturing makes one appear to be more or less than one actually is. Murphy Brown and her pregnancy are social caricatures that are funny precisely because they aren't real or even instructive; rather they are absurd misrepresentations of what is now a common social phenomenon. But it is one thing for a fictional caricature like Murphy Brown, a beautiful, rich, and famous professional woman, to have a baby; the humor is in how different that is from the common experience of young poor women living in urban projects or rural shacks to become single mothers. Her situation is so ludicrous that it is comic, and her character so unusual as to be a caricature.

Such figures in situation comedies (Roseanne's family, Bart Simpson's family, the various "extended" families such as that in M*A*S*H) are strange people in familiar settings doing weird or idiotic things, even though in another way they are familiar people doing strange things in familiar settings. Social caricatures are strangely familiar, although often they are a travesty of social ideals, such as the grotesque families we have mentioned. Mr. Quayle to the contrary, such incongruous figures are objects of humor because of their ludicrousness and deviation from social norms.

A social caricature exemplifies the comic view of life as being a "perspective by incongruity" (see the Prologue): a sitcom character like Murphy Brown lets us see what we are not through the comic bisociation of misrule in familiar settings by characters incapable of serious rule or correct behavior. They evoke laughter not as didactic exemplars but as distorted grotesqueries who are comic fools beyond the norms of mundane life. Quayle may not have considered that Murphy Brown's situation made fun of the pretensions and confusions of the rich, and wasn't a model for the pathetic behavior of very real poor women on the margins of society. The vice president misrepresented the comic meaning of a social misrepresentation, evoking more comedy when the fictional Murphy Brown answered the real Mr. Quayle in a subsequent episode of the show.

The misuse of a straw woman reminds us of the essence of sitcoms: they involve characters who are social distortions in situations that are comic because they haplessly try to talk and act their way out of messes they foolishly create. The typical characters in situation comedies are atypical, we like to believe, because they are either incompetent or immature in some way, while we are not. Some past TV sitcoms we can see in rerun (*Leave It to Beaver*, *My Three Sons*, *The Donna Reed Show*) use social caricatures as part of the formula, and they charm us because they are of another time and myth—the prototypical middle-class family of the 1950s that displayed the comic possibilities of the new suburban and affluent life. Oddly, for all their social success, they are portrayed as remarkably dumb and unimaginative: the husbands are well-dressed executives but in the perplexed and housebroken tradition of Dagwood Bumstead; the wives are domestic beings dealing with dopey neighbors, a wisecracking housekeeper or butler (another rare and unusual feature of ordinary life), and the friends of the children; the kids are an array of essentially nice children experiencing charming and harmless growing pains. In the 1960s sitcoms grew more complicated in their domestic variants—widows with children marrying widowers with children, a single mom forming a rock band with her kids;

and odd and bizarre functional families (*The Beverly Hillbillies, The Addams Family*; and an infusion of magic and genies to liven up domestic relationships in *Bewitched* and *I Dream of Jeannie*). With the 1970s, single mothers, single women, and divorced parents appeared, along with the first comic depictions of dysfunctional families (*All in the Family, Maude*). By the 1990s, dysfunctional family sitcoms were the norm, depicting families characterized by stupidity, grossness, surliness, and destructive behavior (*The Simpsons, Married, with Children, Roseanne*). Added was one other element, namely, the "extended" families—work groups with a mix of caricatures (The Fonz of *Happy Days*, the vain and dumb news personality Ted Baxter of *The Mary Tyler Moore Show*, the dense blonde Corky of *Murphy Brown*), and more recently, even more grotesque and anomic caricatures, such as Beavis and Butthead.

The ritual format of the popular sitcom has been stretched to the limit, perhaps, but it retains its appeal as a way of depicting implausible social characters in incongruous situations for whatever age or taste. The ritual format of the congressional situation, although perhaps not yet stretched to the limit, has mirrored the evolution of all situation comedy.

CARICATURE: H. L. MENCKEN'S
LEGISLATIVE SITUATION

The congressional setting has its own unique absurdity. It is the forum for interaction among politicians (such as in floor debates), but as a group the legislators are acting in a dynamic situation that takes on a life of its own, a striking state of affairs with problematic shifts in the action of the unfolding narrative or drama action. At times, the legislator finds himself or herself dealing with a mix of people, ideas, expressions, interests, public opinion, and so on, that affect behavior as well as the outcome of the situation. A situation is part of a legislative story, a narrative drama in which the anxious solon plays a part and hopes to exercise some measure of power over the ending.

As in situation comedies, there is a long, honored tradition of caricaturing politicians, especially by political cartoonists on editorial pages of magazines and newspapers. American politicians such as Richard Nixon were eminently caricaturable in physical appearance, voice, and word. Nixon's ski-jump nose, dark mein, public voice, and tortuous rhetoric became familiar to Americans in the last half of the twentieth century. Cartoonist Herblock of the *Washington Post* made a career of lampooning Nixon, often depicting him with a shadowy beard and shifty eyes, contributing to the enduring negative image of Nixon as Tricky Dick. Mimics and impressionists such as David Frye and Rich Little performed hilarious impressions of Nixon's public personage and voice, including our sense of his personality. Writers even caricatured Nixon's speaking style applied to the most outrageous fantasy, such as Philip Roth's *Our Gang*, wherein Nixon speaks to the nation about a commando raid into Denmark to bring Curt Flood, the baseball player who broke the reserve clause and fought for free agency for players, to justice for his effrontery against American life.

Many great American journalists have engaged in delightful caricature of politicians and political types. In the latter case, there have always been spoofs on various figures one encounters in politics—the party hack, the ward heeler, the drunken delegate, the wild-eyed radical, the pussel-gutted local sheriff, the naive reformer, the dumb hick voter, the candidate's phony wife, the cynical reporter, the perplexed John Q. Public.

Such figures become part of our popular iconography of politics, perpetuated by the graphic and verbal imagery of journalists. Often such imagery is promulgated to promote some partisan or other editorial purpose, but in most cases the impact is *iconoclastic*, breaking a positive image or forming a negative image of some individual or prototypical figure in politics. The use of caricature allows political iconoclasts to portray their subjects as flawed and unworthy of admiration. But usually journalistic iconoclasts are limited in the scope and depth of their "image destruction." What is rare is someone who, without revolutionary or nihilistic purpose, is able to caricature the idea of democracy, and in particular the democratic politician, as a corrupt and bizarre comedy. The democratic legislator is aboard a ship of fools that always sinks itself.

Of all iconoclasts, few have been as vitriolic as the journalist H. L. Mencken (1880–1956). "Human life," he wrote, "is basically a comedy. Even its tragedies often seem comic to the spectator, and not infrequently they actually have comic touches to the victim. Happiness probably consists largely in the capacity to detect and relish them. A man who can laugh, if only at himself, is never really miserable."[2] Mencken appears to have taken his own advice, since his good humor and German-American *Gemütlichkeit* were well known among his friends and colleagues, and his acerbic wit was famous around the country. He became for many the image of the prototypical journalist. Articulate and cynical, alcoholic and tolerant, self-deprecating and self-important, as a group they felt both superior to and apart from their countrymen. Mencken the iconoclast became an American icon himself, a caricature of the urban front page journalist, famous and admired for his comic treatment of democracy and the democratic politician.

Mencken's long-expressed political criticism of America is clear enough: democracy doesn't work. Modern democracy was the rule of "boobus Americanus," the inferior many who are incapable of self-rule and who always wind up being ruled, and taken, by clever and glib politicians. The fundamental democratic transaction between ruler and ruled is a scam, a fraud, a con game. Politicians, said Mencken, are not chosen by merit in democracies; more usually they acquire high office by "their power to impress and enchant the intellectually underprivileged" in the same manner—this is long before Reagan—as "a radio crooner, a movie actor, or a bishop," for all have discovered that "hooey pleases the boobs a great deal more than sense," knowing that "votes are collared under democracy, not by talking sense but by talking nonsense." But alas, perhaps we should pity the poor politician under democracy, since "his failure is ignominious and his success is disgraceful"; we should object to democracy, for it "imposes degrading acts and attitudes upon the men responsible for the welfare and dignity of the state."

So this is the plight, Mencken says with glee, of the democratic politician. A "servant" put into an impossible situation, having to abandon all dignity and value in order to appeal to the common voter, at the risk of reducing himself or herself to a comic state of puerility. The same childishly idiotic state awaits those who seek legislative office. There are certain ills, Mencken notes with an air of philosophical resignation, that "in all probability the American people are doomed to suffer . . . forever," among them being "executive secretaries . . . Prohibition agents, revivalists, the radio and Congress." Congress, indeed, is the comedy central of what Mencken called "the land of mirth," for in America "the buffoonery never stops." Indeed, he didn't mind paying taxes, he said, because it was cheap entertainment: "Here in this Eden of clowns, with the highest rewards of clowning theoretically open to every poor boy—here in the very citadel of democracy we found and cherish a clown *dynasty*!" The Congress costs him little, yet offers a good return on the investment. He wrote, "The United States Senate will cost me perhaps $11 (in taxes) for the year, but against this expense set the subscription price of the *Congressional Record*, about $15, which, as journalist, I receive for nothing." Hence, "for $4 less than nothing I am thus entertained as Solomon never was by his hooch dancers."[3]

Mencken wrote often about that house of mirth, the Congress, but one example will suffice here. In a section of his collected works entitled "Utopian Flights," Mencken proposed, quite tongue in cheek, that legislators be chosen by lot, like juries,—that "the men who make our laws be chosen by chance and against their will, instead of by fraud and against the will of all the rest of us, as now." The advantages of such a system, he maintained, are several: it would make expensive campaigns unnecessary, end reprisals and fraud, fill legislatures with people who think "public service is a public burden, and not merely a private snap." But most important, such a system of selection would "completely dispose of the present degrading knee-bending and trading in votes." Would such a random "miscellaneous gang" of amateur legislators be up to the job? Sure, Mencken says, for they will see through the scam that vast knowledge and great experience are needed to legislate, and that most veteran legislators of the political class possess such qualities. The ordinary citizen differs from "the two gangs of lawyers" who obfuscate things, and a citizen legislature would bar "experts" from power so that their present advantages as a class would be lost and seem to disappear. This would free us from "the worst curse of democracy," which is that public office is "a monopoly of a palpably inferior and ignoble group of men [who] have to keep on abasing themselves in order to hold it." Since legislators are "men congenitally capable of cringing and dishonorable acts," replacing them with ordinary people would "reduce immensely the proportion of such slimy men in the halls of legislation, and . . . the effects would be instantly visible in a great improvement in the justice and reasonableness of the laws."[4]

Mencken's characterization of legislators is, to be sure, a caricature. Yet his modest proposal amuses us, because it hits a popular chord that reminds us that the professional class of legislators often engage in activities, and produce results, that seem to laypeople to be patently absurd—a taste for power, perquisites, illicit money and sex beyond what we can attribute to ordinary human weakness. There is something about the legislative situation that makes legislators seem more clownish than others. Mencken the iconoclast observes what some won't see, and what others see only with guidance from the comic inquirer: that legislators through self-abasement become caricatures of the solon, a wise and skillful lawgiver deliberating in the great citadel of parliamentarianism. Abasement suggests voluntarily yielding one's dignity, prestige, or honor. As Mencken remarked of one politician, legislators "long ago [became] lost to every decency" and have grown quite willing to "divest themselves of their character as sensible, candid, and truthful men." They learn the first lesson of political survival: "In politics, man must learn to rise above principle."[5] Or as the J. R. Ewing of TV's *Dallas* series said, "Once you give up integrity, everything else is easy."

The democratic legislator is beholden to what Mencken called the "boo-boisie," or the sovereign voter. The legislator is in a tenuous and precarious position, since he or she must sink to the electorate's level of understanding and desire, and cater to the whims of the common herd who vote. The transaction between would-be legislator and electorate is not an intellectual but rather an emotional exercise, appealing to the baser motives and common instincts of the democratic mass. Unlike feudalism, as Mencken argued, wherein the vassal had to degrade himself before his lord, who "was very apt to be a brute and an ignoramus," democracy "imposes degrading acts and attitudes upon the men responsible for the welfare and dignity of the state." The democratic politician is compelled to do homage to constituents, who are certain to be both brutes and ignoramuses. Before such a cretinous multitude, democratic politicians have to "abase themselves in order to get it [power], and they have to keep on abasing themselves in order to hold it."[6] As Mencken understood, much of the political activity of the successful solon consists in perpetuating the fraud of one's own rectitude by directing attention toward the selected transgressions and crimes alleged to have been committed by one's foes. The legislative comedy continues down to the present, Mencken would be delighted to know, centering on the drama of attempting to degrade other people in the legislative situation.

LEGISLATIVE RHETORIC AS SITUATION COMEDY

The legislative situation comedy is a drama of degradation, with actors attempting to use talk and "evidence" to shame or humble someone else whom it is useful to humiliate publicly. The legislator is in a precarious situation as part of the legislative group and the larger political world, since his or her political survival and prosperity depend upon maintaining the fraud of one's reputation. Legislators are willing to do virtually anything to sustain that gas-filled balloon, perhaps most of all using the accusing finger that points to the horrendous and disgraceful behavior of one's fellow legislators and the world at large. If a real or "straw" man or woman can be constructed (an errant legislator caught with his hand in the till, a threatening movement of political or social crimes, such as communism or drug-taking), then the legislator has a convenient and identifiable political *exigency*, an imperfection fraught with urgency. This new malady is so immediate and dreadful that it demands investigation, exposure, condemnation, and public degradation. Since political enemies are without conscience, they feel no guilt for their conduct; but they can be shamed before the rhetorical community. Thus each personalized enemy is unmasked as contemptible and degradable, providing the accusing legislator with a convenient exigency which requires public scrutiny. The typical legislator is always something of a poseur, a political Tartuffe, who succeeds to the extent that he or she can maintain the phony facade of rectitude and power, often shielded in the humbuggery of "toughness" and "strength," like single-combat warriors of the days of chivalry and knighthood. But a major way the legislative warrior can prove his or her mettle is to disprove the worth of others, including one's own colleagues in the legislative "family."

The legislative posturer, then, maintains exalted position, and the political status quo in the legislature, by acting as a voyeur, directing observation toward someone who is the embodiment of foolishness or evil, and of course diverting attention away from one's self. Through the act of political observation, the object of attention is to be seen as guilty of some dereliction as charged. The sorry political and social situation of the country is thus someone else's fault, the "someone" who is discovered and accused. Bad things must be the fault of *somebody*, and much legislative energy goes into seeking and finding those errant somebodies. In the process, all the attributes that Mencken and other critics saw in democratic legislators get pinned on someone else who is *really* to blame. As Mencken charged, this common practice is childish and unproductive, but it does have the effect of finding convenient scapegoats.

With such practices, the contemporary Congress resembles nothing quite so much as a situation comedy about a dysfunctional group of social misfits. The comedy resides in the fact that legislators are in an impossible situation, damned if they do and damned if they don't. To remain part of the "permanent government" in Washington, the solon must participate in the charade that sustains the illusion of work toward progress and happiness for the many he represents, while maintaining the status quo that protects powerful interests from too much public demand, and concomitantly, the congressperson's status in the legislature. Phony action in the form of big talk must substitute for real action in the form of substantive measures. In so doing, the legislator must resort to the typical antics of hypocritical remarks with a straight face, yet continue the voyeuristic scan for enemies of the state. To keep the situation tenable, the solon must both vilify and negotiate with fellow parliamentarians; since they must do the same, the "blame game" becomes an expected and ritualistic part of the legislative drama. Like the characters on a contemporary TV sitcom, the "distinguished gentlemen" must, on the one hand engage in shameless rhetorical potboiling and on the other, negotiate deals or at least get along with colleagues.

But like so many TV sitcoms, the dysfunctional legislature not only engages in destructive character assassination and expressed cynicism about the political system, it poisons the well for members and their constituents through blocking behavior that effectively prevents anything worthwhile from happening. Thus, typically, the debate over health care reform in 1994 deteriorated into sniping, name-calling, threats and counter-threats, plots to obstruct, paranoid constructions of evil motives and secret conspiracies ad nauseum; at the end of this process of "deliberation," the health care reform bill was dead, and everyone could blame someone else for its demise. The trick is to be for change, but to sabotage the efforts of those who are serious about it, thus restoring the status quo ante and reinsuring the flow of campaign money. In situation comedies, plots unfold with everyone scheming against everyone else, but at the climax everyone reunites in the restoration of an abnormal order. Legislators act similarly, by making their negotiated order dysfunctional: in the end nothing happens, so the system works. Here is the "demosclerosis" of the body politic, the increasing inability of Congress to function at all![7]

Thus the contemporary comedy of Congress follows the ritual structure and logic of the popular sitcom. In the sitcom, the characters cannot leave each other alone; they argue with each other, and engage in mutual humiliation and abasement; but in the end, the comic impasses and absurdities that unfold reunite them in their love-hate relationship. Like the TV sitcom, the rhetorical relations among members of Congress involve them in public disputes in which they feign the range of moral indignation (outrage, disgust, exasperation) and simulate a stance of political courage that demonstrates conviction and "strength." After much mutual vilification and public posturing, the issue at hand passes away without unduly upsetting the status quo and the privileged position of the statesmen who guide the republic. During much of the political show, solons engage each other in a rhetoric of execration, with dire warnings and threats of reprisal, contemptuous and condescending remarks, and much solemn alarm about the future if this measure passes. As with Alice and Ralph, Archie and Edith, and Roseanne and Dan, there is much rhetorical conflict, to the point where one might think that the parties and the issue at hand, are irreconcilable. But in the end, the issue goes away, the parties are reunited, and the situation, no matter how dysfunctional (Ralph is still poor, Archie still a bigot, and Roseanne still a slob), is restored to normal abnormality.

Indeed, the characters in the situation comedy of Congress in the 1990s seem to delight in their dysfunctional status, praising themselves for their obstructionism, buck-passing, alibiing, contempt for a presidential agenda or initiative, disdain for party loyalty, and unresponsiveness to popular agony. Their obsession instead is the maintenance of the abnormal situation within the group, no matter how comically pathological that set of relationships may be or how little it has to do with the real world of functional organization, ruled by the principle of the rational adequacy of means to realize ends. Instead, the Congress has become a dysfunctional organization guided by the principle of the irrational inadequacy of means to realize ends, aiming instead toward system maintenance of a pathological group that doesn't do anything. It should be remembered that in situation comedy, the people in the familial group don't seem to do anything (you never saw Ralph Cramden at work, or Roseanne do housework), and work groups do things badly, which is really secondary to the maintenance of group relations (we may wonder how Murphy Brown's news show ever got high ratings).

THE GROTESQUE IN LEGISLATIVE COMEDY

The comedy in the congressional situation is that members have achieved a state of group relations that makes it imperative that nothing happen, so that they may all coexist in a perfect world of inactivity. Better rituals of execration followed by reconciliation than pragmatic activity that threatens the internal bliss and continuity of the group. In situation comedy, the "happy ending" restores the dynamics of the group through the elimination of external threats that excite internal strife; the group wants above all else to continue doing each other dirty.

To prolong a ridiculous ritual for the purpose of continuing to do harm to one another is certainly not the humane ridicule that Aristotle saw as comedy. No, it is a *grotesque* form, one that exposes the incongruity between what a group purports to be about and actually is about; as Kenneth Burke noted the grotesque is "incongruity *without* the laughter."[8] The preeminent example of the grotesque in legislative comedy is the congressional investigations. Such proceedings, on more than one occasion, have served as political degradation ceremonies, where members of Congress can exercise their moral indignation by the ritual destruction of the one denounced.[9]

Public denunciations that lower the status of the person being degraded often have pathetic or even tragic results. Still, hearings have their comic aspect (albeit without laughter), especially when the high seriousness and exalted position of the congressional inquirer are undermined by a witness who will not accept the rules of the degradation ritual. When that happens, the potential for peripety, or role reversal, occurs, threatening to make the witness the hero and the congressional persona a fool or villain.

The most spectacular cases of role reversal often put the congressional inquisitors on the defensive. During the Army-McCarthy hearings of 1954, TV audiences viewed a Senator Joe McCarthy who was no longer a hero, especially when confronted with the sardonic questions of Army counsel Joseph Welch. Welch's avuncular bow-tied image and debonair wit endeared him to the television audience and Washington opinion makers, especially in contrast to the snarling and bullying McCarthy. McCarthy laughed at Welch's quips, but belatedly sensed that Welch was making him look foolish. Early on, Welch caught McCarthy in a lie: the senator had previously testified that he had never seen an application for an army commission for his aide G. David Schine. Welch produced the document, and McCarthy, giggling, asked if he had notarized it, to which Welch replied, "No, you merely signed it," evoking laughter in the packed committee room. McCarthy then began to pronounce these proceedings as "ridiculous," now aware that the joke was on himself. He was transformed from a hero uncovering treachery and treason in government to a brutish lout making a fool of himself in public.

Welch's skeptical quips had a cumulative effect. As the hearings dragged on, the TV audience witnessed McCarthy unmasked as a fraud. When committee counsel, McCarthy's right-hand man, Roy Cohn admitted at Welch's instigation that the FBI had "communists" working under cover in defense plants to search out communists, Welch asked Cohn, "Then what's all the excitement about if J. Edgar Hoover is on the job, chasing those 130 communists?" No longer restraining himself, McCarthy finally exploded, "How long must we put up with this circus?"; time was being wasted while Welch sought "a laugh from the audience."

McCarthy's demise came with his claim that a young lawyer in Welch's law firm had once belonged to a communist-front organization, and that Welch himself was a dupe and fellow traveler:

Uh, whether you knew that he was a member of that Communist organization or not, I don't know. I assume you did not, Mr. Welch, because I get the impression that while you are quite an actor, you play for a laugh, I don't think you have any conception of the danger of the Communist Party. I don't think you yourself would ever knowingly aid the Communist cause. I think you're unknowingly siding with it when you try to burlesque this hearing in which we're attempting to bring out the facts.

As McCarthy badgered on, Welch emotionally, but calmly, exposed the senator's "reckless cruelty." Welch pointedly asked the visibly nervous McCarthy, "Have you left no sense of decency?"

McCarthy had no reply. His senatorial colleagues openly defied and ridiculed him. Later the entire Senate conducted its own degradation ceremony through the formal investigation and censure of McCarthy, who then became a pathetic figure preaching to empty galleries. Ironically, McCarthy the inquisitor and degrader became the subject of senatorial inquisition and degradation.

In the age of television, televised hearings give members of Congress the opportunity to appear foolish, especially in circumstances where normal procedures and protocols break down. They expose themselves as frauds who try to bamboozle Mencken's booboisie. "For it is upon the emotions of the mob," wrote Mencken, ". . . that the whole [democratic] comedy is played. . . . In the main that business consists in keeping alive its deep-seated fears—of strange faces, of unfamiliar ideas, of unhackneyed gestures, of untested liberties and responsibilities. The one permanent emotion of the inferior man, as of all the simpler mammals, is fear—fear of the unknown, the complex, the inexplicable."

Congressional politicians like McCarthy reinforce the comedy of democracy by acting out the citizen's irrational fears, shielding democratic citizens from "the need to grapple with unaccustomed problems, to weigh ideas, to think things out for himself, to scrutinize the platitudes upon which his everyday thinking is based."[10] The McCarthys make a mockery of the idea of democratic rationality and deliberation, since they threaten to turn such ideas into farce. They make legislative activity seem a situation comedy of dysfunctional misfits bent on the expression of paranoid fears and subhuman aggressions, a collection of simpler mammals who imitate not Machiavelli's lion or fox but rather the weasel.

Situation comedies, certainly contemporary TV comedies, feature a form of pathological communication—illogical, contradictory, selective, hurtful, irresponsible, timebound, and magical, hoping that merely saying things makes them so. This is the rhetoric of dysfunctional groups, be they TV sitcom families or legislatures in session. Recall that in situation comedy no one ever seems to *do* anything; rather they live in a perpetual state of absurdity, inveighing against each other and the ills of the world but never really getting anywhere. They are funny because they do not understand their own perplexity at being so immature and incompetent. The audience for their behavior is moved to contemptuous laughter at grown people acting so foolishly in a public group setting. Contemporary situation comedy is a form of freak show featuring the grotesqueries who populate marginal social groups, be they dysfunctional families or political gatherings such as legislative sessions. Neither Roseanne's family nor the U.S. Senate appears well-adjusted, wise, and worthy of respect.

This is not to say that Congress is populated with Homer and Marge Simpsons, only that the behavior of both groups demonstrates the comic incongruity of poorly operating systems of relations. Both sitcom families and the Senate exist in a permanent state of gridlock, in the absurd situation of inharmonious relations and illogical communication that is pathological, neither pragmatic nor productive. The group exists in a situation comedy of mutual torment, acting out the various games people (and legislators) play. Arthur Koestler, writing about families, could as easily be describing Congress:

Family relations pertain to a plane where the ordinary rules of judgement and conduct do not apply. They are a labyrinth of tensions, quarrels and reconciliations, whose logic is self-contradictory, whose ethics stem from a cozy jungle, and whose values and criteria are distorted like the curved space of a self-contained universe. It is a universe saturated with memories—but memories from which no lessons are drawn; saturated with a past which provides no guidance to the future. For in this universe, after each crisis and reconciliation, time always starts afresh and history is always in the year zero.[11]

Proceedings of Congress reveal the similarity. In the surreal atmosphere of the Senate, for instance, the "ordinary rules" do not apply: they are exempt from libel and slander laws through congressional immunity, take junkets, money, and lodging in the nation's pleasure domes at the expense of powerful interests, and obstruct or filibuster to death proposals that many of those interests don't want. With the decline of parties and party discipline, the Senate is a fragmented and shifting group of temporary coalitions, a labyrinth of relations and intrigues. Its members speak profusely various forms of illogic ("All we have to do," said Senator Bob Kerrey of the health care crisis, "is to spend more in order to spend less").

Legislators' values are distorted by their wholly cynical and selective expressions of judgment, the mouthing of meaningless slogans (sound bites) and invective that maintain the pathological divisions within the cozy jungle of the legislative group. For such speakers, it is always zero time, the political now that is addressed through hurled talk—big talk, fast talk, sweet talk, tough talk, loose talk, and most of all, empty talk. The legislative talking shop is full of talk that is hard to take seriously, not so much because it is false, but rather because it is *phony*. Much of what is said is, like the banter of dysfunctional families, a put-on, a con game, b.s. artistry, political platitudes, stuff said for effect that we don't *really* mean. Like schizophrenics, legislators are continually saying things they don't mean (it's my political self rather than me saying that sort of thing, and I can't help myself). And, again like sitcom groups, there is no learning going on, just mouthing the same tired clichés, accusations, outrages, and worries that get the group nowhere. Legislators are treated with comic contempt by popular audiences because, like sitcom families, they are constantly involved in contentious episodes that simply reinforce the internal pathology and dysfunctionality of the group, without learning how to get along and get things done. Sitcom groups are funny in part because they are so powerless to affect their own fate as a dysfunctional unit; in an odd way, legislators are powerless to affect our fate because they seem so powerless to overcome the group dynamics that make them dysfunctional.

The legislative "definition of the situation," then, is inherently comic in that the group effort is to substitute the phony for the real, the delusional for the actual, and the dysfunctional for the effective. Those who identify with a legislative system find themselves defending the institution itself, feeling part of an important group in whose hands the future of the republic lies. Thus they tend to develop and share a group myth that justifies their own existence through belief in their own group efficacy and legitimacy. Watzlawick, Beavin, and Jackson note that "family myths" are prevalent in families at varying stages of pathology, but serve as a "special reality" shared by those inside the system of relations and help to bind relations within the group through a shared delusion.

A popular fictional example is the imaginary child of George and Martha in Edward Albee's play *Who's Afraid of Virginia Woolf?* George and Martha have a classic hate-love relationship sustained by their mutual verbal aggression toward each other, through which, with one another's acquiescence, they express their contempt and loathing for each other and the shared complicity in the imaginary child which becomes the fantasized object of their affection, or perhaps of their delusion that they are, or could be, a "normal" family. The family myth is phony, but serves as a homeostatic mechanism, a unifying symbol that perpetuates the relationship, which otherwise would be based on nothing more than mutually hateful vilification. The group illogic of "I'm not happy unless you're miserable" is complemented, and made sustainable, by the fiction of an "as if" being who serves to remind the couple that group normalcy might have been in reach. George and Martha act out a decadent comedy of situational degradation, relieved only by their private knowledge of what might have been.[12] A situation is decadent when it becomes both useless and delusional, and many such groups seem to populate contemporary America. (The comic groups of Generation X exhibit these traits: Beavis and Butthead make little effort at functionality, and share only mass-mediated delusions of sensual delights and catastrophic events.)

IS THIS HOUSE TO BE LETT?

At the height of American democracy in midcentury, it would have been unthinkable to suggest that someday the Congress would become an irrelevance. But dysfunctional and delusional groups cannot limp along forever (except in reruns on TV: will people someday watch C-SPAN reruns of Congress the way they now watch reruns of *I Love Lucy* and *Married, with Children*?). People may remember Congress as a comic group, worth watching in retrospect for the same reason we watch sitcoms: to watch the group stumble and bumble its way through life, and thus feel morally and socially superior to these lesser beings who collectively display their essential immaturity and incompetence, venality and indecency, phoniness and vulgarity for all the world to see.

Like other reruns, Congress could become a comic sideshow, remembered nostalgically as part of the fun of the past, but eventually relegated to a form of popular entertainment of folk memory, like circuses and comic books and baseball. But like all sitcoms, eventually the comedy of the situation becomes a bore at last, and is canceled from prime time by the authorities. The democratic institution that specialized in the varieties of political degradation would then finally be degraded by a new power who would put an end to their endless and worthless prating and sitting.

In the situation comedy the situation is always hopeless, but never serious. The poor players strutting and fretting upon the group stage are trapped inside the situation, destined to play out the rituals of degradation forever. For Alice and Ralph, George and Martha, and the crews of extended families making a TV show in Alaska or Arkansas, there is no happy ending; rather there is no ending and no exit. They must go on berating and abusing each other forever. Observation of the U.S. Congress evokes the same sense of a declining institution that has become a parody of itself, a mockery of the parliamentary ideals of democratic theory. In the House and Senate, there are no endings and no exits, only the eternal interplay of talk about all the things we shall, or should, do, if only we could. The bizarre, sometimes grotesque, proceedings of the Congress go on as if the world outside still took them seriously.

The English revolutionary Oliver Cromwell said to the English Long Parliament in 1653: "It is not fit that you should sit as a Parliament any longer. You have sat long enough unless you had done more good. . . . I will put an end to your prating. You are no Parliament. I say you are no Parliament. I will put an end to your sitting." After Parliament was dissolved, a wag put up a poster outside that read, "This House is to be Lett; now unfurnished."[13] Any future American Cromwell who dissolves our parliament may have popular support from citizens equally tired of congressional comedy.

NOTES

1. Henry Adams, *The Education of Henry Adams* (New York: Modern Library, 1931), p. 261.

2. H. L. Mencken, *Minority Report* (New York: Alfred A. Knopf, 1956), p. 11.

3. H. L. Mencken, *Prejudices: A Selection* (New York: Vintage, 1955), pp. 125, 258.

4. H. L. Mencken, *A Mencken Chrestomathy* (New York: Alfred A. Knopf, 1956), pp. 388–391.

5. Ibid., pp. 148–152.

6. Ibid., pp. 165–166, 380.

7. Jonathan Rauch, *Demosclerosis: The Silent Killer of American Government* (New York: Time Books, 1994).

8. Kenneth Burke, *Attitudes Toward History* (Berkeley: University of California Press, 1984), p. 58. Emphasis in original.

9. See Harold Garfinkel, "Conditions of a Successful Degradation Ceremony," in James Combs and Michael Mansfield, eds., *Drama in Life*. (New York: Hastings House, 1976), pp. 315–320.

10. Mencken, *Chrestomathy*, p. 183.

11. Arthur Koestler, quoted in Paul Watzlawick, J. H. Beavin, and Don D. Jackson, *Pragmatics of Human Communication* (New York): W. W. Norton, 1967), p. 81.

12. Watzlawick et al., *Pragmatics*, pp. 149–186.

13. Oliver Cromwell, quoted in Antonia Fraser, *Cromwell* (New York: Alfred A. Knopf, 1973), p. 420.

CHAPTER 7

Political Bureaucracies: Comedies of Errors and Intrigue

Jean Molière, master of comedy, said that its purpose is "to enter rightly into the ridiculous aspects of mankind and to represent people's defects agreeably on the stage." Two comic forms, the comedy of errors and the comedy of intrigue, aptly capture both the ridiculous and the defective in the politics of democratic bureaucracies. A comedy of errors depicts characters, acting on seemingly the highest motives, behaving instead at cross-purposes to defeat those noble ends. A comedy of intrigue involves characters manipulating events to their own ends in the name of broader, more socially beneficial interests. Political bureaucrats who routinely err cover their tracks, yet claim they act in the name of the public good.

BUREAUCRATIC FOOLERY

In *Twelfth Night* Shakespeare wrote, "Foolery, sir, does walk about the orb like the sun; it shines everywhere." Certainly the sun of bureaucratic foolery glows everywhere. Consider a few cases in point: news reports of Pentagon potlatch, for example, buying $600 toilet seats; Denver's billion dollar airport delayed endlessly in opening because the exquisite automatic bag handling system didn't work; Chicago's post office, with millions of pieces of mail lying undelivered and piles of mail surreptitiously burned under bridges; or the U.S. Internal Revenue Service demanding taxes from people long since deceased. Bungling of this sort has spawned a lexicon of apt terms. "Boondoggle," "cost overrun," and "red tape" are the accepted vernacular for waste, incompetence, and pettiness, even arrogance.

An ex-bureaucrat, James H. Boren, articulated a comical code of behavior for successful bureaucrats: *When in charge, ponder; when in trouble, delegate; when in doubt, mumble.* He wrote a tongue-in-cheek bureaucrat's handbook advising aspiring bureaucrats to cultivate "dynamic inaction" in the mastery of getting nothing done; maintain the permanent status of the organization through "constructive decision avoidance." "Paper," he intones, "to the professional bureaucrat is as canvas to the artist."[1] Boren belongs to that school of thought that regards bureaucracy as something that *exists rather than functions,* exists to prevent results through artistic circumvention, and to ponder proposals to death. Boren's satire of bureaucracy, both public and private, hits a comic nerve by reminding us of the extent to which our lives are affected, frustrated, and annoyed by the omnipresence of Big Organization.

Underlying a satirical view like Boren's is a comic existentialism, that the plight of humankind in a bureaucratic world is mostly comic, not conspiratorial. We are the tool of our own tools, including the tools of organizational power and procedure. Our entrapment in a bureaucratic world is not so much tragic as absurd. When we find ourselves standing in line endlessly at a bank or courthouse; when we call someone in an organization, only to hear a recording that the person sought is "away from the desk at the moment," and we wait in vain for any response; when we find ourselves filling out a massive form to apply for something as simple as a check-cashing card at a supermarket—at such tedious moments we experience the absurd comedy of bureaucratic life.

We respond by equally absurd oversimplifications: the other line always moves faster; the person we need to reach is never there and never responds; everything simple is transformed into something difficult. Our quotidian experience of the indignities and idiocies we associate with bureaucracies raises comic doubts about the efficacy and wisdom of organizational rationality. We may conclude after a torturous episode with bureaucrats that such rationality is irrational, that what seems quite sane and reasonable from inside the bureaucracy seems equally insane and unreasonable from the outside.

We seem trapped in "trained incapacity," wherein bureaucrats develop habits that make them incapable of seeing that what they are doing doesn't work or brings about unintended consequences. This helps us explain why schools require more staff and money in order to teach students less and less; why we spend more and more money on intelligence to find out nothing of value (the CIA failed to predict the fall of the Shah of Iran or the collapse of communism); and why we continue to provide price supports for tobacco farmers and at the same time spend public monies to urge people to stop smoking. Here is a comic world of ever-expanding and futile effort of human organizations to overcome temporal and social chaos. The belief that order triumphs over chaos, that organization masters human frailty and recalcitrant reality—is the ultimate comic absurdity.

The widespread feeling that organizations don't work well, or at all, that expertise is often fraudulent or misleading, leads to expressions of *comic inanity*. Citizens sense that bureaucrats lack reason or substance, and are useless, silly, or vain. Most of us irritated by bureaucratic requirements don't find them sinister, just inane. After frustrating bureaucratic encounters, we wonder if all organizations are run this way, and whether they are all equally inane and equally comical. The response of comic inanity helps us to adopt a stance of stoic but bemused existentialism in dealing with the line at the bank that never moves and the new and "simplified" income tax form many find inanely complex. Seeing bureaucracy as merely fatuous helps us to resign ourselves to dealing with it all with stolid disposition and grace.

That citizens innately sense how foolish bureaucratic politics is may help explain the popular appeal of the literature that mocks bureaucracy. British professor C. Northcote Parkinson in 1955 published his first formulation of Parkinson's Law: "Work expands so as to fill the time available for its completion." In an effort to explain bureaucratic growth, Parkinson noted that bureaucrats are not lazy; they simply have "justifications" for expanding personnel, equipment, and missions, making bureaucracy itself a growth industry regardless of necessity. Thus "war departments," once established during wartime, also expand in peacetime, transforming themselves into "departments of defense." With no wars to wage, defense departments justify existence through other projects.

Indeed, said Parkinson, the corollary to his First Law is the Second: "Expenditure rises to meet income." If the necessity of expenditure seems urgent enough, nothing succeeds like excess. The "law of extravagance" dictates that spending on, say, defense is justified even if the money is borrowed. Thus American defense spending on the Cold War defeated communism but also bankrupted the state. The United States defeated the threat of communist power by outspending them, but in the extravagant process it was too impoverished to accomplish other ends. Parkinson grasped the comic essence of bureaucracies, namely, they engage in inane enterprises that expand their missions and costs to the point of ludicrousness. The British government of mid-century, he noted, "is not merely cumbersome but ludicrous. Reform may be impossible but we have still (so far) the right at least to laugh."[2]

Following Parkinson came other comic treatments of political bureaucracies. There is now a *maximology* of organizational life, simple truths insightfully put. The most celebrated and enduring are Murphy's Laws;

they posit that the trouble first noted by Parkinson is a much deeper problem: the fact that the universe was not created for our convenience. Organizations do inane and insane things because of a basic existential flaw in the universe, summed up in Murphy's First Law: "If anything can go wrong, it will." From this has been derived a massive array of corollary laws concerning the nature of the world, such as "If there are several things that can go wrong, the one that will cause the most trouble is the one that will go wrong." Murphology is an inexact science, but it apparently grabs bureaucrats where they live. One finds maxims posted on office walls, collected in books, and most of all, kept in the hearts and minds of every poor slob who has had to suffer through the daily grind of bureaucratic inanity.[3]

Particularly apt for any citizen faced with political foolery is Gumperson's Law: "The probability of anything happening is in inverse ratio to its desirability."[4] Like other laws of comic existence, it is immediately and intuitively grasped by frustrated citizens. It explains why the other line always moves faster, why lotteries are always won by someone who haphazardly buys one ticket, why the phone rings just as one is leaving, why machines break down only after the warranty expires, and why authors with deadlines write prolix prose.

Still other axioms speak to the reward system inherent in bureaucracies, a system fraught with mischievous consequences for citizens. For example, the Peter Principle says that organizational hierarchies promote employees to their maximum level of incompetence. Ideally, modern organizations are meritocracies that promote people on the basis of merit in the job they have been performing. The meritorious achieve new jobs up the hierarchical ladder that are different and more challenging; at some point in this upward mobility, they reach a level of incompetence, leaving the work of the organization to be done by those beneath who have not been so rewarded. So a bureau researcher is rewarded with an administrative position, at which she may be mediocre; but on the basis of continued success at continuing research, she becomes research director, where she performs poorly. Yet since the agency secretary runs everything efficiently in the director's stead, the director becomes departmental head, perhaps even a member of the president's cabinet, wherein there is ample opportunity to display ingenious administrative incompetence.[5]

There is a disturbing corollary to the Peter Principle. Call it the Dumbing Down Factor. When competent people at the lower levels of organizations are promoted to higher-level tasks for which they are not competent, who assumes the jobs at the lower levels? When competent lathe operators become shop managers, skilled teachers become university vice presidents, artistic surgeons become chiefs of staff, and effective U.S. Senate majority leaders become overwhelmed U.S. Presidents, what happens? The supply of competent talent in any endeavor is *not* inexhaustible. To promote such talent as does exist beyond its limits produces the ultimate irony of a society, namely, talent no longer exists to make society possible. Society's success proves its demise.

The literature that depicts the degree of America's organizational absurdity offers put-upon citizens a defense in keeping with romantic comedy (recall Chapter 1), saying "the people" are not complicit; they are the victims. Faced with the social fact of having to deal daily with bureaucracy, one can cope with better humor if informed by aphoristic wisdom about what is happening. The popular literature on the informal dysfunctioning of organizations gives us daily mantras to repeat when encountering bureaucratic foolery. Repeating these "fundamental laws" of bureaucracy gets victims through waiting in line, being put on hold, being told to go to another office, or going through a tax audit. Proverbial wisdom acquires the status of adage, timeless and placeless truths that appy to a variety of contemporary frustrations and outrages. When inching along in a choked traffic jam because of road repairs that have lasted for years, auto drivers can repeat Cheops' Law: "Nothing ever gets built on schedule or within budget." Or if sitting in a dreary and unending committee meeting, a worker can recall the Law of Committee Triviality: "The time spent on any item of the agenda will be inversely proportional to the sum involved." And when a deal labeled "guaranteed" unravels (such as a warranty or insurance policy or contract), "There is always a catch, and the catch is Catch-22."[6]

THE COMICAL LOGIC OF ORGANIZATIONS

The modern theater of the absurd, exemplified by writers such as Ionesco, Sartre, Camus, and Pirandello, exploits a comic perspective, using black humor in order to dramatize the absurdity of contemporary life. A world dominated by large, impersonal organizations run by functionaries is, from the point of view of the artist, insane. The only aesthetic response to such a grotesque and lunatic world is to portray the logic, or more aptly illogic, of the organized world in contradistinction to the logic of the individual who seeks survival and freedom from organizational madness. The existential stance of the theater of the absurd is strongly comical, since it sees organized power as not so much evil as misguided, trapped by the logic of organization rather than the humane logic of individuals who must exist in their nexus. What organizations do becomes grotesquely and inanely comical because the individual has little recourse other than to reject organized insanity via comic rebellion against the hierarchy and its logic of power.

The manic and insane view of organizational life has perhaps never received more insightful portrayal than in Joseph Heller's novel, *Catch-22*, first published in 1961. Set in an air force bomber unit off the coast of Italy, it expressed a comic existentialism through its depiction of a cowardly airman's effort to avoid flying more missions, and his struggle with a structure of bureaucratic power that keeps trying to make him fly more missions. The order of the world is a surface reality; beneath it chaos and insanity rule. Organizational authorities are capricious and indifferent— the arbiters of a crazed enterprise where the protagonist knows that the people who command are insane.

In Heller's conception, one writer notes, "sanity in the traditional sense is really insanity; that is, if sanity is the ability to come to terms with reality, then it is insane to act as if the world is coherent and rational. Loyalty to traditional institutions can be disloyalty to oneself simply because the institutions may threaten the people they are ostensibly designed to serve." Heller sees chaos rather than order as the fundamental category of human organization, believing that the world is governed by *crazy laws*, in the Parkinsonian tradition cited earlier. Heller's novel made "Catch-22" part of the language as one of the crazy laws of organization: every bureaucracy uses an elastic clause that negates all rules and rights an individual might have in an organization. Catch-22 refers to "that rider which seems to be attached to every code of the rights of men and which gives those in authority the power to revoke those rights at will."[7]

In a discussion between Yossarian and Doc Daneeka concerning the former's tentmate Orr, they agree that Orr is crazy and should be grounded:

All he had to do was ask; and as soon as he did, he would no longer be crazy and would have to fly more missions. Orr would be crazy to fly more missions and sane if he didn't, but if he was sane he had to fly them. If he flew them he was crazy and didn't have to; but if he didn't want to, he was sane and had to. Yossarian was moved very deeply by the absolute simplicity of this clause of Catch-22 and let out a respectful whistle. "That's some catch, that Catch-22," he observed. "It's the best there is," Doc Daneeka agreed.[8]

Heller's novel has endured as a modern classic. The term "Catch-22" has entered the language because it captures what the maximology on organizations describes: bureaucracies are often neither benevolent nor efficient; they do not necessarily have the best interests or the well-being of the individual at heart, especially when rules get separated from their operational meanings. And as organizations, public and private, have grown to gigantic size and power, the individual often feels pitted, however helplessly, against these mammoth systems of power. What came to be called The System seemed to signal the obsolescence of the individual and the transcendence of organized power. The System pursues the interests of power and uses individuals to pursue them.

During the Vietnam War, *Catch-22* was both a book and a phrase: officers and enlisted men leaving "The Nam" gave their successors copies of the book, telling them that if they wanted to know what this war was *really* all about, read this book. Soldiers who had not read it and knew nothing of literary reputation all understood and used the term "Catch-22." When there was a snafu, a crazy order, an ambitious officer willing to get his men killed, an accident such as "friendly fire" that was then covered up, an inflated body count to prove we were killing the enemy at an ever-increasing rate, the standard mantra was simply "Catch-22." In order to endure the nightmarish conduct of the war in Vietnam, troops relied on a maxim that explained everything, since they knew the war was being officially won while it was being actually lost, that the army saw them as quite expendable in the pursuit of organizational purposes that made no sense, and that the situation was hopeless but not serious.

Indeed, perhaps the larger appeal of the novel and the concept was that it spoke to individual hopelessness in a world dominated by impersonal and indifferent organizations. The comic became an integral part of their speech patterns, offering cynical and wry explanation of what the army system was up to now, a mixture of organizational mendacity and incompetence. For the larger civilian audience of *Catch-22*, there was much that gave fictional validation to the comic maxims of the Parkinsonian tradition. The officers in the novel have clearly reached their level of incompetence; work is done and things are run by the mail clerk, ex-PFC Wintergreen. For Yossarian, the desirability of getting out of flying more missions was inversely proportional to its probability, since Catch-22 dictated that for one organizational reason or another, he had to fly more missions. Even though, explains ex-PFC Wintergreen to him, the 27th Air Force says he only has to fly forty missions, this doesn't mean he can go home, for he still has to obey orders, and his commander has ordered everyone to fly fifty-five missions; so even though he only has to fly forty missions, he has to fly fifty-five because the commander has ordered everyone to do so, and he will be shot if he disobeys orders; thus says Catch-22.

The organizational norm of obedience to rules and authority is used to further the ambitions of the officers, but the desires or even the rights of the individual are subsumed by the manipulation of the generic rule of Catch-22. The organizational role of "good soldier" made you an expendable cog in a hierarchy that relied on an administrative trick to use you. Indeed, Yossarian finally concludes that Catch-22 is a universal principle:

Catch-22 did not exist, he was positive of that, but it made no difference. What did matter was that everyone thought it existed, and that was much worse, for there was no object or text to ridicule or refute, to accuse, criticize, attack, amend, hate, revile, spit at, rip to shreds, trample upon or burn up.[9]

In the labyrinths of power, then, we are all put in the comic position of being at the mercy of organizations through their use of a *principle of exception*. Elastic clauses exist in order to give the organizational powers elasticity. Bureaucratic rules of exception allow the hierarchy to crush hope, blunt aspiration, avoid responsibility, and prevent change. But what Heller discovered was that Catch-22 and all such principles of exception, and the spirit of deception and manipulation behind them, are comic. The comedy is in the absurdity of believing that organizations are on the level and will live up to their obligations, and then discovering that they will not. Organizations live on circumvention and obfuscation, and it is in these lateral moves that much bureaucratic comedy occurs.

Everyone, then, who deals with organizations understands the bureaucratic logic of Catch-22. In high school or college, for example, students can participate in student government, a form of self-government and democracy that allows them to decide whatever they want, just so long as the principal or dean of students approves. This bogus democracy that can be overruled by arbitrary fiat is perhaps a citizen's first encounter with organizations that may profess "open" and libertarian values, but in fact are closed and hierarchical systems. Catch-22 is an organizational assumption, an unwritten law of informal power that excepts the organization from responsibility and accountability, and puts the individual in the absurd position of being excepted for the convenience or unknown purposes of the organization.

The justificatory reasoning is circular, as Yossarian found out when MPs raided an Italian whorehouse: "Catch-22," the old woman told him, "says they have a right to do anything we can't stop them from doing. . . . They don't have to show us Catch-22. The law says they don't have to." And what law is that? Why, Catch-22, of course![10] This "law" is extralegal, a rule that is exempt from rules, an ethic that is beyond ethics, a standard for rulers without standards. The bottom line of organizational power involves the use of any means necessary, which makes the individual expendable. Catch-22 is the mechanism that makes the system rather than the person paramount, an assertion that they have the right to do anything we can't stop them from doing, and that they do not have to tell us the source of that right. Catch-22 is central to the *mystique* of organization, the mystery of their power to do what they want at our expense, and without our permission or control. Catch-22 captures our fear that systems are their own arbiters of what they can do, and that what they do to us is after all arbitrary.

THE COMEDY OF BUREAUCRATIC FAILURE

Perhaps because citizens often do fear and chafe under the arbitrariness of organized power, many develop a strong anti-organizational streak. One can admire Yossarian's rebellion against authority, even if it ends in the quixotic act of rowing in a life raft to Sweden. Most of us cannot escape from having to deal with bureaucracy; instead we engage in equally quixotic rebellions, such as dressing up our workstation with tokens of individuality that assert our identity as not wholly the property of the organization we work for. In popular culture, we enjoy the anti-organizational exploits of figures who are loners that discover truths about the evils of the powerful (such as private detectives) or are rebellious members of a bureaucracy who get things done despite the organization's constraints and displeasure (rogue cops like Dirty Harry Callahan). Most of all, we derive pleasure in poking fun at the major foul-ups and messes of big organizations, enjoying the quiet satisfaction of seeing a bureaucracy humbled and the mighty fall from power and grace.

Such individual enjoyments allow citizens to see bureaucracies as settings for comic bungles, botches, and screwups, mitigating our fears about their demonic intentions and powers, and reassuring ourselves of our individuality. Even though it may cost them money, people enjoy the exposure of a government boondoggle, such as the acquisition of expensive weapons systems that don't work; even though it may not be just, a jury award of a large amount for damages to an individual who has sued a corporation is a victory for the little guy; and scandals, since they confirm popular suspicions about both the venality and the stupidity of bureaucrats, are titillating. Since the organizational world puts citizens, who are supposed in theory to govern, in a position of subordinate absurdity, there is a certain pleasure when bureaucrats get their comeuppance.

This experience helps us sustain a comic image of the organizations that threaten us, making them seem merely dumb, clumsy, and bloated rather than sinister. Unlike Yossarian, most of us have to become resigned to living in the orbit of bureaucracies, but even so we can enjoy the spectacle of organizational absurdity. But like Yossarian, we can assert our belief that worth and even efficiency are properties of living human beings like ourselves, and that the truly absurd comes from vast and inhuman organized power structures. Since we feel that organizations devalue the competence and maturity of individuals, then in turn when we hear of bureaucratic failures, we can think that real incompetence and immaturity reside with organizational authorities. The people that run things are the true architects of idiocy, the comic actors in the unending drama of bureaucratic pratfalls and mishaps, the geniuses who dream up insanities like Vietnam and Watergate.

Thus there is a wry and rueful joy in observing the spectacle of organizational insanity. Like Yossarian, we like to believe that we are sane and that it is the world of organized power that is insane. In so doing, we seek information that validates that self-affirming belief. Thus we are delighted when we find stories in the press that recount, for example, real-life examples of Catch-22. When the Freedom of Information Act was passed, people wrote the Federal Bureau of Investigation to see if it had a file on them; the bureau responded by saying that if it did, the bureau could censor it, and if there was no file on the person doing the requesting, it would open one, on the assumption they were guilty of something! (In the sequel to *Catch-22*, entitled *Closing Time*, Chaplain Tappmann explains the Freedom of Information Act as a "federal regulation obliging government agencies to release all information they had to anyone who made application for it, except information they had that they did not want to release."[11])

Students of the bureaucratic art of Catch-22 also relish the circular logic of President Nixon's Watergate attorney James St. Clair pleading Nixon's case before the Supreme Court with the circular argument that Congress can impeach a president only if there is evidence that he committed a crime, but constitutionally Congress can't legitimately subpoena criminal evidence against a president that might prove him guilty of a crime. Replied one of the justices, "Wait a minute, you lose me there." More mundanely, we all can invoke Catch-22 when we encounter a bureaucratic rule that seems to involve the same sort of logical circularity. For example, people on welfare in states with legal limits on their income are well aware of the letter of the Catch-22 law, for if they do things to make themselves less poor, such as get a job or save money, they lose their welfare benefits, which makes them poor again; they are penalized for attempting to get off welfare, but also penalized for trying to stay on it. The Internal Revenue Service has a rule that a person must report on an income tax form "embezzled or other illegal income"; of course a citizen is in violation of the tax code and subject to prosecution in reporting, for if one reports such income, the citizen will be reported to the proper authorities for prosecution for having illegal income. There are many instances of such bureaucratic imponderables, often involving the rhetoric of hedging, using conditional clauses like "provided that" or "as long as" or "with the exception of." And why is it that your case always turns out to be an exception?

The study of supposedly "rational" decision-making in high-powered administrative groups has demonstrated that they share the common human capacity to make lousy decisions based on bad information, erroneous assumptions and poor advice, emotional prejudices and wishful thinking. They commit themselves to the most idiotic courses of action and the biggest disasters through the most sober and reasoned kind of decisiveness that seems to them to be the height of wisdom, formulating a best-laid plan that cannot go awry. We may not know about or be able to stop such organizational insanities, but in retrospect we can marvel in sardonic bemusement at the collective *hubris* that went into an elite decision, based on the analysis of the best information and the most sophisticated models of decision-making, that led inevitably, as the oracle Murphy would have predicted, to utter catastrophe.[12]

Historian Barbara Tuchman called this "the march of folly." "Why," she asked, "do holders of high office so often act contrary to the way reason points and enlightened self-interest suggests? Why does intelligent mental process seem so often not to function? . . . Why, to begin at the beginning, did the Trojan rulers drag that suspicious-looking wooden horse inside their walls despite every reason to suspect a Greek trick?" She recounts the melancholy history of wooden-headed mismanagement and political grief stemming from governments acting on "preconceived fixed notions," "ignoring or rejecting any contrary signs," and the "refusal to benefit from experience."[13]

Folly, as Tuchman understands it, is an administrative malady as broad as Erasmus long ago envisioned it, including acting out of ignorance, stupidity, impulse, emotion, and rashness, while refusing the use of wisdom, calculation, and foresight. Erasmus satirized the universality of folly by arguing for its necessity, and the foolishness of reason; since, after all, humankind had its origin in folly, and was sustained by the vital force of ignorance, the power of folly to keep us in a state of foolhardiness and stupidity should be praised.[14] However, as individuals, we are limited in the harm done by our own personal folly; in organizations, the commitment of leaders to acts of folly has far-reaching consequences.

BUREAUCRATIC INTRIGUE AS COMEDY

This is especially true when decision makers practice the arts of organizational *intrigue*, the effort to use secrecy and guile in order to achieve some purpose. Organizational life is rife with plots and cabals, conspiracies and schemes, covert deals and double crosses, coalitions and alliances, spying and disinformation, indeed the whole gamut of ways in which people gain advantage over others who are unaware of their plans. As we know from the history of diplomacy and espionage, intrigue is especially difficult to pull off, and should be used sparingly and only by experts. Yet people who should know better, aided by those who don't know any better, can get themselves in big trouble through the inept and inattentive use of intrigue; such maneuvers can easily be discovered and backfire badly. When they do, when the awful truth of another sorry episode of intrigue comes out, there is "comedy tonight." The clowns have arrived, to amuse their folly.

In democracies, elaborate intrigues often produce celebrated scandals. In nineteenth and early twentieth century America, these tended to involve money, with graft and bribery involving public officials and private wealth seeking advantage. Scandals such as Crédit Mobilier and Teapot Dome exposed private money influencing public offices in secret deals benefiting both politicians and plutocrats. Although financial scandals still occur in American politics, they have been complemented by a new and more curious kind of scandal, intrigue to gain control of, or circumvent, the bureaucratic "permanent government" of Washington.

As the federal bureaucracy grew in power and established authority following World War II, presidential aides and allies were increasingly frustrated with what they saw as the reticence of the permanent bureaucracy to cooperate with the president's purposes. Beginning with the Kennedy administration, presidential teams created "countergovernments," a kind of privy council that sought to manage affairs from the White House by making an end run around the reluctant and cautious bureaucrats. Mainly, these efforts involved circumventing the national security bureaucracies. The folly in many of these efforts was that covert operations inherently restricted planning and execution to small numbers of like-minded officials, "team players" whose silence and cooperation could be counted on; if detected, operatives sought "plausible deniability" by hiding from press and Congress, through adept evasion and a phony appearance of cooperation. The inane quality of these palace intrigues resided in breathtaking assumptions that the creation of a countervailing force against the bureaucracy could succeed despite resistance from the permanent government, leaks to the press by team players who defect and confess all, feeding frenzies by journalists sensitive to the popularity of tales of capital scandals, and the unrelenting curiosity of investigators in unraveling intrigues in all their tangled and mysterious weaving.

In our time, the granddaddy of all such scandals is Watergate—ancestor to other -gates (Koreagate, S & L-gate, Iran/contragate, Iraqgate, Whitewatergate, etc.). Nothing can compete with Watergate for sheer comic inanity and inattention in generating a major scandal that surpasses all other such episodes in sheer political folly and bureaucratic ineptitude. It is easy to see Watergate described as tragedy (Nixon as Richard III or Macbeth) or as sad melodrama (Nixon as Willy Loman or Captain Queeg). Yet, Watergate was, at heart, comedy. In the comic version, Nixon is less a sinister or troubled figure than the one *Esquire* magazine has featured every year since 1962 in its Dubious Achievement Awards—a Nixon uncharacteristically laughing hysterically, captioned, "Why Is This Man Laughing?" (In the January 1992 issue, *Esquire* dubbed Nixon "The Most Dubious Man of the Last Thirty Years"[15]).

In fact, the term "dubious" turns out to have comic insight: Nixon himself was always dubious about what to do, as someone fraught with uncertainty or doubt, and he ("Tricky Dicky") always aroused doubt about his motives. He aroused so much suspicion because he was equally suspicious of everyone else; he was as dubious about other people as many of us were of him. Although he was not noted (unlike Reagan) for his levity and wit, this does not mean he was necessarily a tragic figure whose fall was mighty, or a pathetic figure that deserved our pity. He was a figure of *comic dubiety*, a politician whose comic status stems from uncertainty about himself and our uncertainty about him. Throughout his career, he was a politician of dubious achievement, whose triumphs (the opening to China, détente with the Soviets) were always mitigated by the mutual distrust and uneasiness between himself, the public, and the news media.

In a comic view of Nixon, he was neither a fallen tragic hero nor a pathetic little man who overreached himself; he was simply an oddity. What kind of man invokes his dog Checkers in a 1952 campaign speech to keep from being dropped from the Eisenhower-Nixon ticket, as president walks on the beach for journalists' photo opportunities in suit and tie, or asks TV interviewer David Frost, making small talk moments before beginning his first post-Watergate interview, "Well, did you do any fornicating this weekend?"

Many veteran Nixon-watchers followed him in dubious skepticism through his career, but Watergate was a defining comic moment—what the "real Nixon" was like. Presidential conversations caught on audio tapings of the Oval Office revealed vindictiveness, prejudice, and self-loathing. Here appeared a Mafia *capo* plotting his next vendetta against a rival family; or a gloating villain in a Victorian melodrama, plotting all manner of torment for his enemies ("Get them on the floor and step on them, crush them, show no mercy"); or a mad Lear, lashing out at the world and defying the limits of nature. But for those who viewed Nixon as a dubious achiever, he appears as a comic court jester in reverse, a Rigoletto waffling and deferential to his cohorts, yet unfocused and incapable of truly evil planning. The tapes reveal the kind of person to avoid at a party, amusing for his half-baked scheming, but one whose plots inevitably contribute to his being fired at the office.

A comic of dubious character, then, is capable of foolishness but not much more. The grandeur of a truly tragic figure is lacking. The politician may be moved by "vaunting ambition o'erleaping itself," but it is in fact merely blind ambition that knows not what it does. Similarly, a truly villainous figure would have been capable of planning and executing flawless misdeeds, leaving enemies in fear and trembling. But Nixon was neither Macbeth nor Machiavelli. The "backstage" glimpses we have of him are more comical than anything: muddled, shallow, silly, and trifling, easily led by his chief of staff and other advisers, self-absorbed and self-pitying. All the taped sophomoric speculation about vengeance and Mafia hit men and hush money, as well as the prejudiced statements about Jews and African Americans, sounds like undergraduate braggadocio along fraternity row. There was much macho big talk in the Oval Office, but apparently no grand design of someone with Shakespearean ambitions or the attention to detail that might occupy a Richelieu or Bismarck.

Indeed, the source of Nixon's folly was his comically dubious quality; he was capable of neither tragic vaunting nor Machiavellian skill, and thus merely inane lacking either the tragic soul or the cunning sense to score a grandiose reach for more power. The private Nixon saw himself as a victim, acting out of resentment that led him into something clumsy and stupid, compounded by secrecy and greed, and finally unmasking him in the final recognition scene as lacking sense or substance. But Nixon was after all neither tragic nor pathetic, merely silly. Watergate was his ultimate comic creation, a fiasco that emanated from his own folly.

Watergate can be viewed as the comic folly of a band of half-hearted and often half-witted intriguers. Their creepy discussions within CREEP (the

Committee to Reelect the President) convinced them not only of their own tough-guy rectitude, but also of their own efficacy at intrigue. Since the inane are particularly good at outfoxing themselves, they committed themselves to a series of bull-in-a-china-shop covert operations with all of the sophistication of a panty raid. Richard Helms, then head of the CIA, told the U.S. Senate Watergate Committee that the initial break-in was "amateurish in the extreme." Even the alleged professionals in these operations were comic—E. Howard Hunt in his wig, G. Gordon Liddy watching old Nazi propaganda films in the White House basement, James McCord assigned to keep Martha Mitchell from talking to the press and, during the break-in, inexplicably taping the lock on the basement door at Watergate, thus making a night watchman suspicious.

The dramatis personae of the Watergate operatives, with their elaborate code names, aliases, disguises, passwords, and equipment, to the CREEP and White House officials hatching insane plots, all seemed like schoolboy graduates of a Junior G-Man course gleefully engaged in a playful cloak-and-dagger adventure. They seem in retrospect more pranksters than intriguers, conducting break-ins and sabotage and surveillance in the same giggling spirit of adolescent gall and effrontery that one might find with junior highschoolers spiking the prom punch with vodka or putting cherry bombs down school commodes. The Plumbers, Donald Segretti's "dirty tricks" group, hangers-on who included Cuban exiles, New York private detectives, party hacks, partisan ideologues, and college boys, were added buffoons in the comedy of Watergate.

Little, however, equaled the antics of the higher-ups involved in the cover-up. Using every evasion possible to avoid being caught and every lie to avoid being found out, they were like students suspected of cheating who dread the prospect of being hauled up before the principal. The more they struggled, the more comic they appeared: John Mitchell, the imperious attorney general, trying to silence his verbose wife; Spiro Agnew, the attack dog vice president forced to resign for taking bribes; H. R. Haldeman, the crewcut sociopath who tolerated "zero defects," yet presided over botched operations and cover-ups; John Ehrlichman, with his cynical sneer and evasive circumlocutions—a rogue's gallery implicated in what presidential press secretary Ron Ziegler dismissed as a "third-rate burglary."

The most comic ruses characterized Watergate: an eighteen and a half minute gap on a White House tape that would have clearly implicated Nixon, as resulting from "Rose Mary's Stretch"—Nixon's secretary Rose Mary Wood "accidentally" erased that part of the tape while reaching across her desk; a plan to ask aged Senator John Stennis, who could barely hear, to listen to the tapes alone and verify what was on them; and Operation Candor, the White House program to appear to be telling the truth, when in fact it was engaging in obfuscation.

Paralleling Operation Candor were the appearances of Nixon in various comic settings, such as motorcading with the Reverend Billy Graham, and playing the piano and yo-yoing at the Grand Old Opry. He began to look less like a king and more like a clown, asserting, "I am not a crook." The self-assured master of intrigue was the architect of a fine mess, a tangled if highly comic web woven from the first practice to deceive. Nixon's increasingly desperate attempt at disavowal was a Catch-22 argument: misjudgments and mistakes were made, but not necessarily by me; whatever was done was done by the "pure in heart"; the crimes that were committed were in fact not crimes, but politics; and the president is protected by executive privilege: he is immune from prosecution for any crimes he might have committed, for no evidence can be obtained constitutionally. The prolix, complicated, and comical recast the president from hero to villain to self-styled victim to fool, not lion or fox but rather weasel. In the end, he was left with nothing save his dubiety.

Watergate was a bureaucratic comedy of foolish men in intrigue to circumvent and undermine a constitutional system, conspirators caught and exposed in the full pettiness and ineptitude of their effort. What they thought in their insulated groups at CREEP and at the White House, to be easy to control turned into a comic nightmare; what began as schoolboyish capers turned into a wild and idiotic escapade that exposed their own reckless frivolity and folly. They were caught in a situation of delicious irony: they had reviled bureaucratic procedure and caution, yet, like good bureaucrats, they made records of almost everything they did! They left notes, diaries, memos, letters, plans—a paper trail so vast that researchers still sift it.

And, of course, the president himself made the ultimate record, by taping himself in the Oval Office. Once Watergate became a crime, all records were evidence; all illegalities were well documented. Habits of bureaucratic procedure carried over into subversive activities, placing the White House in the curious position of convicting officials of crimes the officials themselves had minutely recorded. And, irony of ironies, officials were ensnared in their own legal Catch-22: if they didn't turn over their records, they were guilty of withholding evidence; if they did, they would be found guilty of the crimes documented in the records. That's some catch, that Catch-22.

The intrigue for an imperial presidency led to a fiasco of true genius, the Frankenstein of comedies of intrigue. The stolid bureaucrats Nixon so reviled had the last laugh. No Hollywood screenwriter could have sold such a story to a studio. After the fall, Nixon rubber masks became a favorite Halloween disguise. Nixon himself tried the rest of his life to rescue his dashed reputation, to be taken seriously again. Even today, after Nixon's death, a stand-up comic or impressionist can twist his face into a scowl, raise his hands in a V-for-Victory sign, and say, "I am not a crook"; audiences howl in gales of laughter. Nixon's dubious reputation remains a heritage of political comedy.

NOTES

1. James H. Boren *When in Doubt Mumble: A Bureaucrat's Handbook* (New York: Van Nostrand, 1972), p. 45.

2. C. Northcote Parkinson, *The Law* (London: John Murray, 1979), p. 36.

3. Arthur Bloch, *Murphy's Laws* (Los Angeles: Price, Stern, Sloan, 1977).

4. Ibid., p. 16.

5. Laurence J. Peter and Raymond Hull, *The Peter Principle* (New York: William Morrow, 1969).

6. See Paul Dickson, *The Official Rules* (New York: Dell, 1978), for a compendium of helpful maxims.

7. Vance Ranney, "From Here to Absurdity: Heller's 'Catch-22.' " in Thomas B. Whitebread, ed., *Seven Contemporary Authors* (Austin: University of Texas Press, 1968), pp. 99–101.

8. Joseph Heller, *Catch-22* (New York: Dell, 1973), p. 47.

9. Ibid., p. 418.

10. Ibid., p. 416.

11. Joseph Heller, *Closing Time* (New York: Simon and Schuster, 1994), p. 61.

12. Dean L. Yarwood, "Humor and Administration: A Serious Inquiry into Unofficial Organizational Communication," *Public Administration Review* 55 (January/February 1995): 81–90.

13. Barbara W. Tuchman, *The March of Folly* (New York: Alfred A. Knopf, 1984), p. 4.

14. Desiderius Erasmus, *In Praise of Folly* (New York: Penguin Books, 1971).

15. "Richard M. Nixon, Always and Forever . . . ," *Esquire*, January 1992, pp. 118–19.

CHAPTER 8

The Mystique of Courts and Judges: Comedies of Ideas and Imagination

When it comes to comedy, politicians are amazingly versatile. In executive roles they play comedies of character; for example, every presidential trait, from Calvin Coolidge's fabled miserliness to Bill Clinton's gluttonous appetite for fast foods, attracts public attention. As legislators they act in comedies of situation, characters in bizarre circumstances; like the celebrants at a masked ball, they know each other, yet use all manner of guile to conceal their intentions and elude discovery. And as bureaucrats they wallow in comedies of errors and intrigue, manipulating procedures and rules to achieve their foolish ends.

There is another comedy that attracts the political actor, a seemingly regal spectacle called the *comedy of ideas*. The distinguishing feature of a comedy of ideas is that it involves actors in conflict over abstract concepts and ways of thinking. No such conflict of ideas is of greater import to the comedy of democracy than the one involving judicial officials over the essence of their craft.

WHAT IS JUSTICE?

This question has vexed political idealists throughout history, among them, Confucius, Moses, Solon, and Hammurabi. On the surface there is little to laugh at when approaching it. Our heritage of law and justice as embodied in courts and legal systems derives from the long, serious development of the English Constitution—the common law, Magna Carta, constitutionalism, *stare decisis*, and so on. In the United States it extends to our unique institution, the Supreme Court, which sets its members in a magnificent temple, like a group of Delphic oracles who glean tribal wisdom inherent in the sacred founding document, the Constitution. We pride ourselves on being a nation of laws, not of men, and on having equal justice under law. American civilization is manifest in the elaborate legal system that safeguards rights, discovers truth, and dispenses justice. Courts, judges, the law, and in particular the Supreme Court and the Constitution, are essential to the mysterious sacral order that imbues the state with legitimacy.

There is dissent from this regal, abstract view of justice in comic quarters. Journalist Finley Peter Dunne's Mr. Dooley, the Irish-American wiseacre pontificating from a late 19th century Chicago bar, had something to say on the subject: "I tell ye Hogan's r-right whin he says, 'Justice is blind.' Blind she is, an' deef and dumb an' has a wooden leg!" (Perhaps Justice wears a blindfold to cover her smile?) Mark Twain said, "We have a criminal jury system which is superior to any in the world, and its efficiency is only marred by the difficulty of finding twelve men every day who don't know anything and can't read" (or in our day, don't watch TV). H. L. Mencken said that a judge is "a law student who marks his own examination papers"; as another wag had it, a judge is a lawyer who knows a governor.

And the majesty of the law? Charles Dickens: "The law is a ass, a idiot." Anatole France: "The law, in its majestic equality, forbids the rich as well as the poor to sleep under bridges, to beg in the streets, and to steal bread." Elbert Hubbard: "Law is the proof of the infallibility of ignorance." And of course lawyers. Shakespeare: "The first thing we do, let's kill all the lawyers." Lord Brougham: "A lawyer is a learned gentleman who rescues your estate from your enemies and keeps it to himself." The Roman satirist Martial: "Lawyers are men who hire out their words and anger." And, perhaps most authoritatively, St. Luke (thought also to have been a doctor, perhaps involved in a Judean malpractice suit): "Woe unto ye also, ye lawyers! for ye lade men with burdens grievous to be born, and ye yourselves touch not the burdens with one of your fingers" (Luke 11:46).[1]

Thus, not everyone is impressed with the majesty of the disputants or the nobility of their ends in the comic conflict of ideas over the nature of justice. Nor do comic critics accept as inevitable the triumph of justice. The law and courts are, after all, social institutions with all of the symbolic conventions that constitute human artifices. Such institutions are part of the moral universe of social good, as guardians and enforcers of the rules of right and the knowledge of the just, pitted against the disorder and negation of the immoral world of chaos and evil it must punish or control. The solemn rituals and procedures of the courtroom remind us of the high seriousness of its institutional purpose. But in actual practice, the judicial institution is the province of fallible human beings, and subject to the existential follies and foibles of the mundane interactive world, the broad realm of the comic.

The idea of The Law is, in social practice, a paragon to be attained and a supposition to be applied, but it always comes up against the brute empiricism of the world of comic existence. The law is often but a Procrustean bed that doesn't fit every experience or desire, a Canutean stance against the tide of human folly. Procrustean law includes the effort to write and adjudicate laws that apply equally to everyone, such as the laws governing sexual conduct, school attendance, and drug consumption; Canute's stance includes efforts to prohibit what authorities consider bad conduct—abortion, drug dealing, and illegal immigration.

The American penchant for seeking to stop people from doing things they will surely do anyway, by prohibitory rules, yields comic overtones. In 200-plus years Americans have banned almost everything at one time or another. Prohibition taught us nothing about the utter futility of stopping human passions from expressing themselves. Contemporary "liberals" try to stop smoking, gun ownership, hunting, sexual harassment (broadly defined to include staring, laughing at sexual jokes, and making off-color remarks, and gender compliments); contemporary "conservatives" try to halt abortions, teenage sex, condom distribution, blasphemy (religious or political, such as flag desecration), X-rated movies, and so on.

All so-called reformers share a puritan fear, as H. L. Mencken said, that somewhere, people are enjoying themselves. The effort to outlaw human folly is of course folly itself, but nothing makes such a mind-set more satisfied than the ability to make someone else miserable. Rather than attempting to make life more bearable through tolerance, such rulers make life more unbearable through intolerance. But, comically, such human folly always goes underground or manages to circumvent the law. One may codify the rules of Leviticus, but human ingenuity in evading the law always lets people slip through the net; we may be sure that most Hebrew adulterers were not stoned to death, simply because they weren't caught.

The comic aspect of legal rules is that people always find ways to get around them; human desire is infinite but the ability of rulers to enforce rules is finite. Even the most totalitarian measures, whether Marxist, fascist, or Calvinist, cannot stop the largest and most enduring of our traits, the pursuit of folly. At this very moment, there are people doing things that social authorities somewhere do not approve; those authorities would halt the violations if possible, and if given the power, would promulgate even more draconian measures to stop such "immoral" behavior. Legal/moral crusades are often comedies of control—would-be controllers are the true fools, using futile meanness to impose and extend "good behavior" to all under their purview.

If we haunt courthouses at the local and county level in the United States, we get an impression of how far from the ideal the actual comic practice really is. Court calendars are jammed with petty cases, many of them dismissed, plea-bargained, or settled in haste; major felony or civil cases may be delayed for years; juries may decide something quickly just to be dismissed, or become deadlocked because of personality clashes in the jury room; judges may prejudice themselves on the bench, or inflict punishments that don't seem to fit the crime (draconian sentences for drug possession, light sentences for wife murderers who caught their spouses in an act of adultery). Corps of lawyers may represent a corporation against an individual who can only hire a local-yokel attorney; a state's attorney's office can pit resources against a poor person who is assigned a legal aid lawyer.

The ideal and the reality give us two competing images of the legal system. On the one hand is the image of justice done, truth discovered, the guilty uncovered. One thinks of movie and TV law: Paul Newman in *The Verdict*, Tom Cruise in *A Few Good Men*, Henry Fonda in *Twelve Angry Men* and *Gideon's Trumpet*, Spencer Tracy in *Inherit the Wind* and *Judgment at Nuremberg*—in these films heroic figures insure that justice prevails. Even when justice isn't quite done, as in *To Kill a Mockingbird*, we identify with the *agent* of justice who, like Atticus Finch, embodies the ideal.

This lordly depiction of justice contrasts sharply with images that provoke outrage when justice is denied, as in *Paths of Glory* (about outrageous military injustice), *A Man for All Seasons* (about Henry VIII's injustice toward his key solon, Sir Thomas More), and *And Justice for All* (about petty courthouse injustice). In contrast with the injustice of justice, the justice of injustice is far more romantic—exploits of vigilantes who pursue rough justice in the absence of legal remedies. Here are rogue cops (Clint Eastwood's Dirty Harry defying the police bureaucracy and the Bill of Rights to pursue evildoers), vengeful citizens (Charles Bronson's *Death Wish* killer icing street punks, Michael Douglas' mad-as-hell ordinary Joe taking the law into his own hands in *Falling Down*); rebellious women (Farrah Fawcett as the abused wife who torches her drunken husband in *The Burning Bed*, or rapist-shooting women on the run in *Thelma and Louise*). The persistent vigilante tradition reveals a lingering popular distrust, a suspicion that the law does not and cannot offer just remedies for individual and social wrongs.

This populist sense that all is not right with the legal system, that there is an incongruity between judicial pretensions and legal ignorance, fallibility, and foolery, provokes comic satire. Satirical renditions of the legal system resemble less the dispassionate search for truth on TV's *Perry Mason*, more the hilarity of *Night Court*. Poking fun at the law is an honorable comic tradition in itself. Aristophanes' *The Wasps* is perhaps the first satire on the law, attacking the Athenian penchant for litigiousness; the ancient Greeks were forerunners of the urge to "sue 'em!" so familiar in contemporary America. Citizens of Athens had an enthusiastic willingness to serve as jurors *for pay*; the Athenians had large juries, and each year a list of 6,000 jurors was compiled. In trials the jury numbered several hundred. In Athens the magistrates' courts had no lawyers per se; instead litigants hired Sophists (professional persuaders) to argue cases. Trials displayed the venality, pettiness, and greed of Athenians (according to Aristophanes). Here was a foreshadowing of TV's *The People's Court*.

In *The Wasps* Aristophanes satirizes a citizen as a "lawcourt lover" who is "so hot I itch to go to court and defendants gloomy to scan," looking forward to "the delicate aroma of lawsuit-stew." He describes jurors as they split up bribes: "They manage the matter like two men at a saw—One pushes, one pulls, and there goes the law." The Greek "wasps" swarm into court, making a mockery of justice. They proceed to try a dog for taking off with a piece of cheese. For Aristophanes the great patriotic accomplishments of the Persian War had been replaced by "the waspish state" of "the rhetoricians' eloquence" and "lawyer's tricks." The high value of justice had been diminished by the actual practice of justice, turning litigation and legal procedure into a corrupt comedy of prejudice, venality, and waspishness, a city and court peopled by "stingless drones."

In a more contemporary setting, perhaps the most delightful depiction of the judicial comedy of ideas is the 1949 film *Adam's Rib* (1949), starring Katharine Hepburn and Spencer Tracy as married lawyers. They try a case wherein a woman shoots and wounds her two-timing husband in the act of wooing his mistress. Amanda Bonner (Hepburn) is a committed feminist moved to defend the woman accused of attempted murder on the moral grounds that a spouse has the right to defend the home from disruption, including sleazy husbands and their negligee-clad illicit loves. But Adam Bonner (Tracy), an assistant district attorney assigned to the case, doesn't think so, arguing that adultery doesn't justify the aggrieved spouse taking a potshot at her errant husband.

The conflict involves not only an interpretation of the law but also a clash of principles, a veritable comedy of ideas. Hepburn perfectly embodies the principles of female equality—the right to protect her family—and legitimate indignation over male neglect, betrayal, and mistreatment. Tracy represents stolid male authority, with a commitment to law and order that transcends feminism or legitimate defense of hearth and home. The Bonners' public battle culminates in a courtroom scene. Mrs. Bonner introduces witnesses who attest to women's ability to do anything, attaining advanced degrees, running businesses, and so on. The witnesses include a circus performer who twirls Mr. Bonner aloft like a pinwheel, to his immense chagrin and humiliation. The verdict in the case does not settle the Bonners' basic disagreement or the social issue of how far rights extend to the use of aggressive action to advance those rights. But the casting of the two Hollywood icons ably illustrates a comedy of ideas, characters in an *agon* of recognition and ascendance.

JUSTICE? JUSTICE? FORGET JUSTICE! SHOW TRIALS AS COMIC SPECTACLE

In the summer of 1994, Nicole Brown, the ex-wife of former football star, successful sports commentator, celebrity-endorser, and film star O. J. Simpson, and her acquaintance, Ronald Goldman, were brutally murdered. When O. J. Simpson became a prime suspect, the double murder provoked such unwavering public scrutiny that for months to come the "O. J. Case" provided a riveting spectacle. A few days after the murders, Simpson suddenly disappeared at the time he was supposed to surrender to police. The O. J. Watch was a major televised spectacle.

Spotted in a white Ford Bronco proceeding north on the San Diego Freeway, Simpson was quickly the focus of TV cameras. Thus began the surreal spectacle of the automotive procession. Simpson, riding in the Bronco driven by a friend, had a gun; TV commentators informed viewers that Simpson was believed to be suicidal. Following the Bronco along the freeways of Los Angeles came a phalanx of police cars, not in pursuit of a fugitive, but appearing on worldwide TV as a royal escort for a celebrated figure. The spectacle was made even more bizarre by TV's depictions of crowds on overpasses holding signs reading "Free the Juice" and shouting in unison, "Go, O. J." By 7:00 P.M. EDT, national celebrity-journalists including Tom Brokaw of NBC and Peter Jennings of ABC were narrating Simpson's parade as Big News and, as an aside, agonizing over "should we be showing this salacious and weird story as if it were really important?"

With this spectacular beginning, it was no wonder that the anticipated trial of O. J. Simpson was billed in the news *and* entertainment media as the trial of the century. It was not the first time in the twentieth century that Americans had been treated to the hype of "The Trial." Nor would it be the last. There had been, after all, such celebrated cases as Sacco and Vanzetti in 1920, the Lindbergh kidnapping trial in 1934, and the Rosenberg trial in 1951. There was yet to come the trial of the accused in the Oklahoma City bombing of 1995.

These trials share with the Simpson trial not only the public ballyhoo of the news media; they are also *show trials*. Superficially a show trial is about true or false, guilt or innocence, justice or injustice. Below the surface, however, a show trial is about something else. Show trials are ritual ceremonies of passion, humiliation, degradation, and subordination. They are, to be sure, comedies of ideas. But they do not debate justice; they contest ideas of superiority and inferiority, who rules and who obeys, and what social and political values will reign and which shall perish. To illustrate the comic spectacle of the show trial, we turn to two celebrated cases: the Scopes trial (1925) and the Sheppard case (1954).

The Monkey Trial

The Scopes trial is a classic example of how an obscure legal dispute can become a symbolic event that dramatizes conflict over basic social ideas in the formal setting and procedure of courts of law. It also exemplifies how ideas are personified in symbolic figures, and how a legal comedy of ideas borders on the absurd. John Scopes was an obscure biology teacher in the Dayton, Tennessee high school, in a rural mountain region. The Tennessee legislature had passed a law making it a crime to "teach any theory that denies the story of the Divine Creation of man as taught in the Bible, and to teach instead that man has descended from a lower order of animals." Since Scopes had allegedly taught that man descended from apes, his trial became, in popular parlance, "the monkey trial."

Similar laws were passed in other Bible Belt states in an effort to thwart the teaching of the Darwinian theory of evolution. Such laws established democratic theocracy among evangelical-dominated states; they instituted official godliness in the form of the infallible and inerrant King James version of the Bible (including all the mistakes and mistranslations) and all of the Mosaic and Pauline prohibitions and punishments. The statutes were, on face, inspired by the idea of instilling in the youths of these states knowledge of the laws of the southern evangelical version of Yahweh. Opponents of these laws viewed them as blows against religious "modern-ism," urban Catholicism, and the advance of biological and genetic science in universities with freethinkers, atheists, and Jews on the faculty. Critics also saw the anti-evolution statutes as a bow to stupidity and ignorance more than a moral gesture; H. L. Mencken opined that support for such laws came from the "anthropoid rabble," who also fervently favored lynchings.

What came to a head in the Scopes trial was a democratic comedy of ideas, the legislated idea of official godliness that outlaws an alien doctrine in the devilish guise of scientific truth, thus taking a symbolic stand against the larger idea of science as itself a modern fundamental. This was a serious issue, to be sure, since it involved questions of academic freedom, the conflict of religion and science, and who decides what is taught in tax-sup-ported schools. The difficulty was that, as Mencken put it, the foes of the fundamentalists "insisted upon seeing the whole battle as comedy."[2]

From the outset, it was difficult for the educated circles of opinion and knowledge (professors, journalists, and other suspicious "evolutionists") to take the Tennessee legislature seriously, given its composition and mo-tives. The Tennessee legislature consisted of politicos all too versed in the sins of illegal booze, illicit women, and the lobbyists' bribe. Yet, they passed such a simpleminded law in total cynicism and without the slightest regard for its educational consequences. Small wonder, for they knew that their Bible-toting constituents outnumbered biology professors at the ballot box.

The Scopes trial was one of the first to become a virtually direct and "real time" media experience. The Western Union office in Dayton set up twenty-two telegraph operators in a grocery store, telegraphs ticked the trial from the courtroom as it proceeded. WGN radio in Chicago broadcast it live; motion-picture cameramen filmed the trial's principals for the new movie art form of the newsreel; major metropolitan newspapers sent major reporters, altogether over a hundred including Mencken from the *Baltimore Sun*. Cable companies reported the trial over transatlantic cable to London, where the story was transmitted to papers in Europe and as far away as China and Japan.

However, rather than reporting a sober deliberation on the great issues the conflict implied, the press portrayed the drama as one that pitted advanced knowledge and metropolitan sophistication against backward hillbilly yokels (whom Mencken called a "forlorn mob of imbeciles" and Scopes' attorney, Clarence Darrow, labeled "bigots and ignoramuses"). News accounts submerged the constitutional and pedagogical issues in the more colorful and amusing characterization of the mountain folk as Anglo-Saxon simpletons and Bible-thumping fanatics.

It was hard for the outside world to take such a law and such a trial seriously, since the principals on one side—the judge, jury, and locals—all seemed determined to live up to the stereotype of ignorant Neanderthals who wished to impose on the educated world their own primitive and reactionary theology. Although the advocates for both sides of the issue articulated the conflict as a melodramatic struggle between good and evil, much of the press and public saw it as an odd comedy of ideas played out in an obscure setting in a carnival atmosphere. The trial locale, Dayton, Tennessee, became a gaudy midway reminiscent of a medieval fair, with religious revivalists peddling every form of salvation imaginable, hawkers selling books and pamphlets on biology, evolution, and Darwin, and vendors merchandising lemonade and hot dogs, souvenirs and quilts, jellies and hams in a main street teeming with curious onlookers and tourists. For many of the bemused observers of this strange little drama, it was much ado about nothing.

The Scopes trial ("the trial that rocked a nation") is a modern media-age landmark in the representation of a legal procedure as a spectacle. Recall Aristophanes' lawcourt-lover savoring "the delicate aroma of lawsuit-stew." Although many famous trials attract interest because they offer us a conflict of important ideas, like Scopes they quickly become defined as an *agon* of celebrated personages who give dramatic force and articulation to the ideas or issues in question. The courtroom becomes in such trials the spectacular stage for a contest of wills, a rummage through the mystery of the case that reveals something about the human condition, an unfolding story that puzzles us by being told from at least two perspectives, like the Japanese tale *Rashomon*; and, if important ideas are involved, a test of the veracity or power of those ideas in open court, including the metaquestion of the rule of law itself. With the power of the mass media to make a trial into an immediate experience, it becomes an integral part of daily life, something that grips us as a mediated reality that makes us take sides or ponder guilt and innocence, right and wrong, wisdom or folly. In the context of legal rules, such a trial becomes a ritual of justice: the drama hangs on the question, Will justice be done?

Romantic citizens love the spectacle of justice as a popular forum for the conflict of values. The trial format focuses on the ideational or cultural constructs that are under scrutiny and challenge in the proceeding. In the case of Scopes, it was a decidedly lowlife comic setting for a highbrow debate over great issues, and it quickly was transformed into the idioms of popular thought. Even if much of the audience for such a trial was perhaps a bit astonished at all the fuss over a silly law, nevertheless it was gripping theater. And for many of them, it was comic spectacle, an exhibit of notable ideas and figures engaged in a struggle for the definition of the legal and constitutional situation that becomes so intensely contested and absurdly argued that it is best seen as a drama of ideational or cultural comedy.

A spectacle is a media event staged for its positive theatrical impact on its auditors, and thus becomes something more than simply a contest of ideas or values; rather it becomes a medium for organizing opinion or sensibility that supports the agenda of the agent. So the issue at hand is translated into understandable idiomatic language delivered with histrionic force, becoming rhetoric rather than logic. But in so doing, it is easily seen by press and public as popular comedy.

A case in point in the Scopes trial took place when defense attorney Clarence Darrow put William Jennings Bryan on the witness stand; the exchange degenerated into an absurd trading of insults and slogans, a mutual degradation society. A comic spectacle of this sort is less than a noble declamation and syllogistic consistency; rather it is rhetorical play, trying to further a cause by couching ideas or values in symbols and metaphors which turn them into parodies of themselves. Darrow made Genesis into a joke by attacking the simpleminded literal interpretation of it, and Bryan made liberalism into a joke by defending the right of the government to teach only the most egregious popular superstition. Attorney and witness engaged in popular levity, that an argument can only be sustained by turning it into something jocular, as if lightness of speech and frivolity of manner comprise the way to sustain an argument.

No matter how "serious" the subject of a legal spectacle, then, it is potentially an occasion for carnival excitement, engagement, and enjoyment. It might be opined that since we no longer have public executions, the trial has become the focus of popular entertainment; if we can't watch convicts hang, at least we can watch them being sentenced to be hanged. But an event that becomes a spectacle is not of interest merely because it is sensational; rather it is attributed symbolic significance. For this reason, the French writer Guy Debord sees spectacles as pseudo-religious: "The spectacle is the material reconstruction of the religious illusion. . . . It is a specious form of the sacred."3

A specious event seems fair and true, but in fact only looks good; it may have the ritual form of a religious liturgy or the legalistic form of a sound trial, but there is more to it than that. The presence of the attentive audience makes it into a popular mega-event of emotional and not merely intellectual interest. For those intense auditors, the search is for *primal justice*, and not the rule of law or legal and constitutional justice. Their emotional involvement is a primitive impulse that is likely the emotional origin of both comedy and tragedy. They wish to see a spectacle of vindication, in which the law serves the function of punishing a victim, who is sacrificed in order to vindicate ideational or cultural values. The law and courts are after all an institutional descendant of more directly tribal justice, and often in that evolution people have taken the law into their own hands in bloody revenges such as lynchings, retaliations, and persecutions. Sometimes, as with Nazi law, the desire for blood sacrifices reaches tragic proportions.

Kenneth Burke has argued that this desire for victimage is a universal social principle of the drama of governance. Legal institutions are part of the symbolic hierarchy of government, and such institutions regularize and rationalize order and disorder in codes of justice. In order to justify the symbols of order, the legal system can identify good and evil, acts of grace and acts of disgrace, what is deemed laudable and what is deemed punishable. But lurking behind all this is the primitive impulse for vicarious sacrifice to purify society, expiate guilt, and punish evil.

As Burke says, "If action, then drama; if drama, then conflict; if conflict, then victimage."4 Vicarious victimage offers in the guise of the law a way to satisfy primitive fears of demonic enemies and forces, desires for vindication and identification of us as good, and plain old sadistic bloodlust for the punishment of the wicked. The victim is always guilty if he or she represents something evil, but always innocent if we identify with her or him. This human practice can result in tragedy, and more commonly in pathetic melodramas such as the death penalty. But since the legal system operates in an irrational and emotional environment, often this desire for victims merely results in the triumph of the infallibility of ignorance unfolding in a comic drama of bungling, miscues, and mistakes that remind comic observers how much authorities and citizens of democracies really believe in and practice the solemn rule of law. Victims are often saved by the mirth produced by the comic fools of legal dramas, such as the political and legal authorities of the sovereign, dim-brained state of Scopes-era

Tennessee and the cretinous democratic folk who adhered to the rule of law as stated in Leviticus, not the Constitution and Bill of Rights. Or so thought Mencken in Dayton, as he surreptitiously watched a firelight evangelical meeting in the hills above Dayton; his description of its athletic fervor and spiritual ecstasy sounds amazingly like the descriptions of rude Dionysian cults in Euripides' *Baccahe* 2,500 years before.[5]

The primitive Dionysian comedy of antiquity obeyed a ritual pattern involving an actual combat or contest between antagonists, discomfiture for the loser (who in the original cultic ritual sacrifice was killed and eaten), ceremonial lament, and resurrection of the spirit of fertility. This evolved into comic drama that reproduced the solemn sacrificial rite in parody, and that was what made it funny. In comedy, the rite of purification that demanded sacrifice and victims changed into a festive ceremony making fun of everything authoritative and solemn, and indeed became a perspective increasingly on the side of the potential victim. The fools are the people in charge and the people themselves; together in a democratic state like Aristophanes' Athens, they remind the comic of the infallibility of judicial ignorance in their legalistic foolishness.

The authorities and citizens of 1920s Tennessee displayed no less foolishness in trying to victimize a biology teacher. For some, the bloodlust was still there; but for others, the whole affair was an occasion for celebratory play. For many locals, it was simply a carnival time for exciting fun and engaging talk, and not to be taken seriously, since many of them weren't quite sure what it was all about but were sure that it was an occasion for out-of-the-ordinary frivolity. And for observers like Mencken, the entire spectacle was comic proof of the delightfully ignorant and astonishingly mistaken nature of democratic institutions and citizenship, a ridiculous travesty of the ideals of rational justice carved in stone in the Temples of Apollo such as the Supreme Court building. For the period of out-of-time that the festive mood and the spectacular event last, one can legitimately engage in entertaining play, at least as an impious voyeur of a social spectacle.

A trial as an entertaining play, then, is a happening that has comic potential. It is not an event of Apollonian earnestness and rationality, but rather one of Dionysian fun. Indeed, the very incongruity between its serious purpose (a trial for murder, for instance) and its transformation into a popular media spectacle makes it over into something dreadfully funny in spite of itself. Beginning with comic spectacles like the Scopes trial and other tabloid trials of the 1920s, the clash of legal principles is superseded by the more popular contest of media metaphors and images. Rather than a serious collaborative quest asking, "What is truth?," such trials offer a playful popular forum in which the disputed question is, "Who is telling the truth?" The proceeding shifts from one dedicated to the task of finding the truth to one centered on the competitive art of making one contestant believable, the other unbelievable. The setting switches from an emphasis on the art of discovering the truth to one that stresses the art of using the legal setting to gain control of the definition of the situation.

Legal contests are comic when the idea of law fades before the idea of using the law as theater. The courtroom offers a theater for popular amusement and press bemusement, and becomes the context for *legal play*, a popular escapade rather than solemn procedure. At this point, it is difficult to take the proceedings seriously; a comedy of ideas is thus transformed into a comedy of performances for press and public auditors. A legal procedure such as a trial acquires comic potential when it becomes something other than a solemn quest for true justice, and serves instead as a travesty of justice, a grotesque imitation of the rule of law, a popular spectacle. Justice appears ridiculous when it is but a search for popular justice, appealing to opinion formed from rhetorical play and performance rather than the principles of jurisprudence. Popular justice is what the mass auditors of the trial want out of it, satisfying the requirements of play with the unfolding spectacle of a contest in a legal setting. Taking sides in such proceedings offers side benefits—voyeuristic participation, primitive vengeance, tribal vindication, and conspiratorial revelations.

The idea of justice is preposterous when capricious, not something ordained by the mystery of the law but by the whims of an arbitrary system, the fancy of the jury, the fickleness of the masses, the humor of the press, or the vagaries of the law. When the blindfold of majestic Justice is removed to reveal her mirth at the fundamental capriciousness of the law, the only real justice is comic justice.

The Scopes trial was a spectacle in which the rule of law and the importance of the issue were dwarfed by its specious power as a symbolic mega-event. Such legal spectacles are not so much about law as they are about belief, wherein people wish to see a fundamental drama of good and evil, innocence and guilt, tribe versus tribe played out to their satisfaction. Believing that the law is capricious and likely unjust, they seek occult signs and wonders, hidden forces and cabals, and scraps of metaphorical information from rumor and press to frame their feelings and preferences. For the comic observer, such as Mencken at the Scopes trial, these irrational desires combine with widespread publicity to make the proceeding into something totally lacking in majesty and dignity, a ridiculous travesty of its original intent. The myth of Justice is undermined when what everyone wants is popular justice stemming from emotion and not reason. The incongruence between legal ideal and popular reality evokes comic realism.

Aristophanes' wasps still buzz around infamous legal settings. With the widespread publicity given sensational trials in the media age, such legal proceedings are increasingly the subject of voyeuristic interest, watched by popular audiences as a specious and even occult form of reality, involving all the trappings of the law but occurring in a surreal world that attracts both our salacious curiosity and our secular worship. For media access to a spectacular trial makes us witnesses to a judicial surreality, a legalistic saturnalia that allows us to exercise our carnival spirit and gain playful entry into a magical wonderland of tantalizing mysteries, strange events, hidden motives, and capricious outcomes.

Such play is an expression not of *Homo sapiens* but rather of *Homo ludens*, humankind the player with justice.[6] Since the comic world is capricious, the judicial world is equally fanciful and inconstant; show trials are comic charades offering the amusements of the popular media arts, not faith in ordained justice. Media spectacles have reversed the world order: it used to be that the gods on Olympus could look down in amused detachment at the comic struggles of mere mortals; now we mere mortals now watch in the same way the plight of those gods who occupy the surreal world of power and fame. But if the gods were sure to watch and see that justice was done, we watch in equal certainty that justice will not be done. Human characteristics—self-interest, perversity, cunning, weakness, ignorance, cussedness, or just our inability to control a capricious universe—defeat, or at least muddy, the cause of justice.

The comedy of justice reflects and reinforces our disbelief in a just universe, and our singular faith in the little faith of all men. This interest is expressed in popular wisdom about the legal system: you can't put big money in jail, you can't fight city hall, justice for the rich is different than justice for you and me, important people get away with murder, lawyers are smart and can beat the system for the powerful, the law is rigged against little people, there's no justice. Popular wisdom about the basic injustice of the world leads to the suspicion that the judicial game, if truly tragic, is fixed—or, instead, one unlucky enough to be caught in its comic nexus is a victim of its foolish caprice.

The Sam Sheppard Case

The Scopes trial reflected a comedy of conflicting ideas held by two clashing cultures. The Sam Sheppard case in 1954 put reigning suburban culture on trial in a publicized frenzy that competed for media attention given in the same year to Senator Joe McCarthy's efforts to try the U.S. Army (see Chapter 6). Sheppard was a Cleveland osteopath whose wife was murdered in their home, while he was knocked unconscious, according to his story. There were immediate suspicions that he might have been the killer, since he had a reputation for violence and philandering. Journalists descended on his family and friends and discovered and publicized his failings. For the emerging 1950s, this was a story the nation found compelling. It involved the new world of suburbia, wealthy professionals, and sexual misconduct; here was a challenge to the brave new world of postwar Eisenhower normalcy. The Sheppard case became the stuff of which a Big

Story was made, in which the press largely decided that Sheppard was guilty, no doubt intuitively aware that this was the conclusion that many readers wanted to believe.

The Cleveland *Plain Dealer* began the public conviction with headlines such as "Why Isn't Sam Sheppard in Jail?" and "Getting Away with Murder." Thereafter the national press converged in force, including celebrated gossip columnists such as Walter Winchell and Dorothy Kilgallen. Like Scopes and other sensational trials before it, the Sheppard case was a media event, a show trial transforming the administration of justice into a comic carnival. The Temple of Apollo turned into the Feast of Fools, an occasion for comic celebration; the courthouse not a citadel of justice but a grotesque stage for a press-led holiday, reveling in the obscene drama in the courtroom. As for public executions of old (and the Simpson trial in 1995), people competed for access to the proceedings, for this legal spectacle was "something to watch." It was the occasion for Dionysian enthusiasm and merriment over someone else's misfortune.

In the Sheppard case, the courthouse was occupied by a waspish swarm of reporters eager to taste the delicate aroma of lawsuit-stew. And since everyone could not be there, they relied on the press to provide them with every gory detail, to analyze the evidence, and to prejudge the verdict. Again, as in the Simpson case, the Sheppard show trial made the mass media audience the jury. "The Athenians," wrote Aristophanes in *The Wasps*, "would judge suits at home. Every man would build a miniature court at his front door, like a Hecate shrine."

An appellate judge would subsequently call the festive atmosphere at the Sheppard trial a "Roman holiday," noting that "murder and mystery, society, sex and suspense were combined in this case in such a manner as to intrigue and captivate the public fancy to a degree perhaps unparalleled in recent annals." And a Supreme Court justice noted with horror the "carnival atmosphere" and the extent to which "bedlam reigned in the courtroom."

Indeed, the entire media event made a mockery of the juridical principle that a "petitioner be tried in an atmosphere undisturbed by so huge a wave of public passion." From the beginning, both local and national media tore at the now notorious celebrity-defendant. Sheppard's refusal to take a lie detector test and have an attorney present at interrogations was reported as tantamount to a confession of guilt. The inquest was held in a school gymnasium, with Sheppard present; the press was seated at a long table, and the proceeding was broadcast live over radio and television; the gym seats were filled with several hundred local spectators, who were allowed to cheer and jeer. When Sheppard's counsel tried to place documents in the record, he was forcibly ejected by police at the order of the coroner, who then received cheers, hugs, and kisses from ladies in the audience.

The atmosphere was like a Jacobin execution during the French Revolution with nice Cleveland ladies in the role of Madame Defarge. Sheppard participated in the spectacle himself, making public statements to the press and even writing feature articles defending himself! When the jury was selected, the Cleveland newspapers published their names and addresses. Not surprisingly, the jurors received hate mail, threats, and opinions; they were not sequestered, and since their pictures ran over forty times in local papers, they became local celebrities.

The press presence, including network broadcasters, dominated the courtroom; jurors readily recognized the celebrity broadcasters (such as Bob Considine and Walter Winchell) who routinely reported rumors about Sheppard's personal life, including the false rumor of his sexual athleticism. Moreover, press accounts offered a paradoxical proof of guilt: Sheppard had a prominent criminal lawyer (the same F. Lee Bailey of O. J. Simpson's "Dream Team" coterie of lawyers). Obviously Sheppard's need for high-powered legal advice proved he must be guilty. Sheppard was convicted and sentenced to life imprisonment. On appeal, his conviction was overturned by the Ohio Supreme Court and the U.S. Supreme Court, but only after he had served twelve years in prison.

Sam Sheppard, of course, undoubtedly did not see the humor in all this, nor did the solemn high priests of the temples of law that reviewed and overturned the case. But the judges were the guardians of civic justice. The press became the agent of tribal justice, crying for blood vengeance and for a fresh victim to sacrifice during the exhilarating holiday period. And this brings us to an astounding *comic paradox*: the cry for blood expressed by the press and the public was in the context of frivolous social play, and the demand for the victimage of the accused was articulated in a comic spirit.

A secular ritual such as a show trial is the playful occasion for the expression of the most primitive desires for revenge, and the ludenic context for a kind of mad judicial bacchanal, with the trial serving as the comic play of tribal justice. The press and public that followed and fantasized and talked about the Sheppard case made the event into a fanciful comic drama, casting the defendant, his lawyer, and anyone who dared doubt his guilt as fools.

Like the ancient feasts involving blood sacrifices (originating in cannibalism and the myth of the eating of the gods), for the auditors of the Dionysian ritual of the trial-spectacle, it was a happy and mirthful occasion for reveling in the fate of the victim and the meaning of his condemnation for the life of the group. Shorn of its ancient mythic trappings and placed in a more "civilized" setting, such a spectacle of sacrifice was still a comic celebration of primal justice. Sheppard was "tried" by the mass-mediated tribe and the shaman-reporters who howled for his blood, and it was only the later intervention of the institution of civic justice that saved him from life imprisonment.

WHO STOLE THE TARTS?

If the phrase "justice in America" evokes for legal romanticists a code of lofty ideals, for comic realists it evokes a comedy of ideas. Drama, not justice, is the basis of judicial spectacular. Legal spectacles have a surreal quality to them. The surrealist school in art taught that life should be expressed as something incongruous and startling, with absurd and unusual arrangements that depicted the fluid and imaginative qualities of experience. It wished to depict realities beyond reality ("surreal," above and beyond reality), since life is not rational, but uncontrolled by reason and immanent order. Life is in this sense comic, as with Dali's melting clocks or Magritte's raining clerks.

The modern spectacle gives media life to what the surrealists only imagined. We now may exercise comic imagination of the most horrific events, from real-time warfare from Baghdad to witnessing mega-events ranging from royal weddings to riots to trials, indeed whatever acquires social definition as an absorbing and lucrative spectacle. Even though witnessing such media events is a new experience, it is one derived from very old impulses, rooted in the origins of comedy. Now democratic citizens may *enjoy* as never before legal conflicts as popular theater, even though citizens' knowledge of the intricacies of the law and legal procedure may be scant. In the age of show business, the omnipresence of media access to such institutions as the law and courts has "made entertainment itself the natural format for the representation of all experience."[7]

By approaching events, even serious ones such as battles, terrorist acts, and murder trials, as comic dramas, the battlefield, the hijacked airliner, or the legal proceeding serves as a setting for *horrific comedy*, drama watched for voyeuristic pleasure. The interplay of legal ideas—the appeal to precedent, the contesting of evidence, the logic of questioning and cross-examination, the careful judgment of factuality—becomes the subject of mass play. For viewers a televised trial belongs to a surreal world above and beyond ordinary experience. Since the media event is of another world and is in a sense not "real," we can then view it without serious involvement. A mass-mediated trial takes place for viewers in a surreal wonderland where the mundane rules of experience, including the propriety of our reactions, do not apply.

Lewis Carroll's Alice would understand our American judicial Wonderland. In her tour of Wonderland, she witnessed the trial of the Knave, presided over by the King and Queen of Hearts. Alice had never been in a court of justice before, so it was quite a sight. The King was the judge, she knew, because of his great wig. The twelve animals who comprised the jury sat in the jury-box writing on slates. Alice asked what they were doing, and was told they were putting down their names, "for fear they should forget them before the end of the trial." "Stupid things!" she exclaims, and discovers that all the jurors are writing down "Stupid things!" The King has the herald read the accusation:

> The Queen of Hearts, she made some tarts,
> All on a summer day:
> The Knave of Hearts, he stole those tarts
> And took them quite away!

The King orders the jury, "Consider your verdict"; but the Herald-rabbit interrupts to say, "Not yet. . . . There's a great deal to come before that!" The first witness, the Hatter, comes in and is admonished by the King to give his evidence, and told, "Don't be nervous, or I'll have you executed on the spot." This doesn't encourage the trembling Hatter, and finally the angry King retorts, "Give your evidence or I'll have you executed, whether you are nervous or not." When the Hatter says he can't remember something, the King tells him he must remember "or I'll have you executed!" When the hatter protests that he is a poor man, the King replies, "You're a *very* poor *speaker*."

After much confusion in the courtroom, Alice is called as a witness. When she professes she knows nothing about who stole the tarts, the King instructs the jury to write this down since it is very important, although the White Rabbit tells them that he really means "unimportant." As Alice continues to grow, the King invokes Rule Forty-two: "All persons more than a mile high to leave the court." Alice protests that this rule is not a "regular rule: you invented it just now." The King says that it's the oldest rule in the book, and Alice replies, quite logically, "Then it ought to be Number One." A poem is found, and a juryman asks if it is in the prisoner's handwriting; it isn't, which prompts the King-judge to conclude, "He must have imitated somebody else's hand." The Knave-defendant protests that he didn't write it or sign it; the King cunningly observes, "If you didn't sign it, that only makes the matter worse. You *must* have meant some mischief, or else you'd have signed your name like an honest man." The court is impressed by the King's perspicacity, and applauds; it was, after all, "the first really clever thing the King had said all day." For the Queen, this proves the Knave's guilt, "so off with—."

The nonsensical verses are read. The King describes them as the "most important piece of evidence we've heard so far," and starts to instruct the jury. Alice, now in the role of the defendant's advocate, argues that if any of the jury can explain the verses, she'll "give him sixpence," for she doesn't "believe there's an atom of meaning in it." But the King notes that if there is no meaning in it, "that saves a world of trouble, you know, as we needn't try to find any." The King scrutinizes the verses and finds the word "swim," and asks the Knave if he can swim. "Do I look like it?" he replies, being made of cardboard. The King continues to ponder the poem, attempting to find culpability in the words. Finally he charges the jury to consider the verdict. "No, no!" the Queen says, "Sentence first—verdict afterwards." When Alice protests, the Queen shouts, "Off with her head!" But Alice, who has grown back to her full size, is not impressed, observing, "You're nothing but a pack of cards!" Then the whole pack goes into the air and flies down upon her, and she awakes from her dream, exclaiming, "Oh, I've had such a curious dream!"

Lewis Carroll's famous fantasy was written before our contemporary media age, but its fantastic quality and convoluted logic remind us of the comic aspects of celebrated show trials that capture the fancy of press and public. Trials as diverse as those of Scopes and Sheppard acquire a surreal quality, as if they are occurring in some kind of strange and alien wonderland where normal judicial rules and decorum are abandoned, and the proceedings themselves seem charged and crazy, like a curious dream.

The comic observer of such judicial comic nightmares is in the position of Alice, the outsider who sees just how insane and preposterous the whole proceeding is, and senses the surreal aesthetics of the occasion. The spectacle of Darrow interrogating Bryan about the inerrancy of the Bible or the Sheppard inquest being held in a gymnasium with a cheering audience is clearly in the absurd spirit of the trial of the Knave. Scopes and Sheppard were obviously the Knaves of their respective communities. Scopes was accused of stealing the sanctified tarts of public piety, Sheppard of murdering his wife in order to consort with (female) tarts. Many of the witnesses made as much sense as the Mad Hatter; intimidated (since they had to go on living in Dayton or Cleveland), they probably feared being "executed" by local popular opinion for what they might testify. The trial records often betray twisted logic and weird rhetoric as the courtroom dialogue unfolds (at one point a befuddled Bryan says, "I do not think about things that I do not think about"; to which Darrow inquires, "Do you think about things that you do think about?"

In the Scopes trial, important pieces of testimony, such as the opinions of distinguished scientists, were deemed inadmissable, but Bryan's childish ideas about the Bible were deemed relevant, which might have led Darrow to exclaim, "If any one of them [the judge and jury] can explain it, I'll give him sixpence." Appellate courts in the Sheppard case ruled that the trial judge should have paid attention to judicial Rule Number One, that a trial take place in an unprejudiced and calm setting with an impartial judge and jury. But that was impossible in this case, since the judge would not enforce Rule Number Forty-one, that celebrated journalists leave the courtroom. Sheppard's private life and his statements in the press and court were subjected to the same dubious but detailed scrutiny the King gave the Knave's poem. As the trial went on, the newspapers, as the Supreme Court later noted, summarized and interpreted testimony and evidence, and often made unwarranted conclusions and dark speculations. For example, one paper ran a front-page picture of Mrs. Sheppard's blood-stained pillow; the picture was doctored to show more clearly an alleged imprint of a surgical instrument. Throughout, the press frantically grasped for atoms of meaning in every scrap of information flowing from the murder trial.

The press in the Sheppard case represented the same attitude as the Queen, who is quick to take scant evidence as proof of guilt. Their editorial contempt for legal procedure and presumption that Sheppard was guilty led them to cry from the start, "Sentence first—verdict afterwards," and thus "Off with his head!" (a sentiment assented to by the bloodthirsty public). The Knave Sheppard protested with a typed statement denying guilt, which was reproduced on the front page of one paper, saying in effect, "Do I look like it?" "How could I who have been trained to help people and devoted my life to saving life, commit such a terrible and revolting crime?"

Both Scopes and Sheppard were presumed by the legal and local community to have stolen the tarts, and no amount of denial could stop the process of sentencing first, with the verdict as an afterthought. Reflection on these show trials later reveals their surreal quality, as if the comedy of justice occurs in an illogical and convoluted universe with as much substance and reason as a flying pack of playing cards. To those who enjoy the comic spectacle of a trial, such mass-mediated episodes are indeed curious dreams. They constitute, like most of the comedies of democracies, what Shakespeare described in *The Tempest*, an insubstantial pageant.

NOTES

1. Quotes from Nat Shapiro, ed., *Whatever It Is, I'm Against It* (New York: Simon & Schuster, 1984).

2. H. L. Mencken, "In Memoriam: W.J.B.," in *A Mencken Chrestomathy* (New York: Alfred A. Knopf, 1956), p. 247.

3. Guy Debord, *Society of the Spectacle* (Detroit: Black and Red, 1983), p. 14.

4. Kenneth Burke, "Dramatism," *International Encyclopedia of the Social Sciences*, Vol. 7, ed. D. L. Sills (New York: Macmillan, 1968), p. 450.

5. H. L. Mencken, "The Hills of Zion," *Chrestomathy*, pp. 392–398.

6. Johan Huizinga, *Homo Ludens: A Study of the Play Element in Culture* (Boston: Beacon Press, 1950).

7. Neil Postman, *Amusing Ourselves to Death* (New York: Penguin Books, 1985).

Epilogue: Exit Laughing

Serious scholars differ, but it is highly likely that the last play written by William Shakespeare was *The Tempest* (c.1611). Generations of readers have "for this reason been tempted to see it as a culmination of Shakespeare's vision," a sort of summing up of the great bard's oft-repeated themes about human potential and depravity, spirituality and baseness.[1] If the readers' judgments are correct, it is singularly interesting that this playwright of thirty-seven dramas—historical epics, poignant romances, and human tragedy—should have chosen as his valedictory work a comedy.

This book, too, has reached a culmination, a final statement summarizing the authors' oft-repeated themes about the seriousness and silliness that reside in the contemporary comedy of democracy. Believing that there is a message in *The Tempest* that students of American democracy might wish to heed, the authors close the discussion of the highs and lows of America's comedies by taking advantage of Shakespeare's teachings about insubstantial pageantry as he long ago exited laughing.

SHAKESPEARE'S TEMPEST AND AMERICA'S POLITICS

As with other Shakespearean dramas, *The Tempest* is open to diverse interpretations. The simplicity of the plot alone has given critics and audiences opportunities to impose a multitude of readings, some compatible, some complementary. That simplicity has also allowed imitators to convert the bare outlines of *The Tempest* into widely different kinds of entertaining fare, ranging from the Hollywood science fiction film *Forbidden Planet* to the slapstick and camp TV series *Gilligan's Island*. Be that as it may, if we confine ourselves solely to Shakespeare's rendering at this point, we find a tale about the Duke of Milan, Prospero, who has been denied his dukedom by his brother, Antonio. In his usurpation Antonio has been aided by the King of Naples, Alonso, and the king's scheming brother, Sebastian. In *The Tempest* Prospero seeks his revenge on the plotters with the help of an airy spirit, Ariel, and a corps of other sprites. Buried in all of this are subplots of romantic, social, realistic, and situation comedy; comedies of farce, humor, manners, wit, character, intrigue, and ideas.

The drama begins on a ship battered about on the sea in a wild storm. Aboard are the King of Naples and his royal party, returning home after attending the wedding of the king's daughter. The ship's master and boat-swain are coping with the chaos as best they can. When the boatswain finds himself confronted by the royal party, he treats the dignitaries with contempt. The king's sage councilor of long standing urges the boatswain to "remember whom thou has aboard," but the veteran seaman rudely responds, "None that I love more than myself," and orders the party below deck. After a brief tirade the royal party finally descends to pray for salvation.

Salvation the distinguished members of royalty receive, but not at the hands of any God who has answered their prayers. Rather it is because the tempest threatening their ship is but an illusion conjured up by Prospero. For a dozen years Prospero and his fifteen-year-old daughter, Miranda, have lived on a remote island. As Duke of Milan Prospero had turned over management of the dukedom to his brother, Antonio, while devoting himself to a study of the liberal arts. When Antonio treacherously seized power, Prospero was destined to die. But Gonzalo, then a noble of Naples, took pity on the bookish Prospero and his daughter, giving them a well-stocked (including Prospero's library) sailing craft, thus enabling them to seek exile elsewhere. Now, by accident, all of Prospero's enemies have been cast up on the shore of his island, where "all torment, trouble, wonder, and amazement inhabits."

As the royal party rides out the storm, Prospero relates the tale of his and Miranda's exile to his daughter, assuring her that the ship now cast upon their remote shores is safe and the crew and party in no danger. He then puts Miranda to sleep and confers with Ariel, his magic and spirit-like agent. It is Ariel who has raised the tempest, frightened the crew and passengers, and brought them safely to the island. For all of this hard work Ariel asks Prospero to set him free from the bondage he has owed the exiled duke ever since the latter released Ariel from a cloven pine where a witch had imprisoned the spirit well before Prospero arrived on the island.

Prospero refuses Ariel's wish, explaining that there is yet more work to be done, but that when it has been completed Ariel will indeed be set free.

At this point another of the island's creatures enslaved by Prospero's magic appears. As described by Shakespeare, Caliban is a half-monster, devilishly ugly; in today's more sensitive and politically correct vernacular Caliban is anatomically and cosmetically challenged. Caliban, the son of the same witch who enslaved Ariel, was led by his mother to understand that upon her death he, Caliban, would inherit the island. With Prospero's arrival, however, Caliban's inheritance has been denied. Hence, although Prospero and Miranda have treated Caliban well, even teaching him to speak their language, Caliban feels no obligation to either master or mistress. Indeed, Caliban at one point had been thwarted by Prospero in an attempt to rape the beautiful Miranda. He mocks Prospero, saying, "Thou didst prevent me. I had peopled else this isle with Calibans."

As the plot develops, Ferdinand, the son of the King of Naples, who is thought by his father to have perished in the storm, arrives at Prospero's camp. In short order Ferdinand falls in love with Miranda and she with him. Although privately favoring the match, Prospero pretends to oppose it; he uses his magic to ensnare Ferdinand and puts the royal lad to work piling logs. Ferdinand's eagerness to serve only increases Miranda's innocent infatuation. As the comedy moves forward Miranda offers to be Ferdinand's wife, he accepts, and Prospero judges the marriage a "fair encounter." Prospero sanctions the union of the two innocents with a masque in their honor celebrating a romantic "contract of true love."

On another part of the island, the ship's passengers (the crew being asleep under one of Ariel's spells) mill around and mourn their fate. Gonzalo attempts to comfort the king in the loss of the royal heir, Ferdinand. However, Sebastian, the king's brother, and Antonio, the usurping duke, mock Gonzalo and blame the king for their troubles. Later, as all but Sebastian and Antonio sleep under yet another of Ariel's spells, Antonio persuades Sebastian to kill the king and Gonzalo, then seize the throne of Naples as Antonio did the dukedom of Milan. But just as the two conspirators are about to strike, Ariel awakens the king and Gonzalo and the treachery must be postponed.

Meanwhile Caliban, fetching wood for Prospero and cursing his master all the while, encounters on another part of the island two highly inebriated (chemically dependent) survivors of the ship's beaching: Trinculo, the king's jester, and Stephano, the king's butler. When Stephano offers Caliban a drink, the latter, new to drink, gets soused, assumes Stephano is a god, and disavows any allegiance to Prospero. Off the three go to Prospero's cave. There Caliban proposes that they kill Prospero, then rule the island. Needless to say, the half-monster, jester, and butler are no match for a magician and a sprite; hence, the assassination plot never gets off the ground. Instead the plotters ultimately decamp in confusion and terror.

At the moment, however, Prospero has other fish to fry. He prepares a feast for his enemies—the king, the duke, and the king's brother. With Ariel's help, just as the banquet is about to begin, all the food vanishes. In a spirit-like fashion Ariel accuses Alonso, Antonio, and Sebastian of the dastardly plot against Prospero twelve years earlier. The king is conscience-stricken and remorseful; Sebastian and Antonio remain unrepentant and lash out with swords, but to no avail.

With all his enemies under his control and his daughter promised nuptial bliss, Prospero decides to be magnanimous. He takes pity and has Ariel release the royal party from magic imprisonment. Prospero summons the royal party before him, indicts his enemies, and expresses to Gonzalo his gratitude for saving his and Miranda's life so long ago. He subtly threatens Antonio and Sebastian that they had best reform, lest their plot to kill the king be exposed. Alonso too gives his blessing to the marriage of Ferdinand and Miranda. In his final chores before winning his freedom Ariel awakens the ship's crew and rounds up the drunken Caliban, the jester, and the butler. All are properly contrite and seek forgiveness. Prospero releases Ariel from service, surrenders his own magic powers, and, in an epilogue, speaks to the audience. In it Prospero seeks his own release from the insubstantial pageant: "As you from crimes would pardoned be, let your indulgence set me free."

THE TEMPEST AS A COMEDY OF AMERICAN DEMOCRACY

Let us now recast the characters and plot of Shakespeare's *Tempest* while also recasting the drama as a closing epilogue on America's comedies of democracies. First, consider the characters as Shakespeare cast them, then as they appear in our tempest of democracy:

Prospero, the rightful Duke of Milan, the Ideal People's President and Realist Voice of Public Opinion.

Ariel, an airy spirit, Propaganda's Voice of Public Opinion, Government *of* Public Opinion, not government *by* public opinion.

Miranda, daughter to Prospero. Also an innocent, romantic citizen.

Ferdinand, son of the King of Naples, also innocent, also a romantic citizen.

Alonso, King of Naples, a failed incumbent president too flawed in character to be successful.

Gonzalo, an honest old councilor, a utopian political reformer.

Sebastian, Alonso's brother, an ambitious U.S. Vice President.

Antonio, Prospero's brother and usurping Duke of Milan, a political kingmaker and professional political consultant.

Caliban, a savage and deformed slave, the News Media of choleric humor.

Trinculo, a jester, the United States House of Representatives, perhaps even the Speaker.

Stephano, a drunken butler, the United States Senate, perhaps even the Majority Leader.

Adrian & Francisco, lords, also political lobbyists and hangers-on.

Boatswain, a veteran seaman, the bureaucrat who survives many presidents, senators, and congressional members.

Granted, such a recasting may seem fanciful. Yet in the fanciful often lie insights into the actual, as Shakespeare knew so well. Here is how the plot plays out as political comedy.

In Act 1, Scene 1 of *The Tempest* a storm rages, a chaos of fact and illusion much like a normal political scene, that is, "crisis politics" is actually "politics as usual." The ship of state's boatswain, perhaps the head of the Joint Chiefs of Staff planning an invasion of a Caribbean isle, encounters the incumbent president, Alonso, Sebastian the vice president, Antonio the consultant, and Gonzalo the reformer (reminiscent of ex-President Jimmy Carter?). As the storm reaches its height, the boatswain warns the royal party, "Keep your cabins. You do assist the storm." "Remember whom thou has aboard," shouts Gonzalo in his best Carter-like manner. "None than I more love than myself," scowls the boatswain in contempt of civilian control of the military.

Both the vice president, Sebastian, and his political adviser, Antonio the usurper, smell intrigue in the boatswain's haughty and contemptuous demeanor; a bureaucracy under partisan control is more to their liking. Hence, rather than follow the boatswain's orders, each hurls an insult his way: "Howling, blasphemous, uncharitable dog," whines the VP; "We are less afraid to be drowned than thou art," challenges Antonio the kingmaker.

Ever the pacifist and optimist, old Gonzalo displays his utopian colors in mediating the civilian-military conflict. Noting that the boatswain's complexion is as sallow as the gallows, Gonzalo senses that the mariner is more likely to die by hanging than by drowning. While Sebastian whines and Antonio rails, Gonzalo pleads with them not to fear. Speaking of the bureaucratic boatswain, he offers the VP and the political hack a realistic assurance: "I'll warrant against him drowning, though the ship [of state] were no stronger than a nutshell and as leaky as a wide-open wench." Sebastian and Antonio yield, and the crisis of authority is averted.

As Act 1, Scene 2 opens elsewhere on the island, the innocent and romantic citizen-daughter, Miranda, frets that Prospero is acting out of character, not at all like the sage, ideal presidential figure she imagines him to be in her political philosophy. "If by your art, my dearest father, you have put the wild waters in this roar, allay them," she pleads. Like Snow White, Miranda is pure of heart and agonizes at the thought that a poor, hapless nation, that is, "a brave vessel" with "some noble creature in her," should be "dashed all to pieces."

Acting as elder statesman and as a realist fully aware of the intricacies of special interest politics and intrigue, Prospero assures Miranda that there has been "no harm." He recognizes Miranda for what she is, a naive citizen untutored in the ways of politics, one "ignorant of what thou art." In a scene reminiscent of a presidential candidate sitting on a high stool surrounded by admiring supporters who ask softball questions, Prospero instructs Miranda on the fine art of political intrigue.

In addition to telling the tale of how he and Miranda were marooned on this Gilligan's Island "in the dark backward and abysm of time," Prospero recounts how he lost his dukedom. His account, continuously interrupted with largely irrelevant questions, echoes Jimmy Carter's memoirs. Like Carter contemplating the Holy Bible Prospero studied his books, leaving Milan and his reputation in the hands of his brother, the "perfidious" Antonio, a man of "foul play." As Prospero was "thus neglecting worldly ends, all dedicated to seclusion and the bettering of my mind," Antonio, like Billy Carter, was cutting his own deals. Unlike Billy, who merely signed on as a lobbyist for a foreign power, Antonio lobbied the King of Naples "to confer fair Milan, with all the honors," on himself. Alas, muses Prospero, "Me (poor man) my library was dukedom large enough."

Fortunately, however, "so dear," says the fallen people's president, was "the love my people bore me" that the usurpers "durst not" assassinate him; instead, thanks to the generosity of the reformist-pacifist Gonzalo, "acting out of his charity," Prospero and Miranda were put to sea to make the most of things. Like many an ex-president, Prospero did very well in retirement: "Here have I, thy schoolmaster, made thee more profit than other princes can." Miranda, like citizens in the romantic comedy of democracy, is so bemused by Prospero's biographical TV spot that she is lulled to sleep.

At this point Prospero summons into conference the real power behind his island throne, his public relations specialist and media consultant, Ariel. Like former President Ronald Reagan summoning his pollster, Richard Wirthlin, and his media guru, Michael Deaver, Prospero is the only one who can actually *see* Ariel, who knows of the spirit's existence. This, of course, in the eyes of the island's dwellers and his own enemies shipwrecked there, makes Ariel's magical propaganda powers appear to be Prospero's. Small wonder that in *The Tempest* Prospero, like Ronald Reagan, has a reputation as "The Great Communicator." Like any ambitious political PR specialist, Ariel reports that he has done a bang-up job in creating the illusion of the storm, wrecking the ship, putting the crew to sleep, and setting the wimp Chief of State Alonso, his vice president Sebastian, Antonio the usurper, and other members of the executive entourage to wandering aimlessly.

Now, says Ariel, again like any good PR specialist, he wants out of his contract with Prospero so that he can sell his services elsewhere, perhaps to an independent like Ross Perot. No, says Prospero, when he generously freed Ariel from a cloven pine, where the spirit had been imprisoned by a former disgruntled client by the name of Sycorax the witch, he signed an ironclad agreement that Ariel could not end until having performed all contracted services. Prospero puts it on the line: no services, no freedom. "If thou more murmur'st, I will rend an oak and peg thee in his knotty entrails till thou has howled away twelve winters." With the threat of that kind of lawsuit over his head, the PR spirit returns to his obsequious self: "Pardon, master. I will be obedient to command and do my spiriting gently."

With that Prospero directs Ariel to "go make thyself like a nymph o' th' sea . . . subject to no sight but thine and mine, invisible to every eyeball." Now Prospero turns himself to another problem, government-press relations. On the scene comes Caliban, who, like American journalists who believe that the First Amendment declares a right to be unmannerly in the comedy of manners, growls defiance of Prospero. "A southwest blow on ye and blister you all ov'r," Caliban offers as an editorial aside. For his own part Prospero, who, like all chief executives, believes that the press should serve presidential interests, commands Caliban as an adversarial serf, "Thou poisonous slave, got by the devil himself."

If Shakespeare had lived in the late twentieth century he could not have more accurately captured the essentials of government-press conflict in the United States than he did in the early seventeenth. First, the honeymoon period that marks the early phase of a chief executive's relationships with the press. Says Caliban, "When thout cam'st first, thou strok'st me and made much of me; wouldst give me water with berries in't; and teach me how to name the bigger light." (Current version: when a chief executive first takes office the press is courted, received at the White House with dignity, and given the Big Picture of presidential plans during frequently called press conferences.) Again, Caliban: "And then I loved thee and showed thee all the qualities o' th' isle." (Current version: press coverage of the new administration made the president look good; his popularity ratings soared.) Caliban: "Cursed be that I did so!" (Current version: the honeymoon's over.) Caliban: "For I am all the subjects that you have" (i.e., your only means to appeal to popular opinion); "which was first my own king" (the press was dignified as a fourth estate when the president took office); now "you do keep me from the rest of th' island" (the president is covering up, withholding information that the People have a right to know!).

Prospero's response only adds to the adversarial government-press relationship. First, he treats Caliban as traitorous: "Thou most lying slave . . . I have used thee (Filth that thou art) with humane care." Hence, like any chief executive, Prospero believes that he delivered on his promise of an open presidency. "And lodged thee in my own cell till thou didst seek to violate the honor of my child." The words echo a complaining Bill Clinton who, after providing journalists with all manner of background briefings on his health care reform package, found reporters carping, violating "the honor of my child."

Miranda, like any innocent citizen of contemporary politics, has no great respect for the press either. She too castigates Caliban as "being capable of all ill," for she had taught Caliban at her own expense (much like taxpayers' dollars supporting schools of journalism) to "speak, taught thee each hour one thing or another, when thou didst not, savage, know thine own meaning, but wouldst gabble like a thing most brutish." And what do citizens get in return? Lies, sensationalism, *bad news*! Caliban, however, remains unmoved and unrepentant: "You taught me language, and my profit on't is, I know how to curse."

By now Prospero has had enough of media criticism. The press conference is over and Caliban is dispatched to fetch wood. In the manner of the love-hate relationship that brings politicians and journalists together, Caliban stalks off—fascinated with an "art of such pow'r," but growling all the while.

Act 1 of *The Tempest* closes with the arrival of Ferdinand, son of the King of Naples, and a citizen every bit as innocent, romantic, and naive about politics as the chaste and unsullied (despite news anchor Caliban's best efforts) Miranda. As Ferdinand mourns the loss of his father in the tempest, the unseen Ariel fashions a campaign song akin to a twenty-second radio commercial, "Full fathom five thy father lies. . . ." This clues Ferdinand that there may be something else on the isle other than his own sorrows. He sees Miranda. There is immediate Good Citizen bonding: "A thing divine; for nothing natural I ever saw so noble," gushes Miranda; "My prime request, which I do last pronounce, is (O you wonder!) if you be maid or no?" asks Ferdinand.

On first meeting the two good citizens are tense. Neither as yet knows where the other stands on the burning political issues of the day (say, pro-life versus pro-choice). And neither knows where Prospero as People's President (i.e., *their* president) stands on the issues. Like two dedicated democrats new to politics but wanting to work for a politician they much admire, they are wary about positioning themselves before knowing what the political leader wants. Like many a politician, Prospero appears to commit himself, but does not. He feigns dislike for Ferdinand, but only as a trick to make the royal son more desirable to Miranda, whom Prospero has spoiled for a dozen years while indulging her petulance. Miranda falls for her Dad's political humbug. "Why speaks my father so ungently? This is the third man that e're I saw; the first that e're I sighed for." Ferdinand falls too: "O, if a virgin, and your affection not gone forth, I'll make you The Queen of Naples."

Privately the sage politician in Prospero is pleased ("they are both in either's pow'rs"), but his wily side says, "But this I must uneasy make, lest too light winning make the prize light." So Prospero continues to criticize

Ferdinand for his shortcomings, and Miranda continues to wail. Prospero has had enough. "Hush!" he orders Miranda, then gives good citizen Ferdinand the ultimate insult by comparing him to a journalist: Foolish wench! To th' most of men this is a Caliban, and they to him are angels." Miranda remains smitten. Prospero leaves the two citizen-lovers to work things out for themselves, ordering Miranda not to speak to Ferdinand but knowing full well that good democrats being good democrats, she will.

The first scene of the second act returns *The Tempest* again to intrigue. Alonso is bemoaning his failed stewardship and loss of a son; Gonzalo tries to pacify him; the ambitious Sebastian and Antonio mock and ridicule both; and the two political hangers-on, Adrian and Francisco, who are mere hacks, stay close so as to protect their selfish interests. They all exchange charges and countercharges over whose fault the wrecking of the ship of state was. The scene reminds one of a group of Bill Clinton's advisers debating why the Democrats lost control of both the House of Representatives and the Senate in the 1994 elections for the first time in four decades.

Two key political scenarios unfold during this scene. The first involves Gonzalo's revelation of his utopian plan to reform politics. Like the plans of other such reformers, from President John Quincy Adams' designs for a national commonwealth in the 1820s to perennial presidential candidate Eugene McCarthy's reformist ideas of the 1960s and 1970s, Gonzalo's grand scheme falls on deaf ears. Yet, to those exposed to the workings of America's comedy of democracy there is something quaint and refreshing about the old reformer's approach. He would allow no trade, no officials, no learning; riches, poverty, and the exploitation of labor would be unknown; agriculture would not be restricted by property boundaries; the environment would be healthy, with no use of metal, corn, alcohol, or oil; people would have ample leisure and have no power over one another, and (to the rage of feminists) women would be "innocent and pure." People would share goods in common. There would be no "treason, felony, sword, pike, knife, gun," or other weapons. Nature's abundance would provide for all. Gonzalo, obviously, was a flower child of America's 1960s.

As Gonzalo outlines his utopia, Sebastian, the ambitious VP, and Antonio, his consultant, snicker. " 'Twas you we laughed at," mocks Antonio to Gonzalo. But Sebastian and Antonio do cease laughing, for they are concocting a scenario for reform far more sinister than that of Gonzalo. As the king, Gonzalo, and others doze off, the kingmaker and the man who would be king plot. At first Sebastian sees no possibility of his ever becoming King of Naples. Antonio, however, is not so sure. In the finest tradition of the professional political boss he outlines a plan. Since Ferdinand, Alonso's son, is probably drowned, and Alonso's daughter Claribel now Queen of Tunis, there is hope for Sebastian. All that needs to be done is to assassinate Alonso, install Sebastian, and let Claribel stay in Tunis. The exchange between the ambitious office seeker and the political consultant has a modern ring:

Sebastian: I remember you did supplant your brother, Prospero.

Antonio: True. And look how well my garments sit upon me.

Sebastian: But, your conscience—

Antonio: Ay, sir, where lies that? If 'twere a kibe, 'twould put me to my slipper; but
    I feel not this deity in my bosom. [Current version: "I have no conscience.]

Sebastian: Thy case, dear friend, shall be my precedent. As thou got'st Milan, I'll
    come by Naples.

The voice of public opinion, however, does not take kindly to such
treachery, as the mourning of the assassinations of Abraham Lincoln and
John F. Kennedy (and the multitude of conspiracy theories surrounding
both) testifies. The public's guide, in this case the spirit Ariel, intervenes to
awaken Alonso and Gonzalo. Alarmed at waking to the drawn weapons of
Sebastian and Antonio, Alonso demands to know what is afoot. The conspirators shrug it all off as merely an attempt to drive away marauding
monsters. A relieved Ariel, with the plot foiled, adds another line to his
professional resume: "Prospero my lord shall know what I have done. So,
King, go safely on to seek thy son."

The Tempest shifts from a comedy of intrigue to one of farce and humor
in the ensuing scene. It is time for the U.S. Congress to enter the picture,
with House and Senate allying themselves with members of the press in
bashing the chief executive. It is a scene all too common in the comedy of
democracy. It begins with our journalist look-alike, Caliban, carrying logs
while cursing the treatment he receives at the hands of Prospero. Trinculo,
the court jester, enters in search of shelter against an approaching storm.
Given Trinculo's gaudy appearance in his jester's garments (something like
the neckties worn by Speaker Newt Gingrich), Caliban mistakes him for
one of Ariel's spirits come to torment him. In the manner of the press fearing
that members of the House of Representatives might stop leaking tidbits of
gossip for daily publication, Caliban pulls his cloak over his head to conceal
himself. Trinculo, a downpour coming, decides "to creep under his [Cali-
ban's] gabardine." Sizing up the situation in the manner of congressmen
inviting political journalists into House offices for private interviews, Trinculo observes, "Misery acquaints a man with strange bedfellows."

At this point a drunken, swaggering Stephano, the king's butler, a.k.a.
the U.S. Senate, stumbles on the scene. Seeing the beast writhing with
Trinculo under the cloak, Stephano marvels at the ugliness of the creature,
estimating the advantages of having Caliban tamed (just as any U.S. Senator
would like to tame the press): "If I can recover him and keep him tame, I
will not take too much for him," that is, there is capital to be made by
charging admission to see the beast. Toward that end Stephano gives
Caliban a drink, then another, then another. The contemporary version in
U.S. politics is a wine and cheese reception given by Senate majority leader
Bob Dole for members of the congressional press galleries.

Caliban is much impressed by Stephano and fancies the latter, who is a buffoon, a king. For Trinculo, who is less buffoon than critic, Caliban has respect, but it is more grudging. The Speaker of the House, Trinculo, has harsh words for the journalistic Caliban: "a very weak monster," "a most poor credulous monster," "a most scurvy monster," "an abominable monster," and "a most ridiculous monster." Yet, Caliban, like the typical press gallery member, promises to follow House and Senate anywhere: "These be fine things, and if they be sprites, that's a brave god and bears celestial liquor. I will kneel to him."

Shortly thereafter the three sots wander off. During the trek Caliban informs Stephano and Trinculo of the presence on the island of Prospero and Miranda. Claiming himself the "subject of a tyrant" now that the press-presidential honeymoon is over, Caliban enlists the support of House and Senate to gridlock the people's president. As Caliban pleads his case, the spritely Ariel intervenes, providing a propagandist's analysis of press sensationalism, "thou liest, thou liest." Although Stephano and Trinculo have doubts about Caliban's scheme, they agree to try to unseat the popular Prospero. Trinculo sums up what is to prove the folly of it all—and the folly of alliances between journalists and congressional officials: "They say there's but five us on this isle; we are three of them. If the other two be brained like us, the state totters."

The entirety of Act 3 of *The Tempest* displays the magic Prospero has as the ideal people's president to bedazzle his enemies—King Alonso, VP Sebastian, Antonio the kingmaker, councilor Gonzalo, and political hangers-on Adrian and Francisco. Prospero, garbed in his cloak of invisibility, which acts like the Teflon shield journalists attributed to Ronald Reagan during his presidency, places in front of the court's eyes an illusory banquet. Just as the royal party is about to satisfy their hunger, Prospero makes the banquet vanish with a "quaint device" (i.e., a bit of stage management akin to that planned by presidential advisers in orchestrating a press conference).

Ariel, democracy's agent of propaganda, then appears to the royal court as a harpy who scolds and indicts Alonso, Antonio, and Sebastian for their plot against Prospero twelve years earlier. The conspirators are dumbfounded. They draw their swords. But Ariel's persuasive message is delivered in stern terms. It is a testimony to the futility of the force of arms when pitted against the force of propaganda:

You fools! I and my fellows
Are ministers of fate. The elements
Of whom your swords are tempered may as well
Wound the loud winds, or with bemocked-at stabs
Kill the still-closing waters, as diminish
One dowle that's in my plume.

King Alonso is conscience-stricken, but Sebastian the VP and Antonio the kingmaker are unrepentant. Prospero, however, knows that he has won the day, for he now controls the agenda of political action, not Sebastian or Antonio: "My high charms work, and these, mine enemies, are all knit up in their distractions. They now are in my power."

It is now time for the people's president to consolidate his victory, bind up old wounds, and move on to greater heights of peace and prosperity. This he does first by showing his magnanimity. He will, in effect, pardon Alonso for his perfidious deeds, much as President Gerald Ford pardoned Richard Nixon for any possible wrongdoing the latter might have committed during the Watergate scandals of the 1970s.

Prospero also deals with the plot against him orchestrated by Caliban. After Ariel leaves Caliban, Trinculo, and Stephano wallowing in a pond, Prospero provides the House and Senate with gaudy clothes, the functional equivalent of presidential approval of pork barrel spending for members of Congress who promise to behave. Caliban, like the news media, is left at the mercy of Prospero's landslide victory.

Prospero moves on to bestow his approval, like the seal of presidential legitimacy, on the planned betrothal of the island's romantic citizen pair, Miranda and Ferdinand. "I must bestow upon the eyes of this young couple," says a sage Prospero, "some vanity of mine art. It is my promise, and they will expect it of me." Hence, for them, like a president promising tax cuts combined with increased government spending to make citizens more affluent, Prospero conducts a masked ball, an artificial and stylized spectacle resembling a presidential inauguration. Like any democratic citizen, Miranda is impressed. "How beauteous mankind is! O brave new world, that has such people in't!" Were Caliban in Prospero's good graces, his journalistic manners would lead to press coverage of the masque as a story of celebration. Alas, poor Caliban, like any journalist out of favor at the White House, is condemned to cover Congress. He is last heard moaning, "What a thrice-double ass was I to take this drunkard [the Senate's Stephano] for a god and worship this dull fool!"

With the republic restored to glory and his presidential administration vindicated, Prospero no longer has need of Ariel's propagandistic skills. Hence, to Ariel he declares, "Be free and fare thou well." Toward the end of the political comedy that is *The Tempest*, the Jeffersonian Prospero, the Ideal President, delivers an apt summary of the American comedy of democracy. It too reminds us as political observers—be we politicians, journalists, analysts, or citizens concerned about the republic's agonies—that the best perspective from which to understand what is going on is the comic:

> Our revels now are ended. These our actors,
> As I foretold you, were all spirits and
> Are melted into air, into thin air. . . .

And, like this insubstantial pageant faded,
Leave not a rack [wisp of cloud] behind.[2]

And in the spirit of Shakespeare, we say to readers, as you from our argument pardoned be, let your indulgences set us free.

NOTES

1. William Shakespeare, *The Tempest*, ed. Robert Langbaum (New York: Signet, 1987), p. xxi.

2. Ibid., Act 4, Scene 1, 148–150, 155–156.

Selected Bibliography

Adams, Henry. *The Education of Henry Adams*. New York: Modern Library, 1931.
Allport, Floyd H. "Toward a Science of Public Opinion." *Public Opinion Quarterly* 1 (Winter 1937): 7–23.
Anheier, Helmut K., Lester M. Salamon, and Edith Archambault, "Participating Citizens: U.S.-Europe Comparisons in Volunteer Action." *Public Perspective* 5 (March/April 1994): 16–18, 34.
Aristotle. *De Poetica*. In Richard McKeon, ed., *Introduction to Aristotle*. New York: Modern Library, 1947.
Atkinson, Brooks, ed. *The Complete Essays and Other Writings of Ralph Waldo Emerson*. New York: Modern Library, 1940.
Beard, Henry, and Christopher Cerf. *The Official Politically Correct Dictionary and Handbook*. New York: Villard Books, 1992.
Berelson, Bernard. "Democratic Theory and Public Opinion." *Public Opinion Quarterly* 16 (Fall 1952): 313–330.
Berelson, Bernard, Paul F. Lazarsfeld, and William N. McPhee. *Voting*. Chicago: University of Chicago Press, 1954.
Berger, Arthur Asa. *An Anatomy of Humor*. New Brunswick, NJ: Transaction, 1993.
Berlyne, D. E. "Laughter, Humor and Play." In Gardner Lindzey and Elliot Aronson, eds., *The Handbook of Social Psychology*. 5 vols. 2nd ed. Reading, MA: Addison-Wesley, 1969, 3: 795–852.
Bloch, Arthur. *Murphy's Law*. Los Angeles: Price/Stern/Sloan, 1977.
Boller, Paul E., Jr. *Presidential Anecdotes*. New York: Penguin Books, 1982.

_____. *Presidential Campaigns*. New York: Oxford University Press, 1984.

Boorstin, Daniel. *The Image*. New York: Atheneum, 1972.

Boren, James H. *When in Doubt, Mumble: A Bureaucrat's Handbook*. New York: Van Nostrand, 1972.

Boulding, Kenneth E. *The Image*. Ann Arbor: University of Michigan Press, 1968.

Brockett, Oscar G. *The Theatre: An Introduciton*. New York: Holt, Rinehart and Winston, 1964.

Brown, Norman O. *Closing Time*. New York: Vintage Books, 1973.

Buckalew, James. "News Elements and Selection by Television News Editors." *Journal of Broadcasting* 14 (Winter 1968–70): 47–54.

Burke, Kenneth. *Attitudes Toward History*. 3rd ed. Berkeley: University of California Press, 1989.

_____. "Dramatism." *International Encyclopedia of the Social Sciences*, Vol. 7. Edited by D. L. Sills. New York: Macmillan, 1968, pp. 445–452.

_____. *A Grammar of Motives*. Berkeley: University of California Press, 1945.

_____. *Language as Symbolic Action*. Berkeley: University of California Press, 1968.

Carpini, Michael X. Delli, and Scott Keeter. "The Gender Gap in Political Knowledge." *Public Perspective* 3 (July/August 1992): 23–26.

Carter, Bill. "ABC News Divided on Simulated Events." *New York Times*, July 27, 1989, p. C20.

Cater, Douglas. *The Fourth Branch of Government*. Boston: Houghton Mifflin, 1959.

Charney, M. *Comedy High and Low: An Introduction to the Experience of Comedy*. New York: Oxford University Press, 1978.

Cornford, Francis. *The Origin of Attic Comedy*. Cambridge: Cambridge University Press, 1914.

Corrigan, Robert W., ed. *Comedy: Meaning and Form*. San Francisco: Chandler, 1965.

Davis, Murray S. "Sociology Through Humor." *Symbolic Interaction* 2 (Spring 1979): 105–112.

Debord, Guy. *Society of the Spectacle*. Detroit: Black and Red, 1983.

de Grazia, Sebastian. *Machiavelli in Hell*. Princeton: Princeton University Press, 1989.

Denby, David. "Queen Lear." *The New Yorker*, October 3, 1994, pp. 88–96.

Dewey, John. *The Public and Its Problems*. Denver: Alan Swallow, 1927.

Dickson, Paul. *The Official Rules*. New York: Dell, 1978.

"Don't Mean Diddly," *The New Yorker*, July 10, 1994, pp. 4, 6.

Downs, Anthony. *An Economic Theory of Democracy*. New York: Harper and Row, 1957.

Duncan, Hugh D. *Communication and Social Order*. New York: Oxford University Press, 1962.

Eckardt, A. Roy. *Sitting in the Earth and Laughing*. New Brunsick, NJ: Transaction, 1992.

Eco, Umberto. *The Name of the Rose*. New York: Harcourt Brace Jovanovich, 1980.

Erasmus, Desiderius, *In Praise of Folly*. New York: Penguin Books, 1971.

Fielding, Raymond. *The American Newsreel*. Norman: University of Oklahoma Press, 1972.

Fields, W. C. *Fields for President*. New York: Dodd, Mead, 1940.

Fiorina, Morris P. *Retrospective Voting in American National Elections*. New Haven: Yale University Press, 1981.

Fraser, Antonia. *Cromwell*. New York: Alfred A. Knopf, 1973.

Freud, Sigmund. *Jokes and Their Relation to the Unconscious*. Translated and edited by James Strachey. New York: W. W. Norton, 1960.

Frye, Northrop. *Anatomy of Criticism*. Princeton: Princeton University Press, 1957.

Gardner, G. *All the President's Wits*. New York: Beach Tree Books, 1986.

Garfinkel, Harold. "Conditions of a Successful Degradation Ceremony." In James Combs and Michael Mansfield, eds., *Drama in Life*. New York: Hastings House, 1976, pp. 315–320.

Gassner, John. *Directions in Modern Theatre and Drama*. New York: Holt, Rinehart and Winston, 1965.

Geyer, Georgie Anne. "Our 'Internal Exile.' " *Dallas Morning News*, December 7, 1993, p. 13A.

Goldstein, Jeffrey H., and Paul E. McGhee, eds. *The Psychology of Humor*. New York: Academic Press, 1972.

Gragert, Steven K., ed. *He Chews to Run: Will Rogers' Life Magazine Articles, 1928*. Stillwater: Oklahoma State University Press, 1982.

Gruner, Charles R. *Understanding Laughter: The Workings of Wit and Humor*. Chicago: Nelson-Hall, 1978.

Gunderson, Robert Grey. *The Log-Cabin Campaign*. Lexington: University of Kentucky Press, 1957.

Harris, Leon A. *The Fine Art of Political Wit*. New York: E. P. Dutton, 1966.

Heller, Joseph. *Catch-22*. New York: Dell, 1973.

_____ . *Closing Time*. New York: Simon and Schuster, 1994.

Henry, William A. III. "Fascism, Fury, Fear and Farce." *Time*, April 11, 1994.

Hess, Robert D., and Judith V. Torney, *The Development of Political Attitudes*. Chicago: Aldine, 1967.

Hickerson, Buddy. "The Quigmans." *Dallas Morning News*, June 25, 1993, p. 7C.

Hyman, Dick. *Washington Wind and Wisdom*. Lexington, MA: Stephen Greene Press, 1980.

Johnstone, John W. C., Edward J. Slawkski, and William W. Bowman. *The News People*. Urbana: University of Illinois Press, 1976.

Joyce, James. *Finnegans Wake*. New York: Viking Compass, 1959.

Kaplan, Abraham. *The Conduct of Inquiry*. San Francisco: Chandler, 1962.

Kelley, Stanley, Jr. *Professional Public Relations and Political Power*. Baltimore: Johns Hopkins University Press, 1956.

Kerr, Walter. *Tragedy and Comedy*. New York: Simon and Schuster, 1967.

Key, V. O., Jr. *Public Opinion and American Democracy*. New York: Alfred A. Knopf, 1961.

_____ . *The Responsible Electorate*. Cambridge, MA: Harvard University Press, 1966.

Koch, Howard, ed. *Casablanca: Script and Legend*. Woodstock, NY: Overlook Press, 1992.

Langer, Susanne. "The Comic Rhythm." In Robert W. Corrigan, ed., *Comedy: Meaning and Form*. San Francisco: Chandler, 1965, pp. 139–140.

Lapham, Lewis H. "Terms of Endearment." *Harper's*, September 1994, pp. 7–9.

Lane, Robert E. *Political Life*. New York: Free Press, 1972. Norton, 1966.

Lasswell, Harold. *Power and Responsibility*. New York: W. W. Norton, 1966.

Lasswell, Harold D., and Abraham Kaplan. *Power and Society*. New Haven: Yale University Press, 1950.

Leiserson, Avery. "Notes on the Theory of Opinion Formation." *American Political Science Review* 47 (March 1953): 171–177.

Levin, Murray B. *Kennedy Campaigning*. Boston: Beacon Press, 1966.

Lichter, Robert, Stanley Rothman, and Linda S. Lichter. *The Media Elite*. New York: Hastings House, 1990.

Limbaugh, Rush. "Liberals Fear Me Because I Am Effective." *Dallas Morning News*, October 13, 1994, p. 25A.

Lippmann, Walter. "The Bogey of Public Opinion." *Vanity Fair* 37 (December 1931): 51.

_____ . *The Phantom Public*. New York: Macmillan, 1925.

_____ . *A Preface to Morals*. Boston: Beacon Press, 1929.

_____ . *Public Opinion*. New York: Macmillan, 1922.

_____ . *The Public Philosophy*. New York: Little, Brown, 1955.

Lord, Carnes. "On Machiavelli's *Mandragola*." *Journal of Politics* 41 (1979): 806–827.

Luttwak, Edward. *The Endangered American Dream*. New York: Simon and Schuster, 1993.

McCroskey, James C. "Oral Communication Apprehension: A Summary of Recent Theory and Research." *Human Communication Research* 4 (Fall 1977): 78–96.

McLuhan, Marshall. *Understanding Media*. New York: Signet, 1964.

Marx, Leo. "Shakespeare's American Fable." In *The Machine in the Garden*. New York: Oxford University Press, 1964.

Mead, George Herbert. *Philosophy of the Present*. Chicago: University of Chicago Press, 1980.

Mencher, Melvin. *News Reporting and Writing*. Dubuque, IA: William C. Brown, 1981.

Mencken, H. L. *A Carnival of Buncombe*. Chicago: University of Chicago Press, 1956.

_____ . *A Mencken Chrestomathy*. New York: Alfred Knopf, 1956.

_____ . *Minority Report*. New York: Alfred A. Knopf, 1956.

_____ . *A New Dictionary of Quotations*. New York: Alfred A. Knopf, 1991.

_____ . *Prejudices: A Selection*. New York: Vintage, 1955.

Merton, Robert K. *Social Theory and Social Structure*. Glencoe, IL: Free Press, 1967.

Molotch, Harvey, and Marilyn Lester. "News as Purposive Behavior: On the Strategic Use of Routine Events, Accounts, and Scandals." *American Sociological Review* 39 (February 1974): 101–112.

Montaigne, Michel De. "Of Democritus and Heraclitus." In *The Selected Essays of Montaigne*. Edited by Lester G. Crocker. New York: Pocket Library, 1959.

Mount, Ferdinand. *The Theatre of Politics*. New York: Schocken Books, 1973.

Mutz, Diana. "Impersonal Influence in American Politics." *Public Perspective* 4 (November/December 1992): 20–23.

Nietzsche, Friedrich. *The Birth of Tragedy*. Garden City, NY: Doubleday Anchor, 1956.

Noelle-Neumann, Elisabeth. *The Spiral of Silence*. Chicago: University of Chicago Press, 1984.

Ozouf, M. "Public Opinion at the End of the Old Regime." *Journal of Modern History* 60 (1988): S11–S12.

Parkinson, C. Northcote. *The Law*. London: John Murray, 1979.

Peter, Laurence J., and Raymond Hull. *The Peter Principle: Why Things Always Go Wrong*. New York: William Morrow, 1969.

Peterson, Steven A. *Political Behavior*. Newbury Park, CA: Sage, 1990.

Phillips, Kevin. *Arrogant Capital*. Boston: Little, Brown, 1994.

Pomper, Gerald. *The People's Choice*. New York: Dodd, Mead, 1975.

Popkin, Samuel L. *The Reasoning Voter*. Chicago: University of Chicago Press, 1991.

Porter, Roy. *Gibbon*. New York: St. Martin's Press, 1988.

Postman, Neil. *Amusing Ourselves to Death*. New York: Penguin Books, 1985.

Pratkanis, Anthony, and Elliot Aronson. *Age of Propaganda*. New York: W. H. Freeman, 1991.

Ranney, Vance. "From Here to Absurdity: Heller's 'Catch-22.'" In Thomas B. Whitebread, ed., *Seven Contemporary Authors*. Austin: University of Texas Press, 1968, pp. 99–118.

"Richard M. Nixon, Always and Forever. . . ." *Esquire*, January 1992, pp. 118–119.

Rowe, Chip. "Chelsea Goes to the Nurse. . . ." *American Journalism Review* 15 (June 1993): 37–39.

Sagan, Eli. *The Honey and the Hemlock*. New York: Basic Books, 1991.

Santayana, George. "The Comic Mask and Carnival." In Robert W. Corrigan, ed., *Comedy: Meaning and Form*. San Francisco: Chandler, 1965.

Shakespeare, William. *The Tempest*. Edited by Robert Langbaum. New York: Signet, 1987.

Shaw, George Bernard. Preface to *Saint Joan*. Baltimore: Penguin Books, 1963, pp. 7–48.

Sices, David, and James B. Atkinson, eds. *The Comedies of Machiavelli*. London: University Press of New England, 1985.

Steele, Ronald. *Walter Lippmann and the American Century*. Boston: Little, Brown, 1980.

Sterling, Bryan B., and Frances N. Sterling, eds. *Will Rogers' World*. New York: M. Evans and Co., 1989.

Stolley, Richard B. "People Pictures." *Columbia Journalism Review* 23 (September/October 1994): 41–44.

Stovall, Calvin, Dick Mallary, and Ashley Weissenberger, eds. *Best of Gannett*. Arlington, VA: Gannett Co., 1993.

Sypher, Wylie. "The Meaning of Comedy." In Robert W. Corrigan, ed., *Comedy: Meaning and Form*. San Francisco: Chandler, 1965, pp. 18–60.

Taylor, John. "Passion Play." *Esquire*, December 1994, pp. 58–60, 65–67.

Thomas, Tony. *A Wonderful Life: The Films and Career of James Stewart*. Secaucus, NJ: Citadel Press, 1988.

Thrall, William Flint, Addison Hibbard, and C. Hugh Holman. *A Handbook to Literature*. New York: Odyssey Press, 1960.

Tocqueville, Alexis de. *Democracy in America*. Edited by J. P. Mayer. Translated by George Lawrence. Garden City, NY: Anchor Books, 1969.

Tuchman, Barbara. *The March of Folly*. New York: Alfred A. Knopf, 1984.

Tuchman, Gaye. *Making News*. New York: Free Press, 1978.

———. "Objectivity as Strategic Ritual." *American Journal of Sociology* 77 (July 1972): 660–678.

Twain, Mark. *The Autobiography of Mark Twain*. Edited by Charles S. Neider. New York: Harper and Row, 1959.

Valency, Maurice. *The End of the World*. New York: Oxford University Press, 1980.

Watt, Homer A., et al. "Shakespeare's Life." In *Shakespeare's Plays*. New York: Barnes and Noble, 1966.

Watzlawick, Paul, J. H. Beaven, and Don D. Jackson. *Pragmatics of Human Communication*. New York: W. W. Norton, 1967.

White, E. B. *The Second Tree from the Corner*. New York: Harper and Row Perennial Library, 1989.

Wilhoit, C. Cleveland, and David H. Weaver. *The American Journalist*. 2nd ed. Bloomington: Indiana University Press, 1991.

Worcester, Robert M. "A View from Britain: You Can Do It Better." *Public Perspective* 4 (November/December 1992): 17–18.

Zaller, John. "Positive Constructs of Public Opinion." *Critical Studies in Mass Communication* 11 (September 1994): 276–287.

Index

About the Authors

JAMES E. COMBS is a former Professor of Political Science at Valparaiso University and is the author or coauthor of 12 books, including *The Political Pundits* (Praeger, 1992).

DAN NIMMO is Visiting Scholar, Department of Political Science, Baylor University, and is the author or coauthor of 15 books, including *The Political Pundits* (Praeger, 1992).

ISBN 0-275-94979-6

HARDCOVER BAR CODE